BROTHER WILFREDO E. LUBRICO, FMS

BIOGRAPHY & TRIBUTES

PRIMA GUIPO HOWER

with

Briccio J. Baynosa, Ph.D.

Foreword by Roberto Borromeo, Ph.D.

LifeRich

PUBLISHING

LifeRich Publishing books may be ordered through booksellers or by contacting:

LifeRich Publishing
1663 Liberty Drive
Bloomington, IN 47403
www.liferichpublishing.com
844-686-9607

Editor: Briccio J. Baynosa, Ph.D.
Foreword by Dr. Roberto T. Borromeo
Cover Oil Painting by Bueno Silva
Cover Concept by Cecille Castillon-Weinstein

ISBN: 978-1-4897-4040-3 (sc)
ISBN: 978-1-4897-4039-7 (hc)
ISBN: 978-1-4897-4041-0 (e)

Library of Congress Control Number: 2022902277

Print information available on the last page.

LifeRich Publishing rev. date: 03/25/2022

Dedicated to my father Elpidio, 89.

He died in peace
knowing that we will take care of our mother, Maria Paz.
He showed us how he dearly loved his honey.

~Brother Willy Lubrico, FMS~

Contents

Foreword

This book is a biography and tribute to a person who has touched the lives of many and made a difference in the course of his life journey. Based on my personal and professional interactions with him, he can be considered an epitome of a consecrated person. In the document, *Consecrated Persons and their Mission in Schools*[1] the consecrated life may be compared in some ways to a *school* that every consecrated person is called to attend for his whole life that he may have the mind of the Son and learn from Him to have a heart that is meek and humble, courageous and passionate. As may be gleaned from his own sharing, the narratives, and tributes from those who knew him intimately, Brother Willy, the subject of this biography, demonstrated that it was possible to convey the school of life's evangelical message while living in today's competitive and challenge filled society.

Snippets from his personal journal and the narratives and tributes from family and friends were deftly woven into a saga by the two authors who knew him intimately from two different vantage points. Guipo-Hower writes from the perspective of a lay best friend with whom, at one time or another, Brother Willy shared his simple joys, dreams, aspirations, and life's frustrations. Baynosa, on the other hand, shares his insights about the subject as a confrere in the religious order who witnessed the ups and downs of his journey as a consecrated person.

As she did in her earlier books (*Tio Doroy's Field, 2004; No Greater Service, 2020*), Guipo-Hower demonstrates her mastery of the use of narratives to bring the subject's personal values and characteristics to the fore. Furthermore, her vivid, clear, and texture-filled descriptions of the context and settings provide the reader with a glimpse of the places where the subject was in the various phases of his life and how the many factors in these environments shaped his way of being and becoming. Through her purposive presentation, she shares with the readers Brother Willy's life journey from a boy growing up on the farm to an adolescent finding his way in school away from home, as a grown-up professional and religious taking on his various responsibilities and the time he spent with friends during his sojourns in many places. Readers get a glimpse of Brother Willy's growing-up years as a child of a family who migrated to the land of promise, Mindanao, with the end view of improving their lot.

As one who had a similar phase early in life, I can vividly see him attending to his share of the farm chores – clearing up weeds, tending to the carabao, fetching water, and on school days walking to school on an unpaved path that gets muddy on rainy days. As may be gleaned from the book, Brother Willy's life on the farm, while blissful and characterized by family love, it was not a walk in the park. Aside from the tedious manual labor required to prod the plants to produce, at times, migrant families had to contend with dangers wrought by lawless elements. I can also personally relate to the experience of Brother Willy's family having to escape and move to another place for their safety after a harrowing and life-threatening experience in which they were divested of their earthly belongings. On one similarly brutal night, my own kin had a narrow escape from the wrath of rebels who burned their house and those of their neighbor for reasons unknown. They spent the cold of the night in the cornfield and left for the barrio at dawn. They came back after a few days to find out, that like the Lubricos, everything they had was gone, including the corn crop that was about to be harvested but was razed to the ground. It can be surmised that the challenges that migrant families face, as in the case of Brother Willy played a significant role in character formation and tenacity that kept him in good stead as he moved on to face life's challenges.

Baynosa's discourse on Brother Willy from the lens of a confrere in the congregation gives the readers insights into his life journey as a religious. He describes Brother Willy's formation stages: from his days in the Juniorate to the Novitiate to when he pronounced his vows and his engagements in the various institutions where he was assigned. Given the stringent requirements for admission and in the different stages of formation, it may be said that not all who desire to enter the order do succeed. That Brother Willy successfully hurdled the challenges and left us with his boots on is a testament that he truly deserved all the accolades he received in life and in death.

This book is an inspiring read. This is an affirmation of the adage that education is the key to social mobility. Coupled with resilience, tenacity, commitment to values, and faithfulness to life purpose and calling, love, and support from family and friends, one can make a difference and touch the lives of many.

The outpourings of love that Brother Willy received shows that amidst the inherent conflicts even in religious congregations (Oswald & Johnson, *Managing Polarities In Congregations*, 2010) he remained steadfast in his vows and, to the end, lived out the Marist virtues of Humility, Modesty, and Simplicity.

From my perspective as an academic with a particular interest in qualitative studies as a lecturer, researcher, and dissertation advisor, I consider this book as an exemplary biographical work. Students of qualitative research can draw insights from the authors' purposive use of narrative to unfold the subject's personal values, characteristics, and achievements. In addition, the presentation of vivid, clear, and thick descriptions of the context and setting gives readers a strong sense of being there. The analysis of how the factors in the environment shape Brother Willy's sense of being and becoming, his strong presence throughout the book and that of his narrators, rather than the authors is an added bonus.

Thank you, Prima and Brix, for this well-thought-out saga.

Dr. Roberto T. Borromeo
President, Eton International School
Author: *Strategies for Effective School Management*
Manila, Philippines 2021

Preface

This project is such an unwieldy child – conceived too soon and born too late. All along, it was also surrounded with doubt and uncertainty. Will it prosper and reach fruition? Will it continue and become a fulfillment of a dream? Will it jump off and spring to life?

The unexpected and early demise of Brother Willy has triggered these questions. He was supposed to write this book but all of a sudden the ship has lost its captain and unexpectedly it has paused and seemingly ran out of steam.

Prima and I mused upon the situation for a while and after witnessing the effusion of sentiments and expressions of loss, love, and sympathy, we decided that the project must continue. We will pick up the pieces and complete the jigsaw and paint the canvass of Brother Willy's life.

This book is born out of FRIENSHIP – friendship that knows no boundaries, not counting any cost, always being there when the need arises, ever the inspiration to a friend even beyond death, and for all eternity.

Now that he is gone, we know that we can only scratch the surface of the immensity and profundity of our friendship with him. But sometimes a mere scratch can open an endless source of inspiration that will keep reminding us that somehow, somewhere in time, someone as great as he is has touched our lives.

This book is written through the lens of those people who found it significant that in this journey we call LIFE they have a friend in Brother Willy, that he made a difference, that for some he was a catalyst for growth, and in others he was an agent for change, and maybe for most of us he was a reason to LOVE.

This book is written because FRIENDSHIP is such a beautiful thing – it makes you realize who the person truly is; it makes you see his worth; it makes you understand his flaws as well as his virtues; it makes you strong, unafraid, bold, and also tender because you know . . . YOU'VE GOT A FRIEND!

BBBaynosa

Briccio Baynosa, Ph.D.
C0-Author
General Santos City, Philippines

A Note from the Narrator

IN THE BEGINNING

"That's impossible. First, I am not a good writer. Second question, who would be interested to read?"

~Brother Willy Lubrico on writing his memoir~

Brother Wilfredo Engane Lubrico, F.M.S. the President of Notre Dame of Marbel University (NDMU) woke up one morning and found himself in a formidable position so foreign to him. The NDMU president for fifteen years, president of Notre Dame of Dadiangas University for eleven years before that, a Parish Worker, in leadership roles of local, national, and international organizations, had dealt with countless adversities his whole life. But this was nothing he had ever encountered before. He was not alone.

On March 11, 2020, the World Health Organization (WHO) declared COVID-19 a global pandemic.

The NDM University, like the rest of the world, went on total lockdown. Coronavirus, herd immunity, masks, social distancing, virtual learning, e-management, Zoom, etc., became familiar bylines. The world made adjustments as it grappled with the "new normal". It still rages on two years later – first as a Delta variant and the latest as the highly contagious Omicron – while the latter is not as deadly, it is no less worrisome.

Immediately after the WHO announcement, the NDM University suspended classes for over 6,000 students from primary grades through graduate school. Even the essential staff was forced to work at home. The university took a significant financial loss from matriculation revenues. However, the probationary teachers that usually didn't get paid during the summer session received their pay as initiated by Brother Willy who regarded the well being of his employees a priority. Under his leadership, virtual classes resumed three months later, albeit in a limited fashion. But the critics were swift and vocal; their discontent seeped into the fake news realm. Brother Willy had to weigh his decisions for the common good versus the self-interest of the vocal few.

"At the height of the COVID-19 pandemic, which I feel strangled me with nothing to do, no people to talk to plus the heightened anxiety about the virus and trying to run the university amidst it all, I started to strengthen my personal prayers," he wrote.

Then he started a journal.

His excitement was palpable when he began writing his life story. The prospect gave him a quiet sense of purpose, a comforting distraction from the pandemic with global reach that adversely impacted his province of South Cotabato, Philippines. For one who seldom displays his emotion, it was refreshing.

The campus of NDMU was a ghost town, but he snapped into action. He strategized with his Administrators and conducted a lot of teacher trainings on how to conduct remote learning. In June 2020, the virtual graduate school classes kicked up in high gear, but not without its toll. He shared his concerns on Facebook Messenger:

"Very discouraging. We are very busy preparing for online modules. But enrollment is slow. We don't know where this COVID will bring us, financially we have to make all kinds of adjustments."

Thus, the veteran of twenty-six years as President of two Notre Dame Universities in the Philippines was engulfed in the challenging task of navigating the pandemic within the academic sector. It was no small feat, but he had surrounded himself with an excellent team; quite quickly and remarkably, NDMU managed to adjust to the new norm in educating its children.

After a long day at his office, some nights, he recalled his childhood on his laptop, his obvious affection for his past with happy personal associations shining through his compositions. Then, on a sporadic clip, he'd send me his progress via text or email. Remotely, during the lockdown, we'd do this, he 10,000 miles away in Marbel, Philippines, and I in Warren, Rhode Island. Brother Willy kept himself busy as well, in the university's gardens, checked on the daily progress of the various construction projects, and was unusually active on social media, his only medium to "talk to people."

His Facebook posts elicited hundreds of likes for the two remaining months of 2020 until January 20, 2021. I followed the stream of Brother Willy's photos of ongoing projects, initiatives he wanted to complete, and the images of the gardens he manicured. Many of his fans shared these posts on their own Facebook account, spreading the beauty of the green revolution unfolding at the campus. Our mutual friend Orman Ortega Manansala noticed the sense of urgency and a tinge of nostalgia about these posts and promptly texted me if I had perceived the same. *"Naga sentimental yata si* Brother W."

"Yeah I agree he is becoming sentimental. I believe he just wanted to document a part of his legacy," I responded.

"This looks like the Garden of Versailles," I commented on one picture of geometrical topiaries that Brother Willy posted taken in front of a building. First, I complimented him for perfecting the art of trimming shrubs or trees into ornamental shapes. Then, I teased him; throwing back at him the line he was fond of saying, *"Ano, pang legacy mo na ina?"* (Is that for your legacy?)

The online banter back and forth with Brother Willy was lighthearted. Entertaining. I knew then that writing his life story in tandem would be one fun ride!

I can still picture that one spring day when and where we first discussed the idea of writing his memoir.

It was a sunny, light sweater kind of day in May 2019 in Alaska. The clusters of rhododendrons in hot pink and pastels, the purple lupine spires, and the late-blooming tulips vied for the attention of tourists newly disembarked from cruise ships docked in Juneau, Alaska. Peonies in the profusion of colors perfumed the landscape where we waited for the tour bus.

"What's this flower, Prim?" he asked as he posed by a bush with brilliant green, shiny leaves covered with pink blooms as big as our faces.

"Rhododendron, Brother" I replied.

"Rhodo, what? *Ka* tongue twister *man sina*," he exclaimed.

(What a tongue twister that is).

"In Rhode Island, we just call it Rhody."

"Rhody *na lang*," he said.

We boarded the tour bus. We took a group picture as soon as we reached our destination. After a few announcements, the Notre Dame alumni contingency dispersed into smaller groups and explored Mendenhall Glacier National Park.

Brother Willy wore his heavy green North Face jacket, black knitted winter cap, and a pair of gloves was stuffed in his outsized pocket. Just the sight of the distant mountains covered with snow chilled him to the bone, he confessed. We stood not many miles away from the Mendenhall Glacier, about thirteen miles long, located twelve miles from downtown Juneau. At elevation 5,184 feet above sea level, the glacier surrounded by verdant mountains sparkled under the blue skies dotted with puffy clouds. I signed up both of us for a kayak trip on the lake. According to our tour guide, the lake was fed by the flowing snowmelt from the dense ice formed by centuries of snow accumulation, constantly moving under its weight.

"That's the glacier? It's like a frozen waterfall," he said.

"Yes, that's it", I responded. "It's a shame the cruise ship canceled the kayak trip. The weatherman had forecast gusty wind, and the kayak operators deemed the water too choppy. The trip would have taken you and me very close to the glacier's edge".

"*Sayang*", he lamented.

(What a loss).

Later, our tour ended, we sat on a bench waiting for our bus. Unfortunately, the bus that was to take us back to our 3,500-passenger humongous cruise ship was running a tad late. As we snacked on Planter's salted peanuts, I shared with him a guarded secret at that time - my husband's manuscript had just been accepted for publishing.

"Congrats to Al, Prim," he said.

"Thanks", I replied. "*Di ba one* of the items on your Bucket list is to write a book? You should publish your memoir".

"That's impossible," he replied. "First, I am not a good writer. Not like you who writes clearly and comprehensively."

"But you are the undisputed guru of delegating work", I teased. "Heard of ghostwriters?"

He smiled that elusive smile and added, "Second question, who would be interested to read?" A year and a half later, I reminded him about the book. He would reiterate and put his argument in writing. (See Appendix A: Conversations with Brother Willy).

On August 27, 2020, our conversation on Facebook Messenger went something like this.

Me: "So many Marist Brothers left this world whose life stories and accomplishments were buried with them. Brother Bernard Curtin gave me an article he wrote about the history of the Marist Brothers Philippine Mission. Then there's a manuscript that Brother Paul Meuten compiled, not widely circulated yet, about the history of the Marist Brothers in the Philippines. Since you have always taken the road less traveled, let's write your book. It will humanize the Religious Congregation. We'll include your collections, unorthodox life, travels, and photos. Do it as a Dear Diary. Just write your thoughts and remembrances daily as if you are writing to yourself. We can always edit later."

"Agreeing with you," he responded. "That's in my heart too, that no one would remember the history, the people, and the turning points of the congregations, and institutions that gave way to the present."

"As you finish writing a chapter," I advised, "send them to me weekly. I will organize your musings and produce the book."

"Yes! Too excited, Prim. *Binubuhay mo ang tulog kong damdamin.*"

(You awakened my slumbering feelings). Then, Brother Willy added a L.O.L. (laugh out loud).

"Al would tell you that if it were up to him, his book would have remained a pile of copious letters, journals, and photos rotting away in dusty boxes in the basement. He admits he does not know how to put a book together. That's my job. After our chat, I will send you the guidelines from the publishing company on how to write an excellent memoir. Let's do it", I egged him on.

"I feel like retiring tomorrow to do this," he replied. "Okay, I'll start with an outline, and let's fill every chapter with highlights. I cannot wait, Prim."

"I cannot wait myself."

"If we can do this, life is over for me. Haha. Everything will be recorded, including my collections – mugs, key chains, coins, and Marist memorabilia, etc."

"Life will be over as a Marist Brother perhaps", I kidded back, "but it will be the beginning of a new journey. Seriously though, think of a personal project you wish to make a reality. It can be the beneficiary of your book sales. Let's find one of your students or friends with name recognition or who has authored a book to write the Foreword."

"I wish the readers will remember in their hearts the stories in the book," he wrote wistfully. "As soon as I receive my copy of Al's book, I will forward my outline that I started during lockdown. I included the area of my vocation, administration, relationships, friendships, success, and failures."

"Everyone loves an honest book that projects the real person. Those of us who know you as Orman, Brix, and I do, see you as a human being. Many perceive you as the Marist Brother, a consecrated man, and the '*El Presidente*'. We thought the Madres and the Padres didn't go to the bathroom when we were in high school. L.O.L.".

"Haha. Let's include all my horror, funny, irrational stories, insecurities, fears, drama, etc! We could ask opinions from my friends from long, long ago (many of them) and my students. O.M.G., you are awakening my interest in writing. Sometimes, too many dark shadows *ang buhay ko* (in my life) and I took the road less traveled. Call me *Rebelde*, emotional, etc. I will send you my outline for your comment."

We sat on the wooden bench that one spring day in Alaska, chatting away like two best buddies. At times, I'd forget that Brother Willy was a consecrated man. Brother Willy was a member of the Marist Brothers, also known as the Little Brothers of Mary (*Fratres Maristae a Scholis* aka F.M.S.), a Roman Catholic congregation of teaching Brothers founded near Lyon, France, on January 2, 1817, by Marcellin Champagnat for the Christian education of French youth.[2] (Saint Marcellin, a Society of Mary priest, was declared Venerable in 1920 by Pope Benedict XV, beatified by Pope Pius XII on May 29, 1955, and canonized by Pope John Paul II on April 18, 1999).

Brother Willy was a man "drawn by the Holy Spirit to follow Christ with greater freedom. They have sought to imitate Him through committing themselves to poverty, chastity, and obedience. Like all vocations, a consecrated life is not an end in itself. Still, it serves to sanctify the individual and to build the body of Christ."[3]

However, on this particular day in Alaska, Brother Wilfredo Engane Lubrico, F.M.S., the Marist Brother, the President of our Alma Mater, was just one of the guys traveling with fifty-five of his fellow Notre Dame alumni and their families. As he was often inclined to do, he "bundled" his travels abroad. This time he was on his way from another continent for an international workshop. He made a stopover in Seattle, Washington State, to attend the 25th Biennial Reunion of Notre Dame of Gen. Santos City Alumni Association International (NDGSCAA, Intl) with many other Marist Brother mentors and Nuns. It was his eighth time to join, twice as a Guest Speaker. He served as President of our alma mater from 1995-2006 until he transferred to Notre Dame of Marbel University as its current President.

The four-day reunion in Seattle included the tours of the Museum of Flight and the Boeing Company manufacturing plant. We stood side by side, wide-eyed and in awe at a rare glimpse of the making of a Boeing 787 jumbo jet. He, a boy from an obscure barrio called Naci, Surallah, who made countless sound and life-changing decisions to become President of two universities; I, a barrio girl, still striving to fashion a perfect river of muscari garden at her son's estate called Juniper Farm.

"Never in my wildest dream, Prim. Wow! To witness the making of a 787," he said, shaking his head left and right in disbelief.

At the Gala Night, he visited his classmates and students from one table to another, posed at the Photo Booth, line-danced with the alumnae on the stage with a live band, and got photographed in a selfie. He was the only guy among the ladies. These were some alumnae, his life-long friends, who chipped in to buy him a ticket to help him cross off one item on his bucket list: to see Alaska.

We spent a lot of time together on that seven-day Alaska cruise. He shared his plans to finish constructing an aquatic center, a swimming pool, and a chapel at NDMU before his term expired in June 2021. He sent photos of each project to my Messenger as if he was highlighting his innumerable accomplishments for posterity. He revealed his dreams to learn how to cook and paint, and write the highlights of his life. He expressed considerable angst about what he'd do with his mug and coin collections when he retired from his post. He looked forward to the idea of a sabbatical and traveling to visit his family and friends in the United States, Canada, the Middle East, and Australia. All sponsored by friends and family working abroad. He was full of plans.

Then COVID-19 hit hard. It was doubly devastating for the Notre Dame Community because on January 25, 2021 at 3:25 AM, sadly, Brother Willy died of a non-Covid cause.

Oh, so suddenly leaving me alone to attempt completing a book without the author, a paralyzing thought. I mourned with the thousands who joined the nightly memorial services streamed Live on Facebook, beamed on Zoom for seven days and made widely available on YouTube. He left an immense void; his demise pierced through the hearts of thousands whose lives changed forever in his life as in his death. Grief blanketed the university landscape and spread across the continents.

One day, Brother Ador (Provincial of the Marist East Asia Province) requested a few others and me to write a tribute for publication in the Marist Brothers Newsletter, *Marist News Bits*. I promptly submitted my piece. Sobbing like a baby as I wrote, it was gut wrenching but cathartic at the same time. Then, on the sixth day of the memorial service, I received another request: to pay tribute to my friend Brother Willy Live on Zoom for the International Theme with speakers from Rome, Malaysia, Canada, and the U.S.A. My first reaction was to decline, as I prefer to remain invisible behind my pen, write rather than speak in front of the public. But in the end, I acquiesced. (My tribute appears as Postscript at the end of the book).

I attended these nightly services and commiserated with friends and family members who spoke in the past tense about Brother Willy. That was difficult to swallow. While he was being taken to his final resting place in Tamontaka, (located near Cotabato City), I resolved his book would be written and published. I knew from the onset that it would be immensely challenging. But the nightly memorial service presented an "aha" moment and provided me with enough materials. I promptly reached out to all the "sharers" who eulogized him, and they happily obliged. They permitted me to add their voices to the story; their testimonials laced the pains with inspiring anecdotes about Brother Willy. I couldn't have written this biography without the help of so many people. They are listed at the back of the book under acknowledgement titled *Contributors: Tributes*. In addition, as if Brother Willy was sending a subliminal message, I found Briccio Baynosa's article written in 1997 honoring Brother Willy. I reached out to the writer and thankfully; he agreed to co-author this book.

And the original author himself made the task less challenging.

Brother Willy, a visionary to the end, armed me with these essential materials before he died: the dedication for his book, outline of his topics, and eight paragraphs – his last deed towards the completion of his memoir. Certainly not enough to fill a book, but they are the vital "warp" of the fabric of his life, metaphorically speaking.

His last act reminds me of a T'boli Dreamweaver of *t'nalak*.[4] The weaver gathers all the basic and significant materials like the abaca fiber, the natural dyes, and the pots used for dying, etc. She lays the abaca fiber out on a backstrap loom. With deft hands using a design born out of her dreams, she prepares the warp.[5]

With the warp before me, all I had to do was gather all the weft materials to finish the tapestry. From the beginning, I knew this project wouldn't be easy. But while challenging, the journey was pure joy. With every testimony I received about Brother Willy from many corners of the world, it was like discovering facets of a rough diamond ready for the final cut. According to the Capetown Diamond Museum: A facet is the flat surface on the shape of the diamond. If you would take a look at the brilliant-cut diamond, you will see the stone consists of fifty-seven facets; the crown of the diamond has thirty-three facets on the top part of the girdle and twenty-four on the pavilion...[6]

He was multi-faceted as a diamond indeed.

Dear readers, throughout this book, this narrator used direct quotes shared through interviews, answers to questionnaires, email exchanges, and written testimonials by family, friends, and colleagues of Brother Willy. Any attempt on my part to paraphrase their story would be a poor substitute for their versions. Brother Willy was prescient when he wrote, "We can ask the opinions of my friends of long, long time ago (many of them)..." Some of the verbatim quotes are in Ilonggo (Brother Willy's native dialect) or Cebuano (a dominant dialect in South Cotabato) or Tagalog (the Philippine National Language), or Taglish (combination of Tagalog and English) followed by the English translation. Brother Joao from Rome even sent an Italian version of his tribute. All tributes are presented in block quote except that of the co-author, Briccio Baynosa, and the narrator.

For the facts about his career and accomplishments, I used the testimonies from people who worked with Brother Willy and his curriculum vitae. (Appendix B – Curriculum Vitae).

For his journey as a Marist Brother my co-author, Briccio Baynosa, provided his own experiences at the Marist Formation Centers. Brother Ted Fernandez, young Willy's Novice Master, Brother Ador Santiago, his Superior, Brother Jong Acosta and Brother Manny de Leon his confreres also shared their impressions. So did friends he met as a Junior, Postulant, Novice, and Scholastic. Finally, Saturnino Bayona and Rodolfo Mapada not only provided some critical timelines but images of their life-long friendships as well; photos only a few have seen.

For the glimpses into his character and inner self, the people who intimately witnessed his life from childhood narrated his story thanks to his sister Teresa Lubrico Golveo, and brothers Rodolfo and Jaime Lubrico. People from all continents except Antarctica contributed as well - his Lubrico family, his classmates in grade school, high school, and college, his colleagues and students, his superiors and subordinates, and his countless friends.

I pulled up his copious emails from the 1990s to the present (500 plus) as a resource for his quotes and perspectives. I also listened again to the twelve videos recorded live on Facebook and Zoom during the seven-day memorial celebration, thus revisiting the tributes of so many people. When I could not secure a copy from the "sharer", I transcribed from the recordings. These are archived under "Videos" on the Notre Dame of Marbel University website for anyone interested in viewing them again. (The collated chart on Chapter 13 - Friendships, captures an impressive picture of viewership in seven days, almost 95,000 views, 5,000+ comments, and emoticons).

These voluminous materials became the "weft" that I used to weave the "warp" together.

As to his nickname-Will, Willie, Willy-the evolution was gradual. There are photos discovered by his niece and included in this book when he was in high school where he signed his name "Willie". My co-author Briccio Baynosa has his own take: "I used to write his name Willie because I thought it sounded classy. In fact, on his door, in NDMU convent, WILLIE was posted prominently, the kind of name sign you buy in novelty stores". Some of his superiors and confreres addressed him as Will. The authors decided to leave all three as they appear in tributes and testimonies.

The majority of photos included here came from Brother Willy. He sent them to me in the last six months before his death. It was as if to tell me to use them for his story, making it easy for me to decide which photos to include. Family and friends provided the rest. I sought permission to include them in this book and duly credited each of the contributors.

The portrait on the cover is a miniature version of the 16x20 oil painting created by the world-renowned artist, Bueno Silva, a very good friend of Brother Willy. They met at the Notre Dame Alumni Reunion in Orlando, Florida in 2005. Brother Willy had visited Bueno and his family in Chicago, Illinois. The painting will be donated to the museum of Notre Dame of Marbel University. (Profile of the Artist is at the back of this book).

The most challenging task in putting this book together was to precisely discern what the original author would have written about his chosen topics listed in his outline below.

I. My Father In Me
II. Road Less Travelled By (Marist Life in Non-Marist World)
III. The Teacher, The Parish Worker
IV. The Discovery and Recovery
V. Friendships
VI. Reflections

My co-author, Briccio Baynosa, and I discussed at length how we could present his story to the best of our ability. So we decided to remain faithful to Brother Willy's plans by following his outline, interpreting it the best we could, and providing appropriate context. If we fall short, there is always someday to write a sequel to correct errors. We presented his story in chronological order as best we could. We either used his words for the titles or created relevant ones for ease of presentation and clarity.

Brother Willy, our mutual friend Noh Dalid Conrad and I returned to our alumni reunion host hotel, the Hilton Seattle Airport & Convention Center after the Alaska trip. We stayed overnight to catch our early morning flights the following day. The three of us were the last attendees to leave. My high school classmate Jose "Pepe" Macariola (a former Marist Brother aspirant) and his wife, Fely, live in Seattle. They took us out for a Filipino dinner at Seafood City, a Philippine Grocery and Restaurant. Brother Willy ordered a grilled tilapia, among other things, and declared, "This tilapia reminds me of my childhood and our fishponds when I was growing up."

Pepe dropped us back at the hotel after dinner. Brother Willy and I walked around the gardens at Hilton and left Noh to her unfinished packing.

The orangey sun was just beginning to set over the outline of a mountain covered with snow behind the hotel.

"Is that Mt. Rainier?" he asked.

I confirmed.

"I played in the snow there last week," he said.

"You should visit us in the wintertime. I'll teach you how to build a snowman."

"Adding 'build a snowman' to my bucket list," he responded with a low chuckle. "Look, there's a Rhody!" he exclaimed as soon as we entered the Hilton courtyard.

"Wow! You remembered. What about that pink one?"

"A puny?"

"Close enough, it's pronounced pee-oh-nee, peony."

"I will remember that it starts with pee." We both laughed.

Then on a serious tone, he said, "By the way Prim, *ang libro di pwede like thesis* ha?"

"What do you mean?"

"You know, we won't write this book like a treatise or dissertation for a master's or Ph.D. degree, formal, dry, boring research paper. Instead, I want a book that the young adults will enjoy reading and learn lessons from it".

"Sure. You are the author; you write it the way you want it. I'll just help publish it", I assured him. "By the way, if I were to list the top three people you admire most, dead or alive, who would they be?"

"Oh, so many of them," he said as we continued our meander at the Hilton courtyard. Then, after a thoughtful pause, he said, "St. Marcellin Champagnat, of course, and Mother Theresa, and Brother Renato Cruz also comes to mind. Can I add one more? Tie for third with Brother Rey is Brother Bob."

"McGovern?"

"Yes," he said.

I could not help noting how Brother Willy cited people who shared a singular trait; they all had a very soft spot for the poor.

The following morning, we were up very early to catch our respective flights homeward bound. We took a quick selfie inside the Hilton Airport Shuttle, and with a handshake and pat on the back, we said our goodbyes. That was the last time I saw Brother Willy.

This book, "Brother Wilfredo E. Lubrico, F.M.S. (Biography & Tributes)", is a collective patchwork of Brother Willy's writing, although scant they are revealing. It is colored by direct quotes from the written compositions of his family, friends, colleagues, and students with whom he invested his life heavily and lovingly for over five decades.

I am only his narrator whose goal is simple. I wanted to record his remarkable journey that ended too soon and to keep his legacies alive for generations to come. Unless his "footprints on the sands of time" are indelibly etched on the pages of a book, an indifferent oncoming tide can obliterate them all.

As I promised, a thesis this biography is not.

Instead, it is a colorful storybook finish to an illustrious life.

Prima Hower

Prima Guipo Hower
January 25, 2022

Brother Willy posed with a group of alumni at the Mendenhall Glacier National Park. L-R: Bernadette Buensuceso Graham, Brother Willy, Shirley Zolina Victa, Noh Dalid Conrad, author.

Brother Willy and the "Rhody"

Brother Willy & author, Star Princess Cruise Ship

Brother willy and the members of Notre Dame of General Santos City Alumni Association International at The Mendenhall National Park, Juneau, Alaska.

Mt. Rainier, Washington State

Star Princess Cruise Ship Welcome Party L-R: author (NDL67, Brother Willy (NDL71), Josie Ferrariz Tizon (NDL67), Noh Dalid Conrad (NDL67)

* * * * *

My Father and Me
Brother Willy and his father, Elpidio

My Father in Me 1

"My sisters told me I was my father's favorite son."

~ Willy Lubrico ~

"My father loved to comb my hair and cut it the way he liked it, a style which I resented when I was a young boy", so began Willy's childhood musings. From the time young Willy was old enough to remember until he began his third year in high school, it was this haircut ritual that forged the bond between father and son. According to Rodolfo, Willy's brother four years his senior, their father was the barber for all seven Lubrico boys in Negros Occidental. So it continued when they moved to the island of Mindanao. They lived quite a distance from the Surallah town center, so the barber set up his "shop" under a tree at the yard of their farmhouse.

"Cutting my hair would take my father two sessions," Willy wrote. "As he chewed his tobacco, he combed my hair until I fell asleep. Then, in the second session, my father cut my hair when I woke up. It would take him at least two hours as he narrated stories and asked me questions. I suspected he took his time to cut my hair to impart advice and to ask about my activities in school."

His father's deft hands grasping the comb and scissors held the young boy a captive listener. Young Willy learned two unforgettable stories from those sessions.

Willy wrote: The first story was about a father and son who went to the forest for firewood. While they were resting, the father pointed out one straight bamboo and another bent bamboo to the boy. The father told the son that a boy is like bamboo. While it is still young, it is flexible that one can shape it to his desired form. But once it matures, one cannot bend the bamboo without breaking it.

His second story was about a father who showed his son a pillow filled with chicken feathers and likened the pillow to a man's reputation. If you tear the pillow at the seams and throw its contents in the air, the chicken feathers will fly all over. Once scattered, it would be nearly impossible to gather all the feathers and put them back to their original form. The moral of the story is not to destroy one's reputation and spread it around. One cannot repair it.

"Without any formal education, I don't know where my father Elpidio got his stories", Willy pondered.

What compelled Brother Willy to begin his story with *My Father in Me*? To find the answer, first, this narrator sent a series of questions to Rodolfo Lubrico. (His children call him Papa Doc because his nickname is Docdoc). Then, with the help of his daughter Cecille Lubrico Longanilla, (a public school teacher), Briccio Baynosa, and I attempted to establish how the father clearly influenced his son. Willy's persona encompasses a myriad of desirable characteristics - his desire to achieve in life through education, his soft heart for the Indigenous People (IP), his concern for the poor, his love for reading, his affinity and respect for his family, his deep love for parents, his perspectives of the arts, his care for the environment, his skill in delegating tasks and responsibilities, etc. and yes, even his bullheadedness. All these traits served him well, which he did not learn through birthright, nor wealth, but from his father through the process of osmosis. A *"gradual and unconscious assimilation of ideas and knowledge"* as osmosis is defined, is possible because young Willy possessed an acute sense of curiosity and keen observation. And he adored his father. Rodolfo asserted that Willy was his father's son in more ways than one. A sentiment echoed by his daughter.

Cecille described his Tiyoy Willy as bullheaded. "Tatay Pidio is very firm *gid daw. Kung mag decide indi mabali, pag gin hambal niya panindigan nya gid daw amo gid na ang nakuha ni T'yoy Brother Willy kay Tatay Pidio*".

(When the father decides, he never breaks his words; he'd stand up for what he believes, which Uncle Brother Willy inherited from Tatay Pidio).

Narrator: How about his soft spot for the Indigenous People, concern for his family, and deep love for his parents?

Cecille: *"Ang gaan-gaan ng loob ni T'yoy sa mga IPs kay ang farm nila diri sa* Little Baguio is near the Lake Sebu community of IPs. *Ang nagapamugon taga panggas, taga panghilamon, abono, harvest halos tanan mga T'bolis. Kung may pagkaon si Tatay Pidio dala, tagaan niya sila. Ang isa nila ka cousin sa side ni Nanay Mayang nga si T'yoy Johnny Engane asawa niya si Auntie Elena Sagan, mabuot kaayo nga T'boli".*

(Brother Willy had a very soft spot for the IPs because their farm in Little Baguio is near the Lake Sebu community of IPs. The laborers mainly were T'bolis who sowed the seeds, weeded, fertilized, and harvested. His father would share whatever food he's got with them. One of their maternal cousins, Uncle Johnny Engane, married Auntie Elena Sagan, a very nice T'boli lady.)

Cecille added that Tatay Pidio was very helpful, generous and did not like boastful people. He would share his rice and corn harvest with his friends who struggled to feed their families, including the fruits from his orchard. He planted so many fruit trees that benefit his children and grandchildren to this day – coconuts, mangoes, *santol*, durian, rambutan, guavas, etc. He had a fairly large banana plantation.

"Mapinalangaon kag malipayon si Tatay Pidio. Palakanta to siya sing mga composo labi na kung makainom sing tuba sige dayon kanta kag namian man kami mamati kay nami iya tingug mag pa laoy-laoy gid. Sobra gid ka palangga niya kami tanan nga apos niya. Mapisan gid kaayo."

(Very loving and cheerful, Tatay Pidio would sing, especially after a few drinks of coconut wine while his grandchildren listened to him deliver his songs with gusto. He loved his apos, and he was hardworking).

Tatay Pidio was more into crafts, but he liked arts too, according to Cecille. He was an expert in basket making. He used to make all the nests for his chickens out of bamboo. He also wove simple mat designs for the family to sleep on, utilizing the reeds he harvested from the forest. He was a nature lover and protector of the environment; he planted many trees, especially fruit trees. He was against *kaingin*. (Kaingin is a technique of clearing land *by slashing and burning underbrush and trees and plowing the ashes under for fertilizer, which has been enormously destructive of valuable timber*— A. L. Kroeber).

Cecille noted, "*basta palatanom gid siya*", that it seemed to her Tatay Pidio spent most of his life always planting something.

"Oh Tatay Pidio is like a manager gid daw. *Siling ni Papa Doc, bag-o daw sila matulog sa gab-i, may* instructions *na daw sang task bawat isa pagka-aga obrahon. Very disciplinarian gid kag dapat mamati ka gid, wala dapat magsabat habang gahambal siya, or akig siya. Natuto gid daw sila sang batas militaria kay sa tingug pa lang ni Tatay Pidio, ga sala-sala na sila. Maski ano lang dakpon nila nga obra, basta naga obra ka gid. Naabtan ko pa ini nga set up kay mga twenty-five years old na ako when Tatay Pidio died. Ang tingug ni Tatay Pidio was booming and powerful pero wala siya nagapanakit. Basta daku gid respito sing mga bata niya. Kung magpaharab o pakaon ka sing carabao dapat busog gid. Kung makita niya nga gutom pa ang carabao, pabalikon ka gid niya paharab carabao maski gab-i na kag dulom na.*"

(According to Papa Doc, before they went to bed at night, their father would instruct each kid with a specific task they had to perform in the morning. He was such a disciplinarian who commanded attention, everyone had to listen and not interrupt while he was speaking, or he'd get upset. They learned the military style of discipline; just the sound of his voice made the kids scramble. They would grab whatever task needed to be done as long as they were working. I had observed these incidents because I was twenty-five years old when Tatay Pidio died. Tatay Pidio's voice boomed and was powerful, but he was not physically abusive. His kids respected him well, and they performed their tasks without complaint. He was a taskmaster who taught his kids by example. He was strict. For instance, when you took the carabao to pasture, you must make sure the carabao was sated. If he noticed that the carabao was still hungry, he'd tell you to go back to the field even when it was late at night and dark).

Narrator: Brother Willy achieved in life through education. What do you think inspired him?

Cecille: "*Sa pag kabalo ni Papa Doc* Tatay Pidio was very supportive in T'yoy Willy's *handom mag eskwela kay sad to say ang Tatay nila hindi marunong magbasa at magsulat kay wala siya kaeskwela. Si Nanay Mayang kaescuela hasta grade 2 lang. Pero damo gid si Tatay Pidio pangarap sa buhay amo na nga pirti gid siya kapisan kag paningkamot gid siya kay gusto niya mag asenso man* pangabuhi *sang pamilya kahit papano*".

(Papa Doc knew that their father was supportive of T'yoy Willy's desire for education. Sad to say, Tatay Pidio did not know how to read or write because he never went to school. Nanay Mayang finished second grade. But Tatay Pidio dreamt big. He worked very hard and exerted great effort to improve the family's lot no matter what).

* * * * *

Brother Willy wrote in his journal: "My father is from Negros Occidental. A farmer by heart who loved animals, he planted trees, fruits, bananas, and coconuts for his children's future and for them to enjoy. His ultimate dream is to own a piece of land in Mindanao".

Mindanao aptly called the Land of Promise is the second-largest island in the Philippines, an archipelago in the South Pacific, comprised of 7,641 islands, the biggest of which are Luzon (in the north), and Visayas (a group of islands in the center), and Mindanao in the south. The country was a colony of the United States, part of the spoils from the Spanish-American War. After the Americans led by Commodore George Dewey defeated the Spanish Armada on May 1, 1898, at the Battle of Manila Bay, Spain ceded the Philippines to the United States of America.

The Philippines, as a U.S. territory, was under the United States system of government from 1898 to 1946. Within this time frame of forty-eight years, the U.S. embarked on a nation-building program successfully. As a result, the United States bequeathed to the island nation a democratic system of government, the Legislative, Executive, and Judicial. The first is comprised of Congress that makes the laws, the second President, Vice President, Cabinet that carries them out, and the third the Supreme Court and other courts that evaluate them.

The Governor was the highest official of the Philippines until the territory gained its Independence on July 4, 1946, when a President was installed. In 1902, the United States established a system of universal Public schools in the Philippines. The Filipinos consider this as the best legacy of the United States. English became the medium of instruction at these schools contributing to the country's literacy rate of 98.18%. (This is based on the adult literacy rate among Filipinos fifteen years of age and above as of 2020).[7] The Mindanao frontier was opened to migrants and Corporations through the Public Land Act of 1903, which introduced the homestead system and provided rules for sale and lease of titles for these lands. "Any citizen of the Philippine Islands, or of the United States, or of any Insular possession thereof, over the age of twenty-one years or the head of a family may...enter a homestead of not exceeding sixteen hectares of unoccupied, unreserved, unappropriated agricultural public land in the Philippine Islands".[8]

In the late 1930s, the National Land Settlement Administration (NLSA) was created as part of the Philippine Commonwealth legacy under the country's first Filipino President, Manuel L. Quezon. This socio-economic program was designed to stem the rising discontent of landless people and address the diminishing food supply in the northern part of the Philippines ravaged by WWII and drought. The NLSA created the Monkayo-Compostela Project in Davao Province and the agriculturally rich Koronadal-Allah Valley Project in Cotabato Province in the southern island of Mindanao. The Projects encouraged the adventurous Filipinos from Luzon and Visayas to become settlers in Mindanao. As a result, families migrated to the land of promise in droves. The exodus started in 1939, and waves upon waves, the settlers came in the 1940s and 1950s including Brother Willy's family. The migration did not stop in the 1950s however; it is still on although without government subsidy.

The Manager of the NLSA Lagao Settlement was Major General Paulino Torres Santos, Sr; a retiree of the Armed Forces of the Philippines handpicked by President Manuel L. Quezon. As a young officer, Major Santos served as the former Chief of Staff of General Douglas McArthur, whose famous promise "I Shall Return" still reverberates through generations of Filipinos. The first batch of NLSA settlers of sixty-two men and their family arrived on Sarangani Bay on February 27, 1939, led by General Santos. They joined many families who populated the southern parts at the turn of the century. However, the steady stream of settlers ultimately displaced the indigenous peoples like the Blaans and the T'boli from their ancestral land. It forced them to relocate to the undesirable and less arable patch on the mountainside.

It is important to note here, dear readers, that young Willy grew up to become the Founder and the Chairman of the Board of the General Paulino Santos Museum (GPS). This was his idea that he brought to life in 1990s long before his extensive international travels. The museum is currently housed at the Notre Dame of Dadiangas University, located in General Santos City, and named after its founder. The GPS Museum is slated to be transferred to and occupy a City Museum to be completed soon. The museum at NDDU is only one of Brother Willy's many diverse initiatives.

* * * * *

1959 was the year that Elpidio realized his fondest dream. He took his family to the Promised Land of Mindanao in January of that year. He packed his worldly goods and sold what he couldn't transport to pay for the family's fare. Then, with his wife and nine children, they boarded a Compania Maritima F.S. inter-island vessel. According to Rodolfo, it was a small vessel, took three days to reach their destination. There was no wharf so they climbed down a twenty-foot rope ladder hanging on the side of the boat onto the waiting *banca* (dug out canoe with outriggers) that took them to the shore. One can only imagine how they traveled on a cargo boat for days from Negros Occidental to the shores of Sarangani Bay located in the province of Cotabato.

It was young Willy's first glimpse of the wide world that was waiting for him to explore. He turned six years three months old before their journey. Elpidio was fifty, his wife Maria Paz was forty-three, and the eight other children ranged from barely one-year-old to twenty-six. Jardelito (the oldest boy) decided to stay in Negros Occidental. He was already employed at Victorias Sugar Company. After Jardelito got married, he raised his family in Victorias, where he remained. The youngest Lubrico child, Rodito, was born in Mindanao on July 15, 1959, six months after the family's arrival.

Like many settlers, Elpidio settled on a farm owned by a relative who had ventured to the southern parts. Five years earlier, his brother-in-law Melecio Engane and the brother of Maria Paz arrived in Surallah. He and his family settled at Sitio Sawmill, Barangay Naci, in 1954.[9] Most of the settlers in South Cotabato originated from the northern islands of Luzon and Visayas. These provinces were densely populated and plagued with agrarian problems, as was Negros Occidental, from where Melecio came.

As a favor to his only sister Maria Paz, Melecio apportioned eight hectares of his wooded land to the Lubrico family. According to Rodolfo Lubrico, Tatay Pidio pre-paid the down payment for the farm by sending Melecio a carabao from Negros Occidental through the cargo ships that plied the ocean during that time. Elpidio gave Melecio a carabao as a down payment and continued to pay by installments until the land was paid off.

Cecille Lubrico Longanilla wrote, *"Siling ni Papa Doc hindi gid daw totally na ginhatag ang lupa sa ila ni Tatay Melecio kay ginkambyohan gali sang carabao ni Tatay Pedio kay halin sa Negros Occidental ginpadal-an cila sing isa ka carabao ni Tatay Pidio. Pag-abot sing pamilya ni Tatay Pidio diri sa Surallah gihatagan dayon cila sing lupa bale 8 hectaria. Ginlinis pa nila sing tudo-tudo kay kakahoyan pa kag dalagku kag pirti gid daw kasi-ot as in virgin forest pa daw."*

(According to Papa Doc, his uncle Melecio did not give the land outright to the Lubricos. It was a part of a barter deal. Tatay Pedio sent his brother-in-law a carabao from Negros Occidental. When the Lubrico family arrived Tatay Melecio gave them eight hectares of land in exchange. It was virgin forest with huge trees. The family had to work very, very hard to clear the dense underbrush).

In time, the farm (approximately 17.6 acres) served as the stepping-stone to a better life for the Lubrico family of twelve. Elpidio and his boys built their first home and farmed the land as the family's primary source of income.

Clearing a patch from the thick forest of overgrown trees to plant sustenance crops of rice and corn was laborious and slow. The older children helped Elpidio in the family enterprise.

Cecille continued, *"May daku pa ini nga sapa (Sapali name of river) kag baras ang lupa nga kon mag kusog ang ulan ang ila lupa nagakatiphag kag gina ab-ab sang sapa hasta daw subong sigi lang tiphag kung mag ulan. Amo ina nga naghalin sila didto sa*

Sawmill Naci kag nangita naman diri si Tatay Pidio lupa sa Little Baguio later on. Pero dugay man ila estar sa Sawmill Naci."

(There is a river that runs along the farm. It looks like a lake called Sapali River. Part of the eight hectares farm is sandy. The rain causes erosion and the river reclaims the land; a natural phenomenon that goes on to this day. That's the main reason why Tatay Pidio was forced to find another piece of land in Little Baguio later on. But, the family lived in Sawmill Naci for many years).

They built a house near the Sapali River; it was made of wood and thatched roof using the felled trees. The area was virgin land and quite remote, but it was ideal for raising a large family. The river served as a water reservoir where abundant aquatic food supplies and edible vegetation covered the riverbank. Maria Paz was fond of fishing with her children with young Willy in tow, using bamboo poles and strings. She gathered *igi* (snails) for their meals. Soon Elpidio and his sons built fishponds and stocked them with fish.

Willy's niece, Cecille noted, *"Dira si T'yoy Willy nagapamunit sing tilapia, pantat, kag paitan."*

(That's where Uncle Willy went fishing for tilapia, catfish, and spotted Philippine barb).

The family added a vegetable and flower garden in the clearing and surrounded it with fruit trees. Then, the pigs and chickens began to roam the yard. In less than two years, Elpidio Lubrico and his family were well on their way to self-sufficiency, earning a modest income from farming through hard work and persistence.

* * * * *

The children attended Naci Elementary School, including young Willy. They walked every day to school for about three kilometers (1.6 miles) and crossed the shallow and lazy Sapali River, barefoot most of the time. When the rains came, it flooded. The kids would get drenched. Rodolfo narrated that he and the other siblings would go home when they got wet, appreciating a valid excuse not to return to school. But young Willy never wanted to miss a day in school. He stayed in class in his wet or damp clothing.

All the boys were expected to work on the farm, especially during planting and harvest seasons. Rodolfo recalled during our video interview, a smile lighting up his face from a childhood fondly remembered.

"Ahay kami iya gaobra sa farm, pero si Willy kag si Jaime naga sibat gid pirmi. Habang ga tanom kami sing mais o palay, didto sila sa escuelahan." (While we planted rice and corn, Willy and Jaime would always escape from the farm to attend school).

Young Willy preferred to help his mother plant flowers, wash dishes, clean the house, and fetch water for the family supply from the river nearby. So he and his siblings created a shallow well a few yards from the river's edge utilizing the sand for the filtering system. It did not remove the invisible contaminants, but the water was clear enough for their drinkable water supply.

According to Rodolfo, young Willy did not participate much in their childhood games. "He was always happy just reading and writing!" Willy once admitted to this narrator that he was not fond of farm work as a young boy. He was glad that being the ninth child in the family of eleven, his older Brothers and sisters did most of the heavy lifting at the farm. But once in a while, Willy was tasked to take the *carabao* (water buffalo) to pasture. Wearing a pair of shorts, he rode astride on top of the *carabao*'s back. He recalled how the rough and wiry carabao hairs scratched ugly red rashes all over his thigh, how they itched!

To ward off the boredom from the drudgery of watching the beast of burden as it grazed until sated, young Willy would imagine a future away from the farm of magical places he read in books. According to Rodolfo, he would read any material he could get his hands on, Reader's Digest in particular. Young Willy was fascinated with the country's national hero Jose Rizal who started reading when he was four and traveled abroad to study. Young Willy's childhood was filled with farm scenes where the future stretched out unchanging. A favorite teacher told Willy that one of the best ways to leave the confines of the farm is through education. Young Willy took that lesson to heart.

* * * * *

There is a mural on the wall of the children's library at the Notre Dame of Marbel University IBED campus. It is a beautiful idyllic pastoral scene of "any farm Philippines" at a glance. A *Bahay Kubo* sits on a hillside, surrounded by verdant trees, rice fields, and above it blue skies and a touch of rainbow. There are fishponds, farm animals that roam freely, pet cats and dogs, and a sunflower blooming in the garden. There is an image of two boys by a table, one is reading, and the other is writing. There is also an image of a boy in a blue shirt. The latter is so incongruous and out of place, a boy sitting on a fallen tree trunk reading while the rest of the children are playing or fishing.

Perhaps Brother Willy would have told me, had I asked him about the story behind the mural. But I didn't. When he died, I was intrigued. I scoured through my emails, texts, and Facebook Messenger chats to unravel the mystery behind the image of the boy in blue shirt.

In his text dated March 20, 2018, Brother Willy wrote:

Thanks to your son Lee and wife Heather for the donation to build the NDMU children's library. I received the funds through Brother Bob [McGovern]. I found an existing room to re-purpose. Ideal gid. I will design the library myself. I plan to have someone paint a mural on the wall, build age-appropriate and colorful shelves, and buy a TV and computer.

On January 10, 2019, he posted on his Facebook news feed, photos of the project while the Children's Library was still a work in progress. He prioritized the library so it was ready for the reunion of the NDMU Alumni Association International hosted by the university that was held ten days later. The conversation thread on his Facebook news feed read:

I commented, "The mural looks great! I love the way you incorporated the games we children used to play. Many of us didn't have books at home then so we passed the time outdoors. When we were not planting rice, weeding rows of corn, fetching water, gathering firewood, taking the carabaos to pasture, etc. we entertained ourselves playing hide and seek, *bagoongay, shatum, bakyaan*, and hopscotch...By the way, my classmates and friends who attended the blessing of the library agreed this is the best children's library they have seen. And you said you are not done yet."

"I conceptualize the mural to teach the children," Brother Willy explained. "See the rainbow? I told the painters what animals to include and to add the bahay kubo. There are flowers and vegetable garden knowing your interest. If the kids are bored they can read or play Pinoy games."

Looking at the mural more closely while writing this book, reminded me of my interview with his brother Rodolfo. It dawned on me that the similarity between the mural and Rodolfo's description of the Lubrico farm in Naci, Surallah, is so spot on to dismiss it as coincidental. Rodolfo also said that young Willy did not participate much in their childhood games. "He was always reading and writing."

As his secretary Dalia Mesias confirmed, Brother Willy commissioned the artist Andy Francisco and his assistant Ranel Rikabar to produce the mural. Every time I look at the picture, my eyes are riveted toward the little boy in the blue shirt sitting on the felled tree trunk.

Did Willy the President immortalize the young Willy of Naci in the mural? The boy in the blue shirt looks to me like a "self-portrait" of the boy growing up at his childhood farm.

But so classic Willy, he did it quietly and in the subtlest way.

Mural by Andy Francisco and Ranel Rikabar at the Alvin and Prima Guipo Hower Children's Library NDMU IBED Campus. Photo by Allan Sumadic.

Naci Elementary School Grade III, 1963-1964
Brother Willy is the smiling boy seated closest to the first girl in middle front row.
Miss T. Pama, Teacher In Charge. Photo by Hernando Celino.

From Naci to Little Baguio 2

"...when you come home, I'd like you to meet my mother. She lives in Little Baguio...it is one of my favorite places on earth."

~Brother Willy's email sent to narrator August 1, 2010~

In the mid-1960s, Elpidio bought eight hectares of farmland in Little Baguio. This place derived its name from the summer capital of the Philippines, Baguio City. Located in the Cordillera Mountain range in Luzon, Baguio City is 5200 feet above sea level, making it a magnet to tourists for its constant cool weather. In January 18, 1961, the lowest temperature was recorded at 43 degrees Fahrenheit and snow flurries fell out of the tropical skies.[10]

The town of Little Baguio in Surallah was so named for its topographical resemblance to Baguio City, its geographical location, and temperate climate. The Calang River runs close to the Lubrico property providing an instant water supply. Currently, many farmers in Little Baguio have constructed rice terraces to mimic its namesake in Luzon.

The Lubrico children and grandchildren frequented the nearby little falls to wash clothes with Willy's mother, Maria Paz. They swam, frolicked, and picnicked by the river. They loaded their soiled clothes on a *karusa* (farm sled made of bamboo) pulled by a *carabao*.

Cecille wrote, *"Gadala kami inasal nga manok kag didto ilagpang tapos kami maglaba."*

(We'd bring chicken roasted on an open fire, shredded, and turned into the soup after we washed our clothes).

The Lubricos retained the original farm in Naci, where the family had lived for eight years. Romeo, the son, took over with his wife Riolita, raising his eight children on this farm. When he died, his son Anecito inherited the house. He currently lives there with his wife Juliet where they raised their six children.[11]

By the time the Lubrico family moved to Little Baguio around 1966, young Willy had finished elementary school and was ready for high school. Fortunately for young Willy, Notre Dame of Surala High School opened in June 1967.[12] Unfortunately, the high school was approximately 10 kilometers (6 miles) distant from young Willy's house in Little Baguio.

Leonisa, the oldest child was married to Cefereno Samonte by this time. Their house was located adjacent to Notre Dame of Surala high school. Young Willy stayed with Leonisa during school days and went home to Little Baguio on Saturdays and Sundays although not too often.

Rodolfo described, *"Ginalakat lang namon from Little Baguio to Colongulo. Tapos tabok sa Allah River kag kung maswertihan masakay sa weapons carrier truck. Pero pirti ka iwat ang salakyan dapat bal-an mo ang schedule kung indi kaabot malakat ka gid paSurallah."*

(We used to walk from Little Baguio to Colongulo. Then we would have to cross the Allah River on foot. Sometimes we get lucky we rode on a weapons carrier truck. But you have to know its schedule and if you miss this only means of transport, you have to walk to Surallah.)

When young Willy wanted to go home to Little Baguio, he'd make it home in four hours one way by walking briskly. In 1967, the dirt roads undulated over the rolling hills and when one was lucky to catch the one and only public transport, it took more than one hour to travel the ten kilometers. The dirt road also traverses the capricious Allah River. Young Willy had to cross the river without the benefit of a bridge because the river changes its course constantly. Today, there is a concrete bridge and the two-lane cement road is being paved into a four-lane highway. Today, it only takes fifteen minutes by jeepney or other motorized means of transportation from Little Baguio to Surallah.

"Sa bahay namin sa Purok 3, Surallah nakatira si T'yoy Willy," Pia Samonte Baysa, daughter of Leonisa texted. *"Sabi ng mama ko si T'yoy Willy daw 4 a.m. gising na tapos magsaing. Tapos magbasa gamit yong lampara. Sabi ng Ate Emelda ko, palagi daw pagalitan*

ng mama ko si T'yoy kasi pagdating galing sa school, libro agad buksan nya. At saka magsabi daw mama ko 'nagwali na naman ang pari' kasi lakas daw magbasa si T'yoy Willy. Si T'yoy Jimmy nakatira din sa amin pero sa Allah Valley High School *siya habang si T'yoy sa Notre Dame of Surala. Si T'yoy Rodito nakatira din sa amin para makapag aral siya."*

(Brother Willy stayed at our house in Purok 3, Surallah. My mother told me that T'yoy Willy would wake up at four in the morning to cook rice. Then he'd read using a kerosene lamp. My older sister Emelda remembers how our mother would scold T'yoy Willy because the first thing he did when he got home from school was to open his book and read. My mother said, he sounded like a priest giving a homily when he read aloud! My uncle Jimmy also stayed with us but he attended Allah Valley High School while T'yoy went to Notre Dame of Surala. Later, the youngest uncle Rodito also stayed at our house so he could go to school in town.)

Brother Willy has traveled to all continents except Antarctica through his leadership roles in the international organizations, Marist related affiliations, and Notre Dame Alumni Affairs. His secretary Dalia Mesias collated his official travel schedule, which she provided to this narrator. (Appendix C - Travel Log). A real people-person with astounding number of alumni connections and relatives all over the world, he accepted offers to visit them along the way, as his schedule would allow. Hosts not only pay for his side trips and accommodations, but also happily turn themselves into his tour guides. He appreciated all these exotic places. But as John Howard Payne declared in his poem, "Mid pleasure and palaces though we may roam, Be it ever so humble there's no place like home!" So it was for Brother Willy as his email could attest:

"August 1, 2010. Happy Birthday to you tomorrow...my mother will turn ninety-four this coming December 25. She could still converse but could not walk by herself, always talking of loneliness. She needs more attention and wants her children always by her side. *Umuuwi ako* every Sunday to visit her. It's the reality of getting old. Soon we will be there too. When you come home, I'd like for you to meet my Mother. She lives in Little Baguio...it is one of my favorite places on earth."

Through the years, Brother Willy and I had made many plans for me to visit Little Baguio. "Santa Cruz Mission is not too far, I can take you there," he'd say.

It never happened. I never met his mother either but he took my siblings Nena, Susan, Josie, and Tito to the Lubrico house in Little Baguio to meet her. He sent texts in real time while they were there eating Filipino fruits *durian, lanzones, rambutan.* Little Baguio, his favorite place on earth is also not too distant from the ancestral land of the indigenous people, the T'boli. I know and understand too well why he loves Little Baguio. Only thirty minutes away, is Lake Sebu where I had taught and lived for two years in the 1970s. Like him, I have a soft spot in my heart for the place and the indigenous people who live there. My husband, Alvin J. Hower, and I worked at the Santa Cruz Mission. We fell in love and got married there.

Our mutual friend Lulut Palacios Chan, current president of our Notre Dame Alumni association based in the U.S.A., narrated that in 2018 she was at the Marist Convento at NDMU when Brother Willy asked, "Have you ever been to Lake Sebu? I can take you there, so you can see where Prima used to live and work."

Lulut was elated; Lake Sebu was one place she's never been. She recalled Brother Willy playing the tour guide as he drove through the rolling hills and country roads to Santa Cruz Mission. He talked about growing up in Little Baguio and how he was exposed to the T'boli culture. It must have fascinated him so and left an indelible mark on his psyche. In 2011, he created an initiative called Abante Lumad Scholarship to support college education for poor and deserving indigenous students of South Cotabato.

Fast forward: 2021. Lulut is spearheading the publication and marketing of this book supported by the Alumni Association officers and board members. When they received the proposal to donate all the proceeds from this book to Brother Willy's scholarship initiative, the association readily approved the project. (Supporters of this book are listed in the Acknowledgment at the back of the book).

Advocating for the poor and the underserved like the Indigenous People of South Cotabato is one thing that Brother Willy did so well.

The Lubrico Ancestral Home in Naci, Surallah. The top floor is the original structure.
The enclosed ground floor was added on. The house is surrounded with fruit trees Tatay Pidio planted that now benefit the children and grandchildren. Photos by Pia Samonte Baysa.

The Sapali River adjacent to the Lubrico's home where young Willy swam, fished, and fetched water for family supply. Through the years, it changed its course and has now claimed six hectares of the original eight. It swept most of the arable Lubrico farm including the rice fields and the coconut trees that Tatay Pidio planted.

Brother Willy's favorite place on earth, Little Baguio, Surallah, Philippines
Photo adapted from oil painting from the cover of the book
with permission from artist, Bueno Silva.

The Lubrico Home in Little Baguio, Surallah.

Later in life, Nanay Mayang and Tatay Pidio were able to go home to Negros Occidental for a vacation. Top: Nanay Mayang posed in front of her son Jaime's house in Bacolod. Below: The Lubrico couple inside Jaime's house with Toto Mark Lubrico (eldest son of Jaime) and Karl Marcellin (son of Rodito) whom the couple took along with them from Mindanao.

An endearing picture of Brother Willy
wearing a rare smile sitting on top of his world.

The Boy Called Bargas 3

"...a plow made of steel, a symbol for durability."

~ Estrella T. Golingay~

"Can you tell me more about Bargas?" this narrator asked Rodolfo during our video interview on Messenger©. Rodolfo paused, smiled, and closed his eyes. He was seemingly lost in his secret memory bank as he recalled a cherished childhood moment with his brother young Willy.

When he came out of his reverie, Rodolfo said with a chuckle, *"Ambot ah kung diin ni Tatay Pidio ginpanguha ang iya mga nicknames sa amon. Basi iban halin pa sa mga Hapon."*

(I don't know where my father got our nicknames, perhaps some of them from the Japanese soldiers).

He enumerated said nicknames, "Tinga, Alo, Mat-an, Deding, DocDoc for me, etc., and ah yes, Bargas."

Allow me to continue young Willy's story in the words of Estrella Tano Golingay.[13] This is based on her interview with Teresa Lubrico Golveo, sister of Brother Willy. Estrella wove her own experiences in the story. Brother Willy is a childhood friend of Estrella, a high school classmate, and a colleague at the university.

Teresa, or "Manang Deding", is a widow. Her house (one hour's drive from the university) became the second "home" to Brother Willy. It was the venue for this interview. Teresa's daughter Annie Golveo Golingay (who now resides in Toronto, Canada), emailed me. "We built an additional room at my mother's house for T'yoy Willy in preparation for his retirement and sabbatical." Estrella began:

I went to Barangay Libertad, Surallah, to hold a formal interview about Brother Willy. It turned out to be a lively conversation in the middle of a beautiful garden on the street named Narra (Philippine mahogany) with Manang Deding (Willy's elder sister) and two other friends Cecilia Biare and Cecilia P. Belaza.

Deding fondly recalls that Willy was dotingly called Bargas when he was a small boy. Deding couldn't precisely tell why or how he got that name, knowing that the word has some negative connotation in some places. In the Lubrico family, everyone has a moniker, as in all Ilonggo families, where a nickname is a term of endearment. I learned from my husband that Bargas in parts of the Visayas where he came from refers to a plow made of steel, a symbol for durability. [After further researches, the narrator uncovered that Bargas might have been coined after the brand of plow called Vargas, a common agricultural implement in the Philippines during that time. But since there is no V in the Pilipino alphabet, it evolved to Bargas].

Bargas was the ninth child to come to the family on October 28, 1952, in E.B. Magalona Street, Alicante, Saravia in Negros Occidental. His parents were Elpidio Sorteya Lubrico and Maria Paz Amparo Galvan Engane. It was a big family, as was the case during the baby boom postwar era, with eleven siblings here presented according to biological order: Leonisa L. Samonte, Jardelito, Romeo, Salvacion L. Demetillo, Teresita L. Enfanta, Teresa L. Golveo (Manang Deding-my storyteller), Rodolfo (narrator's storyteller), Jaime, Wilfredo, Benedicto, and Rodito.

Years later, after WWII, drought came. It made life most challenging in the Visayas and other parts of the country. Then young Willy's parents heard of the Promised Land that was Mindanao. In 1959 the Lubricos ventured to Mindanao, tracing the route of a relative [Melecio Engane] in Barrio 12, also called Naci, Surallah in South Cotabato. It was still a forested area. The pioneer residents like Melecio [who arrived between 1939 to the 1950s] got their land free through the government. Elpidio opted to build a thatched house with wooden walls using the many felled trees in the forest by the bank of the Sapali River.

Bargas grew up loving the water; a much welcome respite from the arid lands everywhere. The terrain was rough which, meant anything that had to do with all kinds of undertakings, his education included. They lived pretty far from the barrio center. The procurement of necessities was challenging because when it rained, the road was almost impassable on foot. However, poverty did not hinder young Willy from dreaming of things beyond the trees and the vast tracts of empty lands.

Bargas loved Manang Deding's cooking. Most of the time, they'd thrive with what the forest or the meadows and the river could offer, for there was aplenty: *gabi or abalong* (a kind of taro plant), and other root crops, *pako* (edible ferns), *tambo* (young bamboo shoots), *igi or kuol* (snails) even fishes. The family cooked many dishes with coconut milk. But the ultimate food he loved, Nang Deding proudly recalls, was Misua soup with *tinapa* (canned sardines) and *patola* (luffa). Nang Deding loved to cook this dish, especially on rainy days. During that time in Mindanao, a much-liked canned good was sardines that were hard to come by on the farms. So house hosts would humbly and regretfully offer guests native chicken *tinola* instead. Reasoning that they haven't bought sardines (*tinapa* or salmon in native terminology) from the town to the delight of the guests, of course.

He was barely seven when he enrolled and was accepted as a visitor in Grade 1 at Naci Elementary School, but visitors had no seat. Despite that, he would attend school sitting on the floor. During writing time, he'd lie prone on the floor so he could write - something he was adept with during study time at night. Hernando "Nanding" Celino, a classmate and friend from elementary to high school, related to me that young Willy's family lived three kilometers away from school. They had to walk that far morning and afternoon, rain or shine. When it rained, the Sapali River overflowed. The path became muddy, making it difficult to walk through.

Nevertheless, young Willy endured it all and remained steadfast and strong.

This staunch character would account so much for the dreamer and the doer in him, definitely, a harbinger of the remarkable journey he would take in the future and what was to become of him. As a young boy, he was taller than most. So he had to be at the end of the line consistently. During recess time, they would play *bagoongay* and *lantay-lantay*, where he was a very effective guard because of his height. His voice boomed, as he'd shout "Out" when an opponent stepped offline. He had a lot of friends, though. But because of his love for feminine company and mannerisms, his classmates frequently teased him. He'd run after them in mock anger. But after elementary, he changed a lot into a morose, soft-spoken, but responsible adolescent in high school days.

We were members of a high school clique from first to the second year at Notre Dame of Surala. In the first year, the boys were separated from the girls staying in different buildings. But during free time, we'd exchange notes and memorize "Clay of Youth" by Jorge Bocobo, one of his favorite poems. Our class checked young Willy's class papers during exams, and they did ours having the same teachers. He'd come bringing the news of who topped the exams or who didn't make it. And mind you, he also played along with the times when forced to do so. He would whisper exam questions or assignments they have taken ahead with matching side-glances and whispers.

In the second year, the school combined our two classes. Young Willy was the unassuming guy at the third row near the wall on the boys' side, not too eager to recite, not wanting to join the fray. But when called upon for an answer, he was always ready and on point. This trait quickly landed him on the honor list. Perhaps by our love for adventure, our group became closer in our second year: Bargas, Rene, Mely, Rosie, and I. On weekends, we'd romp in the farms where he was the fruit tree climber. He was good at that, especially when no one else could reach the bunch of ripe *santol* or star apples at the farthest or highest end of the branch. We were the group of noisy cheerers goading him on. And always, that famous line, "*Hoy! Binli nyo ko*!" (Hey, save me some!). The last tree he climbed was a huge *santol* tree along the highway in Liwanay, Banga. I looked for it once. Unfortunately, the tree was not there anymore.

However, because of the financial difficulty of the times, when Bargas was ready for high school, he had to give way to his elder brother Jaime. [Nicknamed Mat-an, he attended Allah Valley High School, as there was no other high school in Surallah at that time per interview by his nephew Macky.] Quitting school was one bad experience for Willy. But a father's word is the law of the family, so he had to stop and bide his time. But it was probably the Holy Spirit reaching out to him at this stage. He was invited for search-ins and was recruited by our school director, Fr. Raymond Pulvino, C.P., to join the religious congregation [Marist Brothers]. Some of our male classmates went with him too. Nanding Celino, a classmate of young Willy and a former Diocesan priest novice, related to me that one way to get a college education when the family couldn't afford to pay was to join a religious group in those days. However, Nang Deding couldn't tell how and why Willy joined the Marist Congregation. She wished she did.

In December 2020, before he left for Manila for medical treatment, Bargas asked his sister Deding to cook his favorite dish of Misua and tinapa again. She obliged, unknowing it would be his last request.

* * * * *

Brother Willy shared memorable moments with his High School Class 1971 at Notre Dame of Lagao and Notre Dame of Surala. I connected with a few of them on Facebook. Brother Willy displayed seemingly no end to his versatility based on the stories that I had gathered.

He graduated with honors in elementary, his brother Jaime Lubrico shared. He was ranked third in his freshman and sophomore classes, exhibiting an intellectual promise at a young age. His brother

Rodolfo remembers him being such a bookworm and did not show much interest in participatory sports with his siblings or the kids in the neighborhood. However, his friend Saturnino Bayona revealed a different side when he was a teenager. Young Willy could hold his own in the rough and tumble of the playground for teens.

"I tell you he was very good at basketball and volleyball. *Pag siya may hawak ng bola*, be sure one-meter away ka. Otherwise, you'll fall victim to a jab of his elbow. But he was so refined too, like he was afraid to make a mistake."

Nanding Celino added that young Willy had zero tolerance for *daya* (cheating) and always played by the rules. Nanding witnessed a lot of heated debates in the playground when the young Willy turned into the rule enforcer.

He also taught "good manners and right conduct" according to Pia Lubrico Samonte, his niece who wrote, *"Stikto yon si T'yoy Willy kasi pag kumain bawal yong kamay at siko mo sa mesa tapos kailangan di maingay kumai*n."

(T'yoy Willy was strict. During meals your hands and elbow should be off the table and you must chew your food quietly).

Another friend Ely Rizaldo narrated that one of his nieces intimated that Brother Willy was like Emily Post who imparted lessons on etiquette at dinnertime. All the plates, silverware, glassware had to be properly arranged. Everything had to be just so, even something as mundane as setting the table. Illustrating his acute sense of attention to details.

He also told his niece and intimate friends that he believed he was the first Filipino Marist Brother to visit Russia.

Fourteen-year-old Young Willy, seated second from right, posed for this photo in 1968 at the Blessing of Notre Dame of Surala High School (NDSHS). NDS high school opened in June 1967; young Willy's group was the first freshman cohort admitted. The group performed a Philippine Folk Dance.

Seated L-R: Wilfredo Solinap, Alfonso Dimavivas, Alberto Hilado, Mr. Repique, Rene Reyes, Wilfredo Lubrico, Ernie Mallorca

Standing L-R: Merlyn Franco Miramon, Edna Dignadice Frugalidad, Roselyn Oquendo, Madoline Agudo de la Rosa, Ms. Salvacion Tano Pascua-teacher, Cecille Hisolana Pobre, Anȧ Mallo, Estrella Tano Golingay. Photo courtesy of Estrella Tano Golingay.

The Boy Called Bargas grew up to become the President of Notre Dame of Dadiangas College in 1995. NDDC BATCH 79 - Art and William at President's office. Photo from Brother Willy's Facebook Wall, 2018

The Signs of the Times 4

"Brother Willy's mother kneeled in front of the robbers, and begged them not to kill her and her husband. She was seventy, Elpidio was seventy-seven."

~ Cecille Lubrico Longanilla, niece of Brother Willy ~

Brother Willy fondly remembers his parents in his journal. He started writing about them while on lockdown during the pandemic. He planned to write more but sadly, he was not able to do so more than what appears in this book.

> My father liked his coffee and enjoyed his *tuba* (coconut wine) and *shoktong*.[14] Sometimes, he became talkative after a few drinks. He was a fan of *sabong* (cockfight). So he would invite one of his children to accompany him to the *sabungan* (cockfight arena).
>
> He adored my mother so much. He would not eat without my mother. My mother would prepare his clothing, underwear, and towel before his bath. My mother treated him like he was her baby. She would not leave the house for more than one day because my father would not go near the dining table without my mother. He always looked after my mother to ensure she had food on her plate. He would cook chicken setting aside mother's favorites – *atay* (liver), legs, and *ewing*.[15]
>
> He also added, "My sisters told me that I was my father's favorite son."

His nephews and nieces looked up to their uncle as their role model; Willy, too, had an excellent role model ~ his father. I wanted to understand better Brother Willy's claim, "My Father In Me". So I asked Rodolfo to describe their father in three words.

"*Stricto. Relihoso. Mapalangaon.*" Strict. Religious. Very Loving.

"Tatay Pidio was a disciplinarian, hard worker, responsible, friendly, and a giver", described Rodolfo's daughter Cecille. *"Na experience ko po ito kasi almost 25 years old na ako noong namatay si Lolo at age 90."*

(This is my first-hand experience with Lolo as I was almost 25 years old when he died).

"Nanay Mayang, on the other hand," Cecille continued, "was the nicest, simple, very industrious, thrifty grandmother who cared for us very much. Her house was always spotless. She was fond of *gulay* (vegetables), especially *kangkong* (water spinach). Nanay Mayang was happiest when she went fishing and gathered snails in the river close to their house. She took me to the *palengke* (open-air wet market). She'd order from the *carenderia* (eatery) her favorite *dinuguan*[16] over rice; Lolo was fond of *bangus*, (milkfish) cooked whatever way".

* * * * *

1986 was an unforgettable year for Willy and the Lubrico family. For context, I offer a brief timeline.

Willy was thirty-four years old and had ten years of teaching experience as a Marist Brother during this period. He became a loyal disciple of the man he so admired, Marcellin Champagnat, the founder of the Marist Congregation. He tried to model his life after Marcellin.

At this point in his life, Willy began to do a lot of soul-searching. First, he found teaching a noble profession. By all accounts, he left an indelible impact on his students. They not only remembered him but also would become his friends, ardent admirers, and faithful supporters fifty years later. But, Brother Willy felt wanting. He started questioning what more could he do for the underserved people. Most notably, the poverty-stricken young adults bereft of education in the slum section of the city where Willy lived. Moreover, he wondered if he could help alleviate the poor's sad plight and still work within the mission framework of the congregation he professed to serve.

After working as the Director of Student Affairs and Campus Ministry for five years in various Notre Dame Schools, he took a sabbatical in 1986. His curriculum vitae listed his first assignment as a "Parish Worker" at the Sto. Nino Parish Church located in Bula, General Santos City. He ministered to the poor young adults, uneducated and unemployed. (This phase of Brother Willy's life as a Marist Brother is discussed in depth in Chapter 9 – The Parish Worker).

When Brother Willy's thirty-fourth birthday rolled around; his parents celebrated twenty years living on the Lubrico farm in Little Baguio, where life was good for Elpidio and Maria Paz. About two kilometers from the center of the *sitio* (hamlet), they had built a traditional Filipino rural Bahay Kubo, anchored on concrete slabs, a spacious wooden house with a thatched roof. Their grandchildren could walk a short distance to visit them regularly and would always stay for sleepovers.

The Lubrico family loved living in Little Baguio. Its temperate weather, pastoral scenery, and life's unhurried pace suited the elderly Lubricos very well. Everybody seems to know everybody. Here, Tatay Pidio and Nanay Mayang found their comfort zone. However, the area was sparsely populated, not yet well developed, and the other farming neighbors were spread so far apart.

One night, an unfortunate incident shattered their idyllic lifestyle. It was a reflection of the tumultuous years in the Philippines between 1972 and 1986.

*****

Countless history books are replete with stories of the more than twenty years of martial law under then-President Ferdinand Marcos. His protracted authoritarian rule described as a dictatorship inflicted a toll on the way of life in the Philippines as the rich became richer and the poor barely made ends meet. The country was deep in debt—owing $24 billion by 1984.[17] The income of Filipinos during the Marcos years painted a bleak picture. The income was 22.60%

for the poorest 60% and 41.70% for the wealthiest 10% in 1979. The middle class shrunk.

Militant and violent revolutionary movements proliferated before and during the Marcos dictatorship, such as the communist CPP–NPA–NDF and the Moro National Liberation Front (MNLF). The economic and political instability combined to produce the worst recession in Philippine history in 1984 and 1985, with the economy contracting by 7.3% for two successive years. And then there were the opportunists of marauding bandits that terrorized the peaceful countryside where visible police presence was deemed unnecessary.

In this dire economic landscape, even the remote, seemingly safe from crime countryside was the scene of terror for Brother Willy's beloved parents.

As was their daily routine, Tatay Pidio, and Nanay Mayang rose early in the morning, ate their breakfast always with coffee. Then, before the sun beat down on them, they planted, weeded, hoed constantly. Finally, ate their lunch, and while others took a *siesta* (nap), Elpidio plowed the fields.

"Si Nanay Mayang never took *siesta,*" Cecille wrote. *"Nagapangumpay siya para pagkatapos ni Tatay Pidio arado may pagkaon ang carabao."*

(She gathered hay for the carabao, so when Elpidio finished plowing the field; there's food ready for the beast of burden).

Cecille never saw the couple being idle, even in their 80s, they were workaholic. *"Sa naobserve namon mga apo ang mga traits nakuha ni T'yoy Willy kay Tatay Pidio; very strong personality, very strict, mapisan gid kag ang trabaho kung kaya tapuson dayon, palasimba, prayerful, mapagbigay, thoughtful, at higit sa lahat mabinuligon gid".*

(I observed that Uncle Brother Willy inherited from his father these traits: powerful personality, very strict, industrious and if possible finish a task instantly, churchgoer, prayerful, generous, thoughtful and most especially, very helpful).

And while Nanay Mayang and Tatay Pidio slept after a tiring but very productive day, a group of ill-intentioned men was marching down the footpath bent to steal their financial security and peace of mind. Like an arrow, their destination aimed straight into the Lubrico's house, isolated from neighbors.

At sunset that particular day, the Lubrico couple ate their supper and prepared for a good night's sleep. Usually, the Lubrico grandchildren who lived but two kilometers away would stay with them overnight. But on this particular night, the two grandkids could not resist the television that the neighbors had just installed. So they stayed and watched the TV shows instead of going to their grandparent's house for a sleepover.

Cecille narrated, *"Kay manol pa kami sang una sang TV bisan black & white matiyaga kami maglantaw sa amon tupad balay."*

(The gadget called TV was so new to us then that we would watch with great fascination at our neighbor's house even in black and white).

After supper, the couple said their nightly prayers and went to bed.

The group of men arrived at their destination. Heavily armed, they crept ominously towards the Lubrico's farmhouse under cover of darkness. One could imagine them hiding in the bushes until they were sure that the occupants of the farmhouse were sound asleep. Before midnight, the group mounted the steps to the Lubrico home, and the armed men roused the elderly couple from deep sleep. Elpidio was known to keep a bolo by his side when he went to sleep during WWII to protect his family while the Japanese roamed the countryside. However, he was defenseless against their countrymen, crooks all, brandishing knives, bolos, and machine guns. The masked men wearing head coverings warned the couple to keep quiet.

Cecille narrated, *"Habang ginatutukan sila sing knife kag machine gun, nabatian ni Nanay Mayang nga naga hambal sing Blaan kag T'boli ang nagahigot sa ila. Layo gid ang neighbors kag laka gid ang panimalay sa farm. Kung masinggit sila, patyon gid daw sila. Sige lang daw sila pakitlooy sa mga Sipot Gang nga indi sila patyon".*

(While the robbers aimed their machine guns and held knives to their throats, Nanay Mayang heard them speak Blaan and T'boli while they were tying them up. The neighbors lived a few miles away, and during that time, the houses were sparse. If they screamed, the robbers threatened to kill them. So they begged for their lives).

Cecille Lubrico Longanilla explained, *"SIPOT GANG ang tawag sa ila kay gin sipot gid nila tanan nga gamit hasta kaldero, mga bayo, alkansiya ni Nanay kag gamay nga ipon, bugas, asin, duha kabilog baboy, mga manok nga wala ka lupad, sipot gid. Ang baboy kag manok gin katay nila sa yard para indi magahod."*

(They were referred to as SIPOT GANG. They take everything in sight. Pots and pans, clothing, piggybank of Lola with the bit of money she saved, rice, salt, two pigs, all their chicken that were unable to fly away. Then, to silence the pigs and chickens, they butchered them in the yard).

Brother Willy's mother and father kneeled before the bandits. Nanay Mayang begged them to spare their lives. She was seventy, Elpidio was seventy-seven.

After the SIPOT GANG left, the couple found their way back to their son's house in town, still fearing for their lives. They crawled on their hands and knees among the tall cogon grasses away from the footpath, avoiding being seen by the robbers. Their pace was excruciatingly slow. Finally, they arrived back at the town center at past two in the morning. They headed to the cluster of houses occupied by their children and grandchildren. They were in shock, their clothing tattered from the escape; shallow cuts and open wounds covered their arms, legs, and faces. Their fear was so intense it took them very long to calm down even after they reached the safety of their children's house.

"Indi gid nila malimtan ining tragedy hasta sila mapatay," Cecille continued. (They never forgot this tragedy until they died).

The police never apprehended the robbers, according to Cecille. They were wearing masks to cover their faces and caps over their heads. According to Nanay Mayang, they communicated in Blaan and T'boli, the dialects of the Indigenous People. This claim was not saying much to identify the robbers because most area residents learned to speak the same dialects in addition to their native tongue. Other neighbors in the community suspected they were members of the NPA (New People's Army, the communist party in the Philippines).[18] They used to terrorize the rural areas all over the country.

The tragic incident traumatized Nanay Mayang intensely. According to Cecille, Nanay Mayang's hatred for the Indigenous People never waned until she died. She never wavered in her belief that the robbers were Blaan and T'boli based on their conversations.

They were in close proximity as they tied the hands and feet of her husband and her own. Whether justified or not, Nanay Mayang held on to her belief. Brother Willy tried to persuade his mother that maybe the robbers know how to speak Blaan and T'boli and used it as a ruse to deceive them. No amount of explanation from Brother Willy could convince his mother to change her suspicions.

It would seem paradoxical that in 2011 while Nanay Mayang was still alive, her son Willy championed an initiative to create a scholarship fund for the Indigenous People (IP). But perhaps, it was to be expected that someone like Brother Willy, who keenly understood the correlation between poverty and crime, believed strongly that education can alleviate the ills of society and did something about it. The fund provides financial aid for IPs of South Cotabato to go to college. It is called Abante Lumad Scholarship (Onward Indigenous People Scholarship). All profits from the sale of his book will be donated to this scholarship fund. Brother Willy, blessed with a hefty dose of empathy, understood only too clearly the connection between a lack of education to poverty, hopelessness, desperation, and to some extent, committing a crime.

Today, surrounded by rice terraces, the Lubrico farm remains fertile. Elpidio and Maria Paz used the land wisely and sent their children to school through the income from their harvest. The children and grandchildren now continue the legacy of farming the land.

After the incident, the couple moved in with their youngest son, Rodito, and his family, and abandoned their home in the farm. The concrete slabs that served as weight-bearing support for the Lubrico's original house are all that are left of the life Elpidio and Maria Paz carved in Little Baguio. Still visible, the slabs outline a home that once was. A constant reminder to the grandchildren like Cecilia Lubrico Longanilla that this house once sheltered young Willy during his formative years. It nurtured not only his body and soul but also all his aspirations and dreams.

Tatay Pidio and Nanay Mayang, Bacolod City, 1995

Lubrico Family, undated photo
Standing: L-R: Salvacion, Rodolfo, Leonisa, Rodito, Jardelito, Teresa
Seated: Nanay Mayang and Tatay Pidio

Left: Rodito's house, where Tatay Pidio and Nanay Mayang moved after the robbery. They would live out the rest of their days here. It has become a favorite reunion venue for the Lubrico Family. Right: Rodito (Boy) and Judith nee Banson a teacher at their Little Baguio home. Photos on this page by Cecille Lubrico Longanilla.

Left: The Lubrico Siblings during their mini-reunion at Jardelito and Nilda Lubrico's house in Alicante, Negros Occidental. 2018, L-R: Rodolfo (Papa Doc), Jaime (Mat-an), Teresa (Deding), Jardelito (Alo), Teresita (Ate) Willy (Bargas)
Right: Benedicto (Tinga) and his wife Rosemarie, a public school teacher. Photo by Rosemarie Lubrico.

BRO. WILLY LUBRICO, FMS

(A Beacon of Light)

The Master Through the Apprentice's Eyes 5

"I will be forever grateful that we crossed paths in this lifetime."

~ Francis Rey "Macky" Lubrico ~

After the tragic robbery incident at the Lubrico Farm in Little Baguio, Elpidio and Maria Paz swore off living at the farm. All the Lubrico children have carved with relative success, their niche in the world by this time, the young Willy included. The youngest son, Rodito, married a schoolteacher, Judith Banson. When Rodito's first child was born, the Lubrico family decided to move Elpidio and Maria Paz in with the young couple. Rodito built an additional room in his house. He created a semblance of a farm around the house for his parents to keep them busy. Their new role as caregivers to the young couple's children gave Elpidio and Maria Paz a new sense of purpose, a new leash in life.

My dear readers, Macky Lubrico, will now continue the family saga. Macky is a nephew of Brother Willy currently working as a Product Manager in an Airline IT solutions provider in Manila, its headquarters based in the United States. Macky wrote:

> "I consider myself as a travel "junkie". This, I believe, is a way of understanding our purpose in the universe, exploring the depths of our potential, and reconnecting our family values to ourselves. I live the life I would never have imagined I could because of Brother Willy. Most importantly, because of his example, I have traveled the world – Peru, Singapore, Malaysia, Japan, Korea, USA, Vietnam, the Netherlands, Thailand, Cambodia, Hong Kong, Taiwan, and more to

come. Because of this, our conversation had expanded into our travel adventures. Listening to T'yoy Willy's travel experiences made me wonder about the world and increased my eagerness to explore it more.

I treasure the vivid memories of Tatay Pidio and Nanay Mayang, the parents of Brother Willy, the man I call T'yoy Bargas. Tatay and Nanay lived with us during their senior and final years. In short, we grew up with them. But, although they were our grandparents, we did not call them by the traditional Filipino endearment - Lolo and Lola. To us they were Tatay Pidio and Nanay Mayang.

A bit of a background – our father (Rodito "Boy" Lubrico) is the youngest of the Lubrico siblings. As our family tradition, the youngest has the privilege of having Tatay and Nanay live in his home located in Little Baguio, Surallah. Tatay and Nanay were so protective of my four siblings and me. They were so loving and caring to the point that our parents could not lay their hands on us. They were the ones who shielded us, or in their words, "*Ako nalang sakita, indi ang mga apo ko*!" (If you must mete out corporal punishment, wallop me instead but not my grandkids).

I couldn't forget these words. So every time I committed a mistake or a transgression, I let Tatay and Nanay know it first before telling my parents. And that's how you build an Army!

My whole elementary life, I always slept beside Tatay and Nanay. I am amazed by their stories of survival during WWII, how they provided for their eleven children, and their tale of migration from Negros to Mindanao. I would sit and listen while Nanay prepared a meal for me. Tatay called me Macario, and it just evolved into Macky. In contrast, Nanay called me Macan or Mat-an (named after my uncle Mat-an aka Jaime Lubrico due to our resemblance).

Tatay was a strong, hardworking, and a dedicated farmer even in his 80s. He always wanted to have something to do: gardening, planting fruits, or tending cattle. Whenever a tree he planted bears fruits, he made sure we were the first to taste them. My whole image of Tatay was a gentle giant (an Eddie Garcia,[19] look-alike) so loving, so caring, which is the exact opposite of the stories and experiences of my older cousins. To them, we were lucky not to experience the "Tatay Pidio" they knew in his prime years' - strict, authoritarian, and disciplinarian. A man you wouldn't want to cross when you break a rule. I guess Tatay Pidio mellowed a lot with age.

But we all agree that Tatay was the solid foundation of our family. He has built the foundation through hard work, perseverance, values he imparted to us, and love for the family. Unfortunately, Tatay Pidio passed away in the year 2000. I was in the final year of my elementary education.

On the other hand, Nanay Mayang was the queen – a queen bee, if you will. She was Tatay's kryptonite. I am fortunate enough that Nanay lived life in full until I graduated college. She witnessed my first year as a professional pursuing my career, and Nanay was my ultimate fan and supporter. I couldn't forget how she always told me *"Mat-an, mag eskwela ka gid. Indi ka bagay manguma! Ang mga tudlo mo daw tudlo sang manggaranon"*.

(Mat-an, stay in school. Farming does not become you. Your fingers are like the fingers of a rich man).

During my college year at Notre Dame of Dadiangas University (NDDU), I usually went home every two weeks to Little Baguio. This is where we lived. Or I would hitch a ride whenever Brother Willy would go home. [Brother Willy was the President of NDDU at this time].

Nanay was always on the balcony waiting for me and showered me with hugs and kisses. She would always have something for me to eat (she even set aside her food allowance from Brother Willy). So Nanay and I would sit and munch on food and catch up on how our weeks went. Then, of course, I lent my ears to hear her stories of war, survival, and her past life, over and over again.

Of all the great and some funny memories that I had with Nanay, one is a standout. There was this *rambutan* tree that Tatay planted that bore fruit. But, unfortunately, some of my cousins told me that they were not allowed to harvest. Nanay would tell them, "*Para ina kay Mat-an*!" (Those fruits are reserved for Mat-an!) Whenever I'm on study breaks or am home, I would always sleep beside Nanay - I am a Nanay's boy, and I am proud of it.

I have so many favorite stories about T'yoy Willy too. One of which is how valuable time is for him as it should be for everyone. During my college year at NDDU, he always asked me if I wanted to hitch a ride home. And my answer was always yes.

He texted me, "We are leaving at 7:30 AM" during this particular incident. On the day of our departure, I woke up late (around 7 AM). Although it would only take me five minutes to reach our designated meeting place, I haven't packed my things yet. So I immediately packed everything and ran to our meeting place. Not too far from my apartment, I could see him in his car waiting. With all my might, I ran towards him. To my surprise, the car moved.

To make a long story short, I took the bus home that day, frustrated and disappointed. When I reached home, T'yoy Willy was gardening right in front of the house and acted as if nothing had happened. I still greeted him, and he responded with a bit of a nod. I went straight to Nanay and cried like a baby. When things settled a few hours later, T'yoy Willy beckoned me to go to him. He told me, "Time might not be valuable to you, but to others, it is. Therefore, you should respect it".

He may be a man of "tough love", but he always had a soft spot, especially in education. He would give anything or everything for your education. For example, he would provide me with food (whatever he had) when I was in school. Every morning, more than getting my things out of my college locker room, I always look forward with excitement to see what food he had for me for the day. My friends would kid me, "Let's check your refrigerator, and see what's inside".

Brother Willy or T'yoy Bargas or T'yoy Willy to us named my four siblings and me. Our names were derived from the saints: Michael John, Francis Rey (me), Karl Marcellin, Maria Angela (named after Nanay), and Mark Joseph.

Because Tatay Pidio and Nanay Mayang lived with us, T'yoy Bargas went home often, he was very involved in our lives. And I must add he was also on top of every family member's life. So I considered it a privilege in a sense that, aside from our parents, we had him to look after us. He was our backup "parent".

When I graduated from high school, I didn't plan for what course I should take in college. I asked T'yoy Willy what he thought was best for me. He said, "You should take IT. Years from now, IT would become a hit." And so I took up Information Technology in college.

Right after graduation, I got a call from a company based in Manila. So I asked my parents' permission to explore outside Little Baguio – work in Marbel or even in General Santos City. But my parents were protective too. They were hesitant to let me fly far from the nest. I can't blame them, as a "*probinsyano*" [country boy] Manila was a vast and dangerous place to be in at that time. But I was motivated to go after the opportunity, and I needed someone to advocate for me.

Without hesitation or doubt, I went to T'yoy Willy and told him about my plans. He simply answered, "When do you need to be in Manila?"

My face lit up like the heavens had opened up for me. I hurried home to tell my parents that T'yoy Willy gave his blessings and permitted me to go to Manila. The next thing I knew, we were busy preparing and packing stuff for my trip to Manila.

Fast-forward to today; I live the life I would never have imagined I could because of him.

If he did not persuade me to take IT, I wouldn't have landed a job in an International/Multinational IT company. If not for his encouragement to explore outside my comfort zone, I wouldn't be earning well and providing for the family.

I consider myself a "Family Man". I believe that we should not consider taking care of or giving back to our family as an obligation, but we should do it out of gratitude instead. It's a blessing not everyone has been fortunate to do so. I believe the reason was, I had a solid role model in my life, and T'yoy Willy was one, if not the most significant, model I had. I grew up seeing how he was so selfless towards his own parents Tatay Pidio and Nanay Mayang, and the whole Lubrico family. T'yoy Willy moved mountains so he could give Tatay and Nanay what they deserved. He lived the simplest and modest life, but his impact was enormous.

If I could rewrite certain parts of my life, I'd meticulously choose the ones T'yoy Willy are in it (over and over again).

I could not thank him enough for what he had done for me. I will be forever grateful that we crossed paths in this lifetime.

* * * * *

Another nephew, Lester Lubrico Tugade delivered his tribute to Brother Willy on January 30, 2021 during the seven-day memorial celebration held at the NDMU gymnasium. Lester is the director, manager, and editor of Brother Willy's photos and posts on Social Media. His tribute was heartfelt as it was moving. He highlighted the generosity of an uncle toward his family even playing match maker to his parents, his versatility in relating to all ages – Gen Z (9-24), Millenials (25-40), Gen X (41-56), Boomers (57-66), and older. Lester also set the record straight regarding some misconceptions, that Brother Willy was unapproachable and standoffish. He wrote:

First, let me tell you about my relationship with Brother Willy. He is the reason why my mother and father met. My mother, Gloria Lubrico, is the first cousin of Brother Willy. He invited her to visit Mindanao from Bacolod, Negros Occidental, to meet my relatives after her graduation. After that invitation, my mother never returned home after meeting my father, Bernabe Tugade Jr.

I remember last November 20, 2020; it was a holiday. We played volleyball in NDMU gymnasium and shot the Tik Tok video with Brother Willy riding on his bike. I asked him about our Christmas bonus. He was so very happy in that video. So after I uploaded it on social media, I told him, "Brother *damo na nag like sing imo video.*"

(Brother, so many already liked your video).

He asked, *"Ano hambal nila da?"* (What did they say?)

I read some of the comments. One said, *"Ay, kabalo man gali magkadlaw si Brother Willy"*. (Wow. So Brother Willy knows how to laugh.)

If you know him, he is actually a very happy person. But playing his role being the President of the institution, he felt the need to show his outer self. *Medyo suplado but pinapanatili ang pagiging gwapo.* (He is kind of standoffish, but he was always trying to look good).

Brother Willy offered to cook the rice for the group after our volleyball game. He shared with me a long time ago, that *indi siya kabalo magluto.* (He does not know how to cook). One of the personnel of the Senior High School, *nagsukad sing iya kan-on and said, "Hilaw man ining kan-on".* (... spooned out some rice and said, this rice is uncooked).

I whispered to him, "Brother Willy cooked that rice". So *siguro nahadlok, gin kaon man niya maski hilaw.* (Fearful, he ate the rice anyway even though it was uncooked).

Brother Willy and I had our last interaction on December 22, 2020, during our NDM University personnel party. After the short program, I approached Brother Willy and greeted him with "Merry Christmas". Then I invited him to attend my birthday tomorrow. [Note: Lester delivered this tribute on January 30, 2021 the day before his birthday, January 31).

He said, "I cannot attend because I am going to Manila for medical reason. But I will try."

Indeed being with you as I celebrate my birthday tomorrow is a blessing, although in the saddest of circumstances. Thank you for coming, Brother I will never forget our shared experiences. You are a friend to me. You are my big Brother. You are my *Tatay* here in Marbel. You are my best mentor, constantly reminding me what to do.

After we celebrate the memorial of your death, I hope you will be happy. I hope you will always guide us, individually and as an institution.

Damo nga salamat Brother *Kuntani happy ka kung diin ka man subong.*

(Thank you, Brother I hope you are happy wherever you are).

* * * * *

Brother Willy's death devastated thousands but nowhere was this loss more profoundly felt than in the Lubrico family circle. He was the anchor that kept the family grounded from the storms of life. He was the cheerleader who encouraged his nephews and nieces to reach the height of their potentials or to experience life to the fullest.

His niece, Cecille Lubrico Longanilla, will never forget how Brother Willy convinced her and her aunt Rosemarie (wife of Benedicto Lubrico) to go to Bacolod for a week in March 2019. Not only so they could attend the graduation of cousin Jim Benedict Lubrico, son of Jaime. But specifically more so they could both fly on an airplane for the first time in their lives. Cecille admits it was an experience of a lifetime, in spite of being nauseous all the way and feeling so *manol* through it all. Aunt Rosemarie was 54-years-old. Cecille celebrated her 50th birthday when they arrived in Bacolod!

Brother Willy insisted that his family in South Cotabato gather during the Christmas holiday before he left for Manila. There were joyful celebrations as each family gathered at the beach, their respective houses, or on an excursion to Lake Sebu. No one, of course, suspected it would be his or her last family reunion with Brother Willy.

His nephews and nieces who have kids had the most challenging time of all, trying to explain death to all their little children. Mhelanie Baguna Golingay (married to Brother Willy's grandnephew Gerwin Golveo Golingay) agonized over her daughter Aning turning five last October 26, 2021, two days before Brother Willy's birthday. Aning misses his Lolo Brother so much because they used to celebrate their birthdays together. Mhel texted, "How does one explain death to five-year-old Aning? I told her that when one dies he turns into a butterfly so it could fly to heaven. So every time there's a butterfly here at home she believes it's Lolo Brother visiting her. It makes her happy."

Lucas Gabriel Lubrico is the five-year-old grandson of Brother Willy. He called him Gab-Gab, his very articulate English speaking *apo*. Gab's mother videotaped him recently as he was "talking" to his Lolo Willy. The video was posted on the family member's Facebook and shared with me. Gab is the son of Michael John Lubrico [brother of Macky] and his wife, Michelle. They live in Manila. From January 9 until he died on January 25, the nephews, nieces, and Gab spent as much time as they could with Brother Willy.

"Lolo Brother, can you please be alive again?" Gab asked wistfully one day. The video was rolling as he gazed up to the heavens from the window of their house. "I will give you a gift," he said. "I will buy you ice cream."

"Do you think Lolo Brother will come down if you give him ice cream?" asked his mother, Michelle.

"Yes," Gab said with a giggle. "Lolo Brother, I will think of you."

"Where do you think he is, is he in heaven?" his mother asked.

"Is he in space?" Gabriel answered with a question of his own.

"Ask him."

"Lolo Brother, what kind of cloud that you land on? I don't know. Can you tell me please?"

Little Gab mumbled some words softly.

"Are you talking to Lolo Brother?" asked Michelle.

"Yes," said Gab.

"So what did he say?"

"He said he is in stratocumulus."

Oh, if we could only see death through the eyes of children.

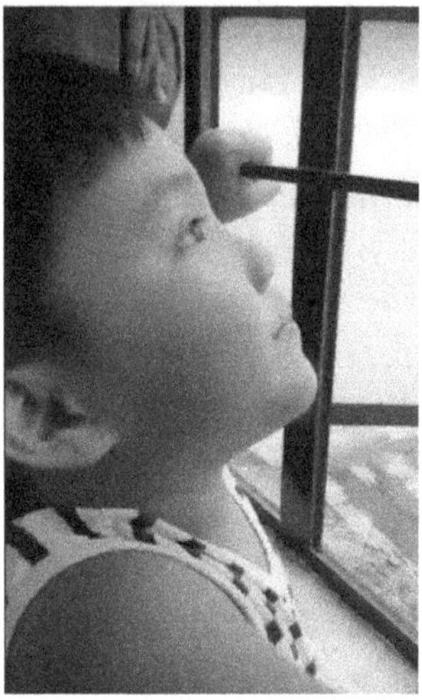

Gab "talking" to Lolo Brother Willy

Gonyong, Macky, Pia, Norberto, Dolly, Ligaya, Romel, and JM. Front: Gab, Brother Willy, Vince, and Hanna

Brother Willy with his siblings, in-laws, and nieces
Standing: Cecille Lubrico Longanilla, Rodolfo Lubrico, Nancy, Hazel, Jennifer, Rosemarie (wife of Benedicto Lubrico not in picture), Susan, Judith (wife of Rodito Lubrico not in picture), and Maria Angela. Seated: Renz Wendyll, Brother Willy his great granddaughter Glessy on his lap, and Teresa Lubrico Golveo.

Brother Willy with the Lubrico Family at the Susan Beach, Glan December 28-29, 2020.
L-R back: Nancy, Peter, Brother Willy, Susan, Judith, Jennifer, Charliemagne, Sherlyn, Rosemarie, Luzviminda, and Rodito
L-R front: Cecille Lubrico Longanilla, Renz, Wendyll, Rudy, Rowena, and Ezel

Rodolfo Lubrico (Papa Doc) and his daughter, Cecille Lubrico Langonilla, who interviewed him for this book and the primary contributor to Brother Willy's family history.

FOLLOWING ST. MARCELLIN CHAMPAGNAT

In 1999, Brother Willy attended the Canonization Ceremonies for St. Marcellin Champagnat in Rome with a delegation from the Philippines. He would live out his life following Marcellin.

At the Tomb of St. Marcellin Champagnat. Photos from Bro. Willy's Facebook.

Le Hermitage, France

Following Marcellin 6

"I procured clothing for him from spare and old shirts and our mother mended them so he would have something to wear."

~ Teresa Lubrico Golveo interview by Estrella T. Golingay ~

Teresa Lubrico Golveo wishes she could remember exactly when and how her younger Brother Willy decided to join the religious order of the Marist Brothers. Or who inspired him. But there are two things she will never forget, procuring clothing for her brother from spare and old shirts and their mother mending them so he would have something to wear. Just in time before he left home to begin his Marist journey.[20]

In the summer after his sophomore year in high school, Willy and his classmates attended "Vocation Promotion" as it was called during Brother Willy's time and conducted by the Marist Brothers at the Notre Dame of Surala. At these events, members of a religious congregation speak before the attendees to encourage them to answer the divine call to religious life. After this particular meeting, the young men were invited to a weeklong workshop at the Marist Juniorate formation center in General Santos City. Young Willy promptly informed his parents that he was interested and asked for permission.

Initially, Elpidio and Maria Paz opposed Willy's plan to become a Marist Brother, according to his brother Rodolfo. It was justifiably so. They were being asked to entrust the life of their favorite son to a religious community they did not know much about, their interactions with the Marist Brothers nil, and General Santos City seemed like another world away. But young Willy had a gift of persuasion, according to his brother Rodolfo. Willy told them everything he heard about the Marists during the workshop. Also, Fr. Raymond Pulvino, CP., the director of Willy's high school, and their parish priest recruited their son according to his classmate Estrella Tano Golingay (Chapter 3 A Boy Named Bargas). Finally, Willy convinced his parents, and they gave their son their blessing.

Young Willy wrote in his journal, "I entered the Juniorate in the summer of 1969 when I was about sixteen".

The Marist Brothers formation center was located at the campus of the Notre Dame of Lagao High School (NDLHS). The Juniorate building was situated behind the Marist Convent in Lagao, General Santos City, about five hours bus ride from Lubrico's home in Little Baguio, Surallah.

Rodolfo Lubrico recalled that it was young Willy's first trip out of town. It is easy to imagine young Willy riding the Yellow Bus from Surallah to General Santos. The municipality of General Santos achieved cityhood in September 1968. Young Willy had been there once before when his family first arrived in 1959 from Negros Occidental. He was six years old. The town was then a sleepy settlement transformed by tremendous growth in just ten years by Dole Pineapple Company. Dole moved its operations from Hawaii to the province of South Cotabato in the early 1960s.

What an exciting time it must have been for young Willy to explore places beyond the hills of Little Baguio, his first small step to see the world. He left behind the tight-knit Lubrico family and became a member of a religious community of young boys living together and sharing the same goal, aspiring to be a Marist Brother.

Saturnino Bayona, a member of Brother Willy's Juniorate cohort related his experiences in the Marist Formation Community. Raised in Lamsogod, Surallah, South Cotabato, Sat (his nickname) lived six kilometers from the Lubrico family home in Little Baguio, Surallah.

Sat recalled quite enthusiastically:

> I attended the Marist Vocation lecture at Notre Dame of Surala together with Brother Willy and the late Joe Torrecampo. After that lecture, we were invited to visit the Juniorate Formation Center in Lagao. I vividly remember going to Lagao using our own money for *pamasahe sa* bus to

attend the seven-day Marist vocation workshop. Those from South Cotabato may have taken the Yellow Bus, and those from Cotabato City took the Dulawan Bus. Unfortunately, I can't precisely recall the names of those who influenced us to join. Still, I remember there were three presenters, possibly Scholastics from Marbel Scholasticate; because of its proximity to our high school NDS.

I will never forget the weeklong Workshop held around March 1969. The Marist Brothers served good food and delicious *merienda* [snacks] too. We attended morning mass daily at the Saints Peter and Paul Parish Church, a five-minute walk from our Juniorate Center. In addition, we went to morning and evening prayers daily at the Marist Convent chapel. In between, we went to school. It made us realize the significant difference between our lives "outside" and "inside" the Juniorate. We routinely spent hours in sports and study periods, which were not part of our daily lives at home. Yes, we played basketball, volleyball, American football, and soccer. After the Workshop, we were given money for our bus fare to go home and a generous allowance for personal use.

Classes started in June 1969. Willy, Joe, and I reported to the Juniorate Formation Center. There were eighteen in our group of young boys searching for the right answer to our calling, the largest batch ever of Marist Juniors. We attended high school as juniors at the Notre Dame of Lagao, Boys Department, where we graduated in 1971. Next door to our campus (divided by barbed wire fence) was the Notre Dame of Lagao, Girls Department. We were the first batch of boys and girls chosen for the experimental program to make the school co-educational. Before that, the boys and girls were taught in separate classrooms/campus and were not allowed to mix and mingle except during Athletic Events, Notre Dame Day celebrations, and Graduation Ceremonies.

As Marist Juniors, we were allowed to go home during a family emergency such as illness or death and on semestral break for one week. The Marist Brothers are very generous. They gave us substantial allowance whenever we went home. And on some Sundays *may* pa *sine* (movie house) *kami* sa downtown Dadiangas if not, swimming. However, we don't always go to the movie house. I would usually tell Willy, "Tago na lang natin ang allowance na pera, let's go out to eat, and save our money for rainy days."

Willy didn't discuss his family life openly. So I never knew about his family situation. He was always well dressed; perhaps he saved his allowance to buy those clothes. We lived together in a community setting at the Marist Formation centers from 1969 until I left the congregation in 1973, but he never did once borrow a cent from me. *Nakikita naman nia at alam niya damo ako kwarta.* (He could see and was well informed that I did not have a shortage of pocket money).

Regarding your question about the wristwatch he was wearing in the photo taken when we were in the Juniorate in 1969. He could have bought it from his Marist allowance because he was so conscious about time and a stickler to punctuality. Or I can't precisely recall if I have given him one because I started to love watches even then and have over 100+ now in my collection. The first time I showed my collection to him, God, *inarbor nia ang iba.* (God, he took a few!). We shared that kind of friendship.

He and I had planned in September 2020 to visit the East and West Coast of the U.S. and my three sisters in Ontario, Canada. He said we would stay with friends and family, which could have meant a stop at your place. Europe and Switzerland were also in our itinerary. But Covid-19 happened.

In 2019, he was in Canada. I requested my sisters to take an emergency leave when Brother Willy's schedule changed. My sisters picked him up from his niece's house, and they threw a welcome party for him. They hosted him and prepared delicious food. *Weakness kasi nia na kumain ng masasarap na pagkain.* (He was partial to delicious food). We did Facetime while he was in Canada and I in Manila; he kept pointing to his belly. He enjoyed his stay because he knew my sisters very well. He used to sleepover at our house in Lamsogod, Surallah, where he met my family and siblings.

Young Willy and Sat's friendship goes back to 1967 as freshman at Notre Dame of Surala (NDS) High school. Their friendship endured the test of time. Brother Willy felt so blessed that he was a part of two Alumni Group, Batch NDL and NDS 1971. [Notre Dame of Lagao 1971 celebrated their 50th High School Anniversary this year 2021 but Notre Dame of Surala canceled theirs on account of COVID-19].

* * * * *

Brother Willy's early life was "simple and unspectacular", much like Saint Marcellin Champagnat, founder of the Marist Brothers. Marcellin grew up in a region badly affected by the destruction wrought by the French Revolution. His community was severely "run-down, materially poor, and opportunities for education were sadly lacking".[21] His biography published on the Marists of Champagnat website[22] describes Marcellin as one who "performed all the chores with enthusiasm, revealing a very active character, a love of work, a spirit of initiative, a practical intelligence, and physical strength. Children and young people are his friends; they relate to him with special affection".

The same could be said about the barrio in which young Willy was raised and about the essence of Willy himself.

Saint Marcellin Champagnat, a newly ordained priest, raised in France during the French Revolution, founded the Marist Brothers of Schools on January 2, 1817, now referred to simply as the Marist Brothers. The Marist Brothers came to the Philippines resulting from the congregation's international missionary mandate.

The Marist Brothers' first international missionary mandate was to the Pacific. They accompanied Marist Fathers in evangelizing and education ministries. The Marist Brothers arrived in Australia in 1872, where they opened their first school at the Rocks, New South Wales. The Province of the United States of America traced its roots to 1905 when the Marist College in Poughkeepsie, New York, was established. The Marist Brothers of the Philippines started in 1948 and are members of the Province of East Asia, comprised of the countries of the Philippines, Hong Kong, South Korea, Malaysia, Singapore, and Japan.[23]

Meanwhile, in the Philippines, the Catholic Church had asked the Oblates to take over the ministry for the people of the then empire province of Cotabato and the Sulu Archipelago; predominantly populated by Muslims. As a result, the Oblates Fathers founded Notre Dame Academy in July 1941. It is now known as the Notre Dame of Midsayap College. It was the first Notre Dame School affiliated with the Notre Dame Educational Association (NDEA), which grew to over 190 members. It includes the Notre Dame of Surala. The same Oblate Fathers would also invite the Marist Brothers to manage the educational system they had set up at their growing parishes. [Of note, young Willy would grow up to become President of NDEA].

When the Oblate Fathers congregation celebrated its Silver Jubilee in the Philippines in 1964, an article was submitted to the Canadian Catholic Conference Information Service entitled "It's All In The Name". It read, "Canadian-born Fr. Gerard Mongeau discussed the question of a name for the school in Cotabato City with his fellow Oblates, all of whom were Americans. They decided promptly and unanimously to call it 'Notre Dame' after the famed University in South Bend, Indiana. A tremendous spirit of unity developed among all the Notre Dame padres, students, and their parents."[24]

* * * * *

Brother Joseph Damian Teston narrated his personal story as the leader of the four pioneering Marist Brothers in the Philippines in a YouTube video produced by Chris Gammon during the Notre Dame Alumni USA reunion in 2011.[25] The reunion was held in the historic Arlington, Virginia/D.C. area. In 1948, the first four Marist Brothers from the United States arrived in Cotabato City at the request of the Oblate Fathers of Mary Immaculate (OMI) - Brothers Peter Leonard Thommen, Maurus James Doherty, Herbert Daniel Dumont, and Joseph Damian Teston. Brother Teston turned 100 years old on January 24, 2021 (one day before Brother Willy died), he wrote:

> Our first assignment was to take over the Notre Dame of Cotabato City High School management, teaching with the Oblates and the RVM Sisters. In the evenings, we taught at

the Oblate's College, now called Notre Dame of Cotabato City University. After two years, I was sent to Notre Dame of Marbel with a new batch of four Brothers. In 1952, I was assigned to Notre Dame of Lagao. Lagao was the headquarters of the LASEDECO (Land Settlement Development Corporation) under General Paulino Santos to open and develop Southern Mindanao, which was our Marist Brothers territory. During that time, the Province of Cotabato (corresponding to a state) was referred to as the Texas of the Philippines because it was the largest province. Today [2011], it is five provinces. The development politically and civilly has been fantastic. So has been the investment of the church through religious orders. There were three religious orders then; today, there are forty religious orders. There used to be four schools named Notre Dame. Today, 115 Notre Dames are in different towns. That is, from Elementary to high school and college to university. The involvement of Notre Dame and the progress of that part of the country have been extraordinary. Notre Dame Alumni had been involved in every profession. Notre Dame Alumni had been engaged in the work of the church. The growth of the religious order of local Filipino people had been phenomenal.

Over time, the Marist of the United States sent over thirty-eight American Brothers. Today there is precisely one American there [this video was taped in 2011]. Because the American method was "you are not there to perpetuate yourself. You are there to have other people take over."

Today, the Filipino Brothers are running the whole show. They are running all the Marist Notre Dame schools. It is the most significant and proudest investment that we American Brothers ever made. So I, right now, after having spent 25 years in the Philippines, look upon my experience as my most significant contribution to the Philippines. And after that, my most important contribution is my absence because the Filipinos, willing and able, are there to run their country.

Brother Damian left the Philippines in 1973 when Brother Willy was still in the Novitiate. Brother Damian's last sentence, "And after that my greatest contribution is my absence because the Filipinos, willing and able, are there to run their country," strongly supported Brother Willy's trailblazing skills that he demonstrated in the late 1980s in what Briccio Baynosa termed as the "Filipinization" of the Marist Brothers in the Philippines. Today, there are no American Marist Brothers left in the Philippines. The last was Brother Robert McGovern, who died on May 19, 2021. All the Marist Schools are administered and managed by Filipino Marist Brothers. The American mentors taught their students well.

Brother Ted Fernandez, the Novice Master of Brother Willy in Tamontaka in 1972 noted a reversal of role even among Filipino Brothers. Both men made their mark within the Marist Community, accepting their assignments with a tenacious sense of obedience and went wherever the call of duty took them. Forty-four years later, their path converged. Brother Ted shared,

"I came back from Australia in 2015 and my former novice, Brother Willy became my President at the Notre Dame of Marbel University and my Superior at the Marist Community House."

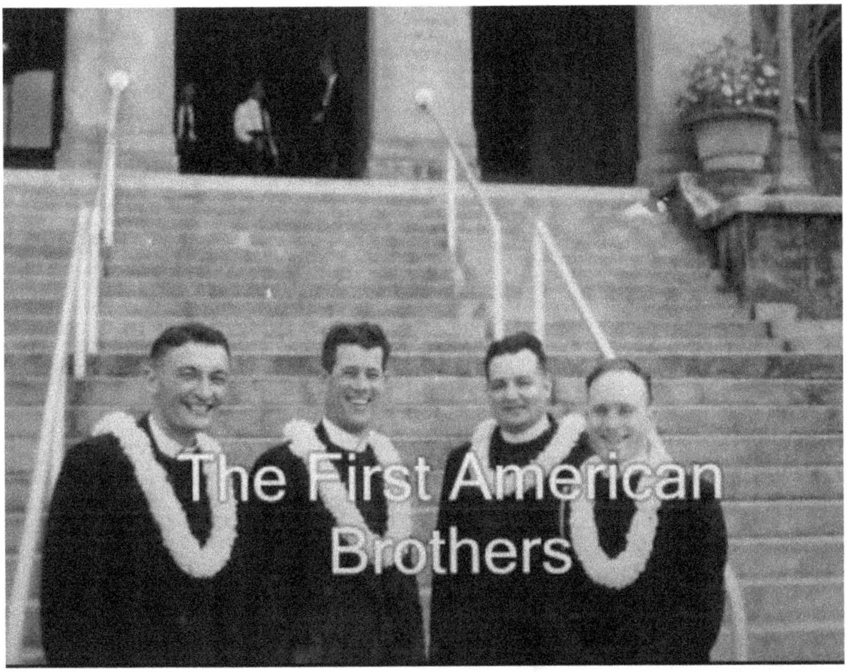

Brothers Peter Leonard Thommen, Maurus James Doherty, Herbert Daniel Dumont, and Joseph Damian Teston. Photos from the Marist Archive.

The Immaculate Conception Marist Novitiate in Tamontaka, made of concrete was plain but an imposing structure by the 1960s standards. Brother Willy spent his Postulancy and Novitiate years here. Brother Ted Fernandez was his Novice Master.
Photo from Notre Dame University Archive

The first four American Brothers together with the faculty members

Becoming a Marist Brother 7

"...to be a Marist Brother is to live a truly wonderful life. It is a life that connects you to so many people and allows you many opportunities to influence and impact others."

~Bro. Bernard Curtin, FMS~[26]

Briccio Baynosa, my co-author, was himself a Marist Brother until he voluntarily and officially left the congregation in December 2015. He held many leadership positions including as the President of Notre Dame of Dadiangas College from 1992-1995 preceding Brother Willy. (Appendix D – NDDU & NDMU Presidents). He illustrates the life of young Willy during his formative years in the religious congregation based upon his own experiences, from Juniorate through Postulancy, Novitiate, and Scholasticate. This rite of passage for young Willy as an aspiring Marist Brother occurred from June 1969 to June 1978. Briccio wrote:

Challenges are there to meet him, as soon as an individual decides to join a congregation. There are many qualifications and requirements needed. For the Marist Brothers, they are looking for candidates who can pass the rigors of formation.

One is intellectual – a candidate must be able to survive the expectations of the congregation. As educators, the candidate must have above average I.Q. to enable him to endure the competitive world of the academe. He is given an I.Q. test to ascertain this qualification.

Next is psychological – a candidate is given a battery of tests by a professional psychologist to measure his mental health. As far as I can remember, we were given these following tests: personality, psychological, emotional, vocational, etc. Family background is also investigated.

There is physical examination to determine the candidate's suitability to do rigorous physical activities such as hard labor and sports. Those with congenital ailments are usually not admitted in formation.

For the spiritual aspect, the candidate must be a practicing catholic and displays moral attitude and behavior. References by reliable people are needed for this.

As early as the Juniorate (this formation stage does not exist anymore) the candidates live in community. This process will test the candidate's capability to live harmoniously with other people in a community and in a multi-cultural setting.

I remember that one of the most important things that the Marist Brothers look for in a candidate is good judgment. A person with good judgment will not put himself or the organization where he belongs in jeopardy. Good judgment minimizes embarrassing situations for the individual and the company.

The candidate must be able to display satisfactorily these expectations within the formation period. The following are the stages of formation during the time of Brother Willy. [Included on the left is Willy's timeline].

1. 1969-1971 Juniorate (3rd and 4th years high school)
2. 1971-1972 Postulancy (after high school -1 year)
3. 1972-1973 Novitiate (after Postulancy – 1 year)
4. 1973-1976 Scholasticate (after novitiate about 3 years until he finishes his bachelor's degree)
5. June 29, 1973 Temporary Vows (after graduation– assigned to different Marist communities or schools–3 years)
6. June 29, 1978 Final Vows end the process of formation

POSTULANCY & NOVITIATE

Brother Willy did his Postulancy and Novitiate in Tamontaka, (located just outside Cotabato City) according to his friend and fellow novice Saturnino Bayona. Brother Ted Fernandez was their Novice Master. He provided some timeline and added his impressions of Brother Willy:

Willy was a junior in Lagao while I was teaching in Jolo in 1969. So I never got to know Willy during his early years in the formation center. It's only in May 1972 that I first encountered him along with seventeen novices and eight postulants. It is unfortunate that I lost lots of pictures taken that year. All my things got burnt soon after I moved to Dadiangas in 1988 during a fire that razed our convent. So my knowledge of young Willy was just limited within those seven months when I was his novice master.

Let me just explain first what Juniorate is as well as the Novitiate. Our Marist Juniorate during his time was intended for at least third year till high school graduation. It was a phase of accepting high school candidates to become Marist Brothers. This is somewhat akin to the minor seminary of the priesthood. But here, our juniors are mere high school students living in Lagao as a community and studying/graduating at Notre Dame of Lagao Boys' Department. His co-juniors must have been the late Brother Joe Torrecampo and Brother Rene Reyes (now assigned to NDMU community). After the first phase of formation (the Juniorate), the candidate is evaluated to determine if fit to continue on with his religious formation.

This is what happened to Brother Willy after he graduated high school in Lagao, Class 1971. He moved to Tamontaka, near Cotabato City, for his initial phase of religious formation in 1972. In between the Juniorate and Novitiate, there is a year of Postulancy.

The Novitiate: At that time of Brother Willy this stage was for a year. Presently our Novitiate goes for two years. The Postulancy during Willy's time was either in Tamontaka or anywhere else where you have a full-fledged Brother guiding the postulants. They start college studies as postulants.

From Jolo, I was assigned to the novitiate to teach Catechetics, a systematic course in teaching religion. I started in the summer of 1972 (about May-June). The regular course was supposed to start in mid June of that year, but then the present Novice Master, Brother Leonard Sonza was elected as Provincial, and he cannot be Provincial Superior of the

Philippines and Novice Master at the same time. So I, being the only Brother assisting him, was to assume his former position as Novice Master. Usually an elderly Brother acts as Novice Master, not a neophyte who was only 25 years old. So then I was on an "acting" capacity. I had to leave for Rome in December of that year to have my formation. So my contact with young Willy was merely from June till December.

The Novitiate is a phase in religious formation (formation for religious life that will soon take the three vows of poverty, chastity, and obedience) a way of following Christ more intimately and effectively. This is what Willy tried to do in this phase. It was supposed to be a life of silence and prayer; but the situation in North Cotabato that year was not conducive to "silence and prayer". The conflicts between the Muslims and the die-hard Christians escalated to an all-out war. Occasionally bombs would land in our property. This could really be scary especially that during the same period unknown persons would enter our property and steal what they could. [According to Rodolfo Regacho Mapada who was in Tamontaka with Brother Willy, they caught a few kids stealing pili nuts and were taken to the Superior, chastised and released to their parents].

So the Novices that year learned to police the property and be security guards at night. This was the situation Willy experienced in his novitiate life. To escape from danger, the group of novices would go to several high schools and promote vocation for the Marists. That was a tough year for those eighteen novices, Willy included. For this group, their novitiate year was definitely far from ideal.

Brother Willy celebrated his "Habit Taking" on June 29, 1972 and professed as a Marist Brother on June 29, 1973 according to his friend Rodolfo Mapado who was in the formation a year ahead of Brother Willy. Brother Ted continued:

Looking at Brother Willy up close and personal, I was struck with two things: First as a novice in 1972, I found him quiet, respectful, studious and a POET by heart. He used to show me his poems written in the chapel, in the garden that he tended, and in moments of reflection, like "desert days". His poetry generally speaks of his feelings and longings, his prayers and love of nature. In a group of eighteen novices where most of the extroverts dominated, Willy is hardly noticeable and appreciated. It was through his poems that I started to like the man for his deep intelligence. I even asked him to keep these poems and perhaps publish these at a right time. But I never heard of it since then.

Secondly, I see in Willy through so many years that unending desire to go to the poor, help them in their plight and even sacrifice his vocation to be with them.

* * * * *

Young Willy developed and nurtured countless enduring friendships during his religious formation and all through his apostolic experiences as a teacher, director of campus ministry, director of community extension services, later as administrator and president.

He introduced this narrator to many, some of them I met after his death. Saturnino Pulido Bayona entered the Juniorate in March 1969, in the same group as Willy. Rodolfo Regacho Mapada met young Willy at the Juniorate Formation Center in Notre Dame of Lagao in 1969. Rodolfo was then a high school senior. They would spend many years together at every stage of their religious formation and later as teachers in the same schools.

Both Saturnino and Rodolfo left the Marist order but later became members of a group that Brother Willy "founded" for former Marist Brothers who became Marist Mission Lay Partners. It is discussed in Chapter 12 - The Marist Experience (MAREX).

Brother Willy died before he could record his personal account of his experiences during his formative years. As authors, Briccio and I cling to every memorabilia we could find and included them in this book. The memorabilia is the next best thing; a collection of photos Brother Willy gave to his friend Saturnino Bayona and some from the collection of Rodolfo Mapada. Each photo "paints a thousand words" and some are captioned in the handwritten messages of the man himself.

Brother Willy received his Bachelors of Science degree major in Economics at the Notre Dame of Marbel University in 1976, he started his teaching career the year before he graduated and Professed as a Marist Brother on June 1, 1978.

Brother Willy once brought my attention to Brother Bernard Curtin's obituary after the latter died on December 23, 2014. Brother Bernard served in the Marist Philippine Mission for over forty years and he came back to the United States in 1992. In 1999, both Brothers attended our Notre Dame alumni USA reunion in New York/New Jersey area. So Brother and I reminisced about those bygone days and he mentioned the quote in the obituary from Brother Bernard speaking about his life as a Marist Brother.

Brother Dan O'Riordan, the author of the obituary posted on the Marist Website[27] that he consulted Brother Bernard about his own work in the promotion of Vocations. Brother Dan asked if he had any advice for young men that might be thinking of joining the Marist today.

Brother Bernard responded, 'Tell them that to be a Marist Brother is to live a truly wonderful life. It is a life that connects you to so many people and allows you many opportunities to influence and impact others."

Above: Young Willy's life at the Juniorate includes structured studies, sports, time for prayers and meditation, shared chores – such as tending to the garden, mowing the lawn, etc. In this picture, Angelito Sonico and Antero Lacia took turns mowing the lawn of Notre Dame of Lagao High School campus where the Juniorate Center was located. The author graduated with Angelito and Antero at NDL H.S Class 1967. Photo by Angelito Sonico.

Below: The boys at the Juniorate in Lagao joined a Boy Scout event. Instead of taking PMT (Philippine Military Training), the Juniorate Group opted for Boy Scouting. Brother Willy was in his 3rd year in high school. He is shown in second row kneeling, third from left. Photo by Rodolfo Regacho Mapada

Saturnino Bayona and Brother Willy, Juniorate 1969. Photo by S. Bayona.

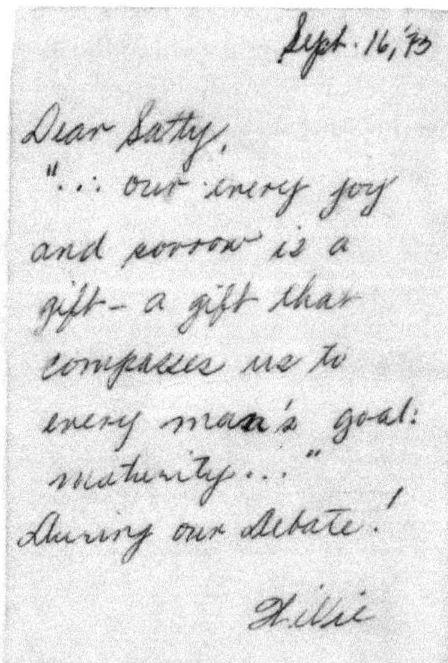

Sept. 16, '73

Dear Satty,
"... our every joy and sorrow is a gift – a gift that compasses us to every man's goal: maturity..."
During our debate!

Willie

Left: During the debate "Women's Liberation Movement is Justifiable", Satur took the affirmative and Brother Willy took the negative viewpoint. Right: Message: Sept 16, '73 *"Dear Satty...our every joy and sorrow is a gift – a gift that compasses us to every man's goal: maturity. During our debate! Willie"*

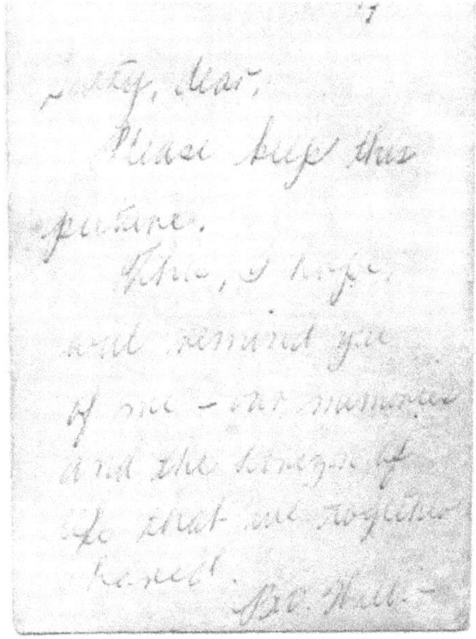

Satty, dear,
Please keep this picture.
This, I hope, will remind you of me – our memories and the horizon of life that we together shared.
Br. Willie

1973 Caption: *Satty, dear, Please keep this picture. This, I hope will remind you of me – our memories and the horizon of life that we shared.* Brother Willie

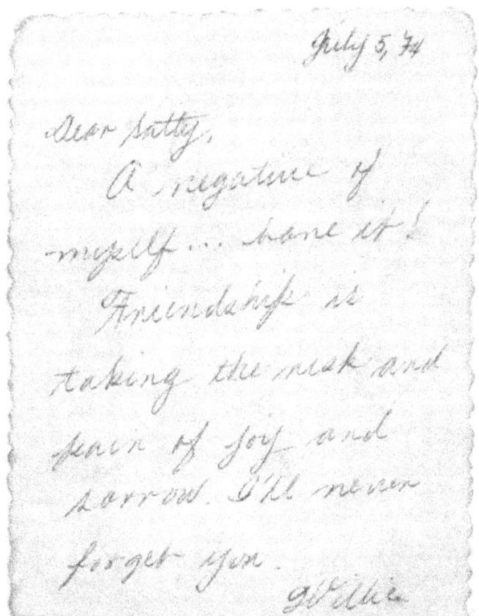

July 5, 74
Dear Satty,
A negative of myself... have it!
Friendship is taking the risk and pain of joy and sorrow. I'll never forget you.
Willie

July 5, '74 Caption: Dear Satty, A negative of myself...have it! Friendship is taking the risk and pain of joy and sorrow. I'll never forget you. Willie

Marist Retreat 1973. Brother Willy seated front row third from left.

1973 Novitiate, Tamontaka, Cotabato City. Brother Willy seated second from left.

1978 Scholasticate at Notre Dame of Marbel. Brother Willy at back row, 3rd from right.
The old and decrepit Scholasticate building was demolished replaced by a new one now called Marist Formation Center.

Marist Retreat 1974
2nd row, third from left is co-author Briccio Baynosa
Brother Willy is fifth from right last row, between Pat Corpus (left) and Brother Romulo Porras (right).

The Lubrico Family during Willy's Profession as a Marist Brother, June 29, 1972
Back l-r: Rolando Golveo (husband of Teresa), Tatay Elpidio Lubrico, Reneta Lubrico (wife of Jaime), friend of Reneta, Rodolfo Lubrico. Front l-r: Editha Lubrico (wife of Rodolfo), Annie Golveo (daughter of Teresa), Teresa Lubrico Golveo, Brother Willy, Nanay Maria Paz, Leonisa Samonte, Salvacion Lubrico Demetillo. Only Rodolfo, Teresa, and Annie in this picture are still alive.

Brother Willy with his siblings, circa 2020
The Lubrico Siblings, November 29, 2020. Back: Rodolfo (Doc) & Brother Willy
Front: Rodito (Boy), Teresita, Teresa (Deding)

The Teacher 1976-1986 8

"We are his happy pills"

~ Orman Ortega Manansala~

Brother Willy stayed true to Marcellin Champagnat's simple but powerful philosophy on Education, "to teach children one must love them". For the first ten years of his life as a consecrated individual, he was the penultimate teacher. Brother Ador Santiago, FMS, the current Provincial of the Marist East Asia Province and Brother Willy's Superior, delivered his praise during his tribute at the Marist Marikina Memorial Service. He met Brother Willy when he was a high school student at the Notre Dame of Dadiangas College (now a university). In his senior year, Brother Willy advised him to see an eye doctor and helped procure his eyeglasses. He was diagnosed with juvenile cataract that resulted in a surgery that corrected it. Brother Willy influenced him to become a Marist Brother, he said. Brother Ador shared:

> "He was a model teacher who made a great impact on my life, not only as my mentor in high school but also as a fellow Marist Brother. My admiration for him grew when he worked at the Socio-Pastoral Institute (SPI) as an activist, an admiration that I hold to this moment. SPI was always on the side of the poor, the farmers, and the people treated unjustly, because of that my admiration for him went through the roof. A compassionate and passionate visionary, may he remain as an example for us how to ran the school, as a teacher, a Brother, and mentor".

The Marist Brothers Community in the Philippines was primarily involved in teaching the youth in the classrooms. However, as the need arises, some were encouraged to pursue other majors aside from Education based on aptitude. Rodolfo Mapada was one of the first in the Scholasticate phase to enroll in Bachelor of Science, major in accounting in the early 1970s. Rodolfo, Brother Willy, and his Novice cohorts were enrolled in basic subjects at Notre Dame of Marbel University while in the Novitiate living in Tamontaka, Cotabato City. Brother Willy entered the Scholasticate at Notre Dame of Marbel College and chose Economics as his area of specialization.

He started teaching in 1975 at the Notre Dame of Dadiangas College one year before graduation and stayed in that position until 1979. It was followed by one year of teaching at Notre Dame of Kidapawan (1979-1980) and the Notre Dame of Marbel College (1980-1981). In the intervening years, he described himself as a Parish Worker. In 1987-1988 he was sent to Notre Dame of Cotabato Boys Department to teach. Briccio Baynosa remembers Brother Willy's teaching style:

During our younger years, in the late 1980s, I had the privilege of being assigned at Notre Dame of Cotabato, Boys' Department (NDCBD) with Brother Willy. When he arrived, he was tasked to teach the 4th year religion classes, which were previously assigned to me before he came to NDCBD. He only stayed for one year, but he truly made a significant impact among his students.

His teaching was outside of the box – not the usual catechism type where students are taught the tenets of the church but how these tenets translate into their realities and lives. He was incarnational in his approach, meaning the church teachings are not proclaimed in a vacuum but in the specific lives and situations of those who hear the Good News. He does not dichotomize his students. They are not body and soul but integration of flesh and spirit - one entity, one person.

At first, the students were confused about where he was leading them; the approach was quite unusual. He would assign the students to do surveys about the realities surrounding them. Then, they would discuss the results in class, discern, interiorize, and plan for action. Sooner than later, the students got the feel of his style and approach, and suddenly, he became an overnight sensation. Up to now, these students still adore him and look up to him.

*****

Orman Ortega Manansala, one of Brother Willy's high school students, became his best friend and staunchest supporter. When Brother Willy was the President of Notre Dame of Dadiangas University, Orman served on the Board of Trustees for many years. Because of his stellar qualifications and proven track record for being an alumni unifier, his robust support for Notre Dame schools, an impeccable sound judgment, he was nominated and was voted by the members of corporation to serve as Board member at Notre Dame of Marbel University as well. For many years, Orman was the President of the Notre Dame Alumni Association. Born and raised in General Santos City, he finished his primary and secondary education at the Notre Dame of Dadiangas University. Attended Mindanao State University in Marawi City for three years on full scholarship. He transferred to University of San Carlos for his Bachelor of Science degree major in Accounting. He is a banker since 1985, and is presently the Vice President and Sales Director of Mindanao Asia United Bank. The special bond between student and teacher is highly evident in Orman's tribute to Brother Willy.

> Brother Willy was our class adviser during our 3rd and 4th years in high school [1977-1979]. It was his second year of teaching. He was ten years our senior. I vividly remember his disappointment when our section chose "Headache 301" as our class moniker. Despite being the first section of the Junior Class [all kids in this section belong to the top tier of four junior classes], we became every teacher's headache. To our class adviser, that moniker would be an embarrassment. Surprisingly Brother Willy respected the decision of the class and supported us every step of the way.
>
> During those years, I felt hurt when some of my *barkada* (clique) got a 100% rating in GMRC (Good Manners & Right Conduct). All I got was a 91%. I was never the complainer; I just took it all in stride and tried to forget all about it.
>
> In one of our high school reunions many years later, I finally mustered the guts to ask him why I only got 91% in GMRC. Brother Willy just said: *"Para ka kasing kiti-kiti!*

Ang ingay-ingay mo palagi!" (You're like this hyper kid. You were such a chatterbox). My batch mates had a good laugh with that response! I rest my case! He was right.

I looked up to him as a learned adviser. Stern but calm. Aloof but caring. During our 4th year in high school, he became a better listener. Although he allowed us to be boys enjoying our last year as high school students, he also pushed us to participate in different organizations. He chose me to become one of the first members of the Blessed Marcellin Champagnat Core Group. My leadership perspective began to widen with his guidance.

When we graduated from high school in 1979, communications between Brother Willy and I stopped. Fortunately, our high school batch made a pact to hold a class reunion every December. Brother Willy never missed a reunion with us, beginning in December 1979. Every December for forty years, he looked forward to reconnecting with us – sharing both past and present stories. We relived the bygone days and planned future reunions.

The last reunion we had with Brother Willy was in 2019. As always, he never asked for special treatment. He dined and drank with us, laughed and cried with us. Brother Willy just became everyone's Big Brother, our go-to guy when marriages are failing, when our children go astray, or when we were just broken as individuals. He was our sponge, taking in all our cares, pains, and joys. During that December 2019 reunion, I knew he was undergoing his personal concerns. Still, around us, he was one of us just having a good time.

Our friendship developed through the years. Brother Willy invited me to join the reunion of the U.S. and Canada-based Dameans in Orlando, Florida, USA in 2005 in my capacity as the Alumni Federation President. I never thought about it very much, but he was persistent. He kept reminding me to apply for a U.S. visa. Finally, to get him off my back, I went through the process and luckily was granted one.

From thereon, our relationship strengthened from student to teacher to good friends. Brother Willy expanded my network of Damean friends. These people have supported his many projects for the Marist community. Brother Willy began complaining about his health issues during the international alumni reunion in Seattle 2019. He wasn't as sprightly as before, but he didn't look physically sick either. We just laughed about our getting old and sharing the names of our maintenance medicines. Around friends and students, Brother Willy was always happy – we were his happy pills.

When Brother Willy was the President of the Notre Dame of Dadiangas University, it developed and prospered. Spirits were high. The school's image dramatically improved, but I never heard Brother Willy brag about it. He just worked and worked and worked. It was enough to see him smile to know that he was satisfied with the goings-on around him. Everyone knew how it broke him when he was transferred to Notre Dame of Marbel University (NDMU). But like a good soldier, he abided. When we spoke that time, there was a reversal of roles. I became the listener. I became his sponge. I felt his pain, but I just knew that this man was going to prove his worth more than ever. I just knew that, Brother Willy would rise to the challenges and take the higher ground. We saw how NDMU has evolved into a premier University under his Presidency in the last fifteen years. And with the opening of the College of Law, a project close to his heart, Brother Willy has come full circle.

Ten years ago, Brother Willy and I started our Breakfast Tradition every January 1 of each year. He invited other Marist Brothers to join us at my house for breakfast. His only request was that I serve him a healthy meal only – so that's basically vegetables and fish.

It was always a fun time with Brother Willy. He has become part of my family. My Kuya Avel and sister Mara look up to him as our surrogate Big Brother. He was "lolo" to the young ones in the house. We have not broken this breakfast tradition, and the last we had breakfast was in January 2019. That's when I noticed something. He seemed burdened. I thought it was about his health issues. But, it was a different thing. I remember telling him to be ready for any eventuality – reminding him that he has nothing to prove anymore. I offered to adopt him to live with me on our farm upon my retirement.

He just said: "Sus sa pagka-arte mo mag-retire ka gid sa farm? Ambot lang ah!" (My what a ham you are. Retirement at your farm? I don't know about that).

I asked him if he was ever proud of me in one of our pep talks. He looked at me and said:

"Ano naman ng drama mo? Siempre eh! Proud ko sa una pa!"

(What's all this drama? Of course! I've been proud of you from the start!)

* * * * *

Abednego Adre, a member of the Notre Dame of Dadiangas Boys Class 1980, Abed graduated from De La Salle University in Manila. In 1993, he migrated to the United States. He worked with several firms in Los Angeles until his entrepreneurial spirit took over and he opened his own business, Spartanburg Group, a garment industry. He lives in Anaheim, California with his wife Xyl and they are blessed with two children. In 2003, Brother Willy attended the NDGSC Alumni Association USA in Anaheim and Abed's family hosted his former teacher. He wrote:

> Notre Dame of Dadiangas College (NDDC) is the academic home for many in General Santos City. My family joined the N.D. community in the late 1960s. We can proudly say this institution paved the way for so many of us to accomplish so much in life. Therefore, it is fitting to recognize the many sacrifices and relentless efforts of the Marist Brothers (FMS) and Oblates of Mary Immaculate (OMI). They provided us with an education that meets the continuing challenges of an ever-evolving world.
>
> Brother Willy Lubrico, FMS, was arguably one of the more prominent figures that led the effort to make what has been a vision into what we have now. Most remembered him as a very soft-spoken mentor who made all those around him feel comfortable. He always espoused working together

towards a common goal. I was among those who had the privilege to be his student in 1978.

We met again during the Golden Jubilee celebration at the NDDC campus in 2003-2004.

Through friends, I followed his many accomplishments as President of NDDC since he was appointed in 1995. Brother Willy was able to pull the entire community together to meet the ever-growing challenges present at that time. Reaching out to the alumni and garnering their unwavering support was a testament to his leadership. The Homecoming during the Golden Jubilee Celebration was a success. Reunions became an annual event locally and in North America. He paved the way for NDDC to be granted University status in 2006.

He honored my family on those many occasions by accepting our invitations to stay with us while he was in Southern California. I realized more than ever how selfless this man was. He wanted nothing more than making NDDC the beacon of modern Education that caters to the needs of everyone.

The transformation of NDDC under his leadership was his legacy.

He was a man on a mission. Even when he was appointed President of Notre Dame of Marbel University, he did not lose a step. He did what he did best. He once again led the way in bringing Notre Dame of Marbel University into the consciousness of its alumni and the local community. He inspired the establishment of the NDMU Alumni International in the USA. His goal was no different from when he was at NDD University.

His untimely demise touched the hearts of so many. Yet, his accomplishments shall be an inspiration to all of us. He was a true friend, a leader, a Notre Damian.

* * * * *

Brother Willy continued to be an academic adviser in formal and informal settings throughout his life. According to Dr. Allan Farnazo, Regional Director of the Department of Education (DepEd) Region

12, Brother Willy was an active on-line tutor of DepEd SEAMEO (South East Asian Ministers of Education Organization) graduate program for distance learning. But his last classroom teaching post was at Notre Dame of Cotabato City Boys Department where my co-author Briccio Baynosa was also assigned. Briccio observed how Brother Willy, the teacher, navigated his way through a tumultuous time with such creativity and ease. Briccio remembered:

During the late 1970s into the 1980s, the students were still restless. It was a big headache for the administrators and teachers to contain students writing on walls to vent out their feelings and sentiments of anger and hatred. These were troubled times and extremely difficult for schools.

Brother Willy provided the students with a "graffiti" board. They can write anything they "want" provided they do it on this "wall".

Problem solved!

Undoubtedly he loved children the most. His secretary for fifteen years Dalia Mesias intimated, "And despite his busy schedule, he took time to randomly observe classes himself, as he wanted to know first hand how instruction is being conducted and delivered in the classroom".

When he was the President of NDDU, the former Principal who worked with Brother Willy for eleven years, Alma Hordista, related this anecdote,

One of the preschool teachers told me the story when Brother Willy came to observe her Kindergarten class. Brother Willy sat on a vacant seat beside a pupil.

The boy asked him, "Are you our new classmate?"

In his usual humor and wit, he answered, "Yes, I am your classmate, I enrolled today".

The boy stared at him and said, "You are old, why are you in Kinder?"

"Ask your teacher." He answered the boy.

The boy raised his hand to catch the teacher's attention. The teacher explained who Brother Willy was and why he was in their classroom.

That was the beginning of his lasting friendship with the class. They continued calling him "classmate" and warmly welcomed him during his visits.

Orman Manansala's Class with Adviser Brother Willy front row extreme left. Orman, the kid striking a pose like a model is immediately behind the boy seated in the front row fifth from the right.

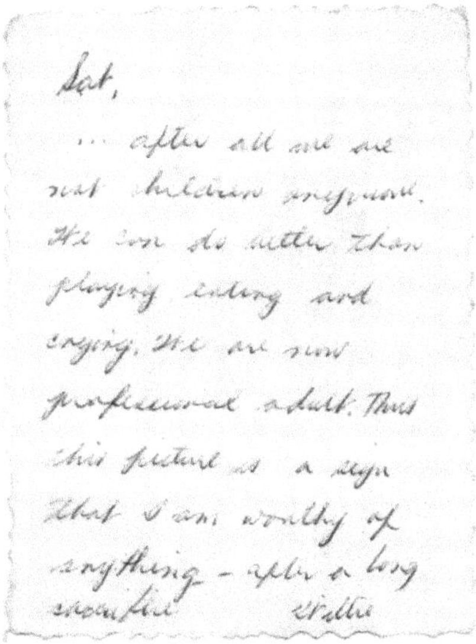

Sat,
... after all we are
not children anymore.
We can do better than
playing eating and
crying. We are now
professional adult. Thus
this picture is a sign
that I am worthy of
anything - after a long
sacrifice Willie

Left: Brother Willy graduated from Notre Dame of Marbel College with a degree in Bachelors of Science, major in Economics in 1976 but started teaching in 1975. Right: Caption: "Sat...after all we are not children anymore. We can do better than playing, eating, and crying. We are now professional adult: Thus this picture is a sign that I am worthy of anything – after a long sacrifice." Willie

Clockwise

1. Notre Dame Intramural Meet in Kidapawan. Brother Willy and Rudy were athletic advisers.
2. The Scholastics attending a Retreat at Calumpang with Rudy Mapada, Pat Corpus, and John Panzo.
4. Rudy visited Brother Willy when he was teaching at the Notre Dame of Cotabato City High School.
5. Teaching at ND of Dadiangas College in the 1970s photo taken near the NDDC Marist Convent.
6. Taken in General Santos City Park in front of Iglesia ni Christo Church.

The Parish Worker (Discovery and Recovery) 9

"...he wanted to give importance to this part of his contribution to the Marist Brothers."

~Briccio Baynosa~

As a narrator, I wrestled long and hard with myself about this chapter. First, I thought about using Brother Willy's intriguing titles, "Road Less Traveled", "Marist Life in a Non-Marist World" and "Discovery and Recovery". However, all three are so vague that each begs for an explanation. I was concerned that neither Briccio nor I could fully and satisfactorily paint the picture that the original author envisioned. Or, even if we did, we may not come close to what he intended. So after we discussed these topics at length, I decided that "The Parish Worker" is the appropriate title. Brother Willy created his outline during the lockdown, which served as our guide in presenting his story. In one of our email exchanges, he confessed, "Sometimes, too many dark shadows *sa buhay ko* and I took the road less traveled".

"Why do you think Brother Willy listed in his notes three topics out of six with similar subject matter?" I could not help but ask my co-author. "You know – Road Less Traveled, Marist Life in a Non-Marist World, and Discovery and Recovery."

"I guess he wanted to give importance to this part of his contribution to the Marist Brothers", was Briccio's response.

To which I totally agreed. Perhaps, we will never set our eyes on the chapters that Brother Willy intended to highlight. Nor read what he had to say about these intriguing titles as he had planned. Unless someone, somewhere, someday unearth a hidden treasure trove of his writing. Until then, all three, especially "Discovery and Recovery", will be forever open to debate.

I reached out to people I know who are very close to him. Still, only Briccio Baynosa and Orman Manansala proffered their opinions. Therefore, our diverging viewpoints are presented here. Each of us has known Brother Willy for fifty years or more. In the end, I believe Briccio's version makes the most sense.

Orman speculated that perhaps it pertained to his "discovery" in early 2019 that he had to step down as the President of NDMU and be relegated to join the retirees. Of course, he was saddened upon hearing the news, but Willy, being Willy, soon "recovered" and started a course of action to mitigate the shock. First, he told friends he planned to take a year of sabbatical and enjoy the company of his siblings, nephews, and nieces and their children. Then, a year later, in 2020, he began to chart the next phase of his life.

On the other hand, this narrator interpreted the title as his "discovery" that he had prostate cancer. He went to Manila, aiming to "recover" fully from it. But knowing how intensely private he was about his health; I deduced it could not have been that.

Briccio, put forward yet another thought. He is privy to information about Brother Willy that, while known to some within the Congregation, was not common knowledge to the public, perhaps even to his family. Briccio reviewed the outline that Brother Willy had left me and shared his observations and conclusions. Briccio opined:

I feel that Discovery and Recovery could not be related to his discovery that he had cancer. For me, "Discovery" relates to his re-discovering his role in the Congregation as a full-fledged Marist Brother. There was a time in his life when he was literally marginalized, cornered, and pushed against the wall. So he left the Congregation for three years to "find himself", and when the Marist leadership called him to go back or ship out, he stayed true to his vow of obedience. Brother Willy was so frustrated with what was going on in the Congregation and how the superiors were handling the societal situation. We were then at the quagmire of the Marcos dictatorship. We felt that we either had to speak our minds out or be swallowed by the apathy and frustrations engulfing most religious congregations at that time. Brother Willy had had enough, so he requested a leave of absence from the Congregation and its mission.

He applied to and got accepted by the Philippines' Socio-Pastoral Institute (SPI) based in Davao City. This group is more to his liking because it leaned more towards the progressive or communistic philosophy or mindset. He stayed with this group for two years and wanted to stay longer if allowed. But unfortunately, after this long period of being "outside" of the Marist congregation, he was given an ultimatum – come back or leave.

I had a long talk with him. I was a member of the Provincial Council then, and I knew precisely his situation and the Council's mindset. So, I told him to come back. He wanted to stretch his luck and asked me: Is it possible to make his work with SPI an official apostolate of the Marist Brothers? And he mentioned some foreign Brothers who were in such situations. I relayed this to the Council, and the answer was a BIG, FAT NO! I told him to come back and "let's do our battle inside rather than outside". He finally agreed to come back and from then on worked as Extension Service Program Coordinator in some of our schools. He soon discovered that he could be a part of an educational system and still be an activist in the area of social service. (This, I believe, was the "Discovery" factor.)

As an extension worker, and especially as an advocate of empowering the poor through community development, Brother Willy "recovered" his status, fame, and popularity with the Marist Brothers in no time at all. He transformed the Community Extension Program of the Notre Dame of Kidapawan College (NDKC) into a progressive and relevant school arm for development. Under his leadership, he connected and networked with foreign stakeholders to make NDKC's Extension program one of the most substantial areas in school accreditation. Brother Willy soon regained his credibility, slowly but surely. He was appointed President of Notre Dame of Dadiangas College (now NDDU), and as they say, the rest is history. His popularity increased to the point where he was appointed as the sector head of the Philippine Marist Province. I guess he wanted to give importance to this part of his contribution to the Marist Brothers after he executed his "second" entry into Marist life. (This was the "Recovery" factor.) On Orman's thoughts, Briccio offered his take:

Yes, he would indeed have liked to continue as the President. However, he told me during our last meeting that he requested the Board of Trustees for another extension. He reasoned that he still had some unfinished business, which involved a relatively considerable amount of money. But in fairness to him, he humbly accepted it when he was told that there would be no more extensions. Instead, he planned to request a year sabbatical and then retire entirely from administration and live simply as a Marist Brother.

* * * * *

Brother Willy arrived in Manila on January 9, 2021 very optimistic about the planned robotic surgery for his prostate cancer. He told this narrator that he would be staying with his two nieces, Pia Samonte Baysa and Dolly Lubrico Fenis, at a condo near his doctors in Manila. Brother Willy thought that the Marist House in Marikina was quite a distance away and could pose a commuting nightmare considering the horrendous traffic jam in Manila. And he did not have a car at his disposal and was not inclined to impose on anyone. He mentioned that the surgery could cost upwards from P800 thousand to close to a million pesos. The fundraiser person in me kicked into gear and asked if we, the Notre Dame Alumni Associations in the United States, could do something to help. "Brother Allan already told me that the Marist Brothers would take care of all my medical expenses", he assured me. He planned to stay in Manila for a few weeks after his surgery and go home to Marbel at the end of January.

Briccio concluded: True, his untimely death is so sad and perhaps could have been avoided. But there are always two sides to a coin. If properly informed, the Marist Brothers would never renege on its obligation to take care of the health of its members. I know for sure that the amount set aside by the Congregation for health purposes is more than sufficient for the needs of its members...At this point in time, there is no room for casting aspersions on anybody – just a time for healing and a time to learn lessons from past mistakes.

Having resolved the "Discovery and Recovery" dilemma to our satisfaction, this narrator began to dissect "Marist Life in a Non-Marist World". I concluded that Brother Willy could have been referring to himself as "the Marist" when he lived "outside the Marist World" for many years. Again, I leaned on the people who knew him best for help. We could approximate our explanation since it would be impossible to truly discern what he meant.

Someone in authority opened the discussion about the topic of activism perhaps quite by accident or perhaps by design. Brother Willy was highly esteemed in the religious community. His Eminence Cardinal Orlando Quevedo concelebrated his burial mass assisted by half a dozen of Willy's clergy friends. Archbishop Quevedo gave a heartwarming tribute. (Video of this is available at the Notre Dame of Marbel University website, under "Videos"). He mentioned that during his stint at SPI (Socio-Pastoral Institute), Brother Willy became an activist.

In the 1970s and 1980s, being an activist had a negative connotation. Today social activism is held in a more positive, even admirable light. Defined as "an intentional action with the goal of bringing about social change", a person, who feels strongly about a cause and fights towards a change in society, could be considered an activist. Or perhaps the better word is "advocate".

As Brother Willy had suggested, I sought the "opinions" of many of his intimate friends. From communications with people who knew him best and by his own admission, Brother Willy had a "*rebelde*" streak. He was passionate about helping the poor; he fought for his initiatives to that end. It defined him and his own relevance as a Marist Brother in this century and the last.

Briccio Baynosa shared:

We used to spend sleepless nights discussing things that matter most for the Marist Congregation. We were sort of "rebels with a cause" then. Brother Willy's most famous quote: *Brix, ang iban nga congregasyon naga martsa na sa mga karsada; kita iya, ang aton gina diskasan, kung mag sutana kita o indi, kung ano ang mga prayers nga i-recite naton, pwede ba kita mag-speak sang dialect sa dining table, etc.*

(Brix, other congregations are marching on the street to protest, while we are discussing if we should wear soutane or not, what prayers to recite, if we be allowed to speak dialect at the dining table, etc.).

It was difficult for us "rebels" during the early 1970s. But we fought for the "Filipinization" of the Congregation and succeeded. [Today, there are no American Marist Brothers in the Philippines. All the Marist Schools are now administered and managed by Filipino Brothers as Brother Joe Damian opined, "his absence is his greatest contribution to the Filipinos"].

Briccio continued: Brother Willy was a significant part of this group with a new awareness and perspective. I think people need to know him deeper.

After Cardinal Quevedo mentioned Brother Willy being an "activist", I received several texts in my personal Messenger chat room. I mean, in real time, as the burial service was going on. All who texted were sixty-something who grew up in the 1970s when being an activist could land one in jail.

"Hey, did you catch that word activist from the Archbishop?"

"What did the Archbishop mean by it?"

"Why did he describe Brother Willy as an activist?"

It triggered some highly philosophical and sometimes uncomfortable discourse, as I was not really informed about that phase of Brother Willy's life. So this is my attempt to answer the questions by way of the most articulate and sensitive essay provided by my co-author:

Why did Brother Willy become an "activist?" Briccio began:

I could trace my friendship with Brother Willy, way back in the middle to the late 1970s, at a time when some of us Marist Brothers in the Philippine Province were struggling and grappling with our identity, vision, and mission as Marist Brothers within the context of the Filipino Catholic Church.

The Martial Law era was turbulent and fraught with anxiety and fear. Our students were restless; some became secular in their thinking and questioned everything the Church hierarchy and the educational system were doing. Specifically, they challenged the triumphalistic Church with its elaborate liturgical trimmings, gilded chalices and vestments, vast properties, and preferential options for the elite. In addition, they questioned the high cost of education perpetrated by catholic schools; reinforcement of elitism that favored the well-to-do students; the implementation of a curriculum that was alien to the realities of the times.

During this period, the by-word or by-phrase was "signs of the times". Some religious congregations recognized the signs of the times and exerted serious efforts in aligning their vision-mission towards the direction where the modern Church was heading and became progressive. Some remained wary and decided to be on the safe side by being traditional. Some congregations decided to march on the streets; some chose to pray in the chapel. Some congregations lost their members mysteriously or brutally; some congregations hid safely in the cocoon of their soutane or cassock.

Brother Willy later joined some progressive members of the clergy and religious. He organized the local communities and youth in the spirit of the *aggiornamento* – the Church in the modern world. They organized rallies and protests. Brother Willy decided to effect change from the outside. I decided to stick it out from the inside. It was difficult warding off the rallyists and protesters. Still, I truly believed then that change must be effected from the inside. Up to the end, we respected each other's views and beliefs. We maintained our friendship.

The 1970s were fraught with political turmoil in the Philippines. The tumultuous radicalism that pervaded the times was even more exacerbated by the rising popularity of the "theology of the laity" as expressed in *Gaudeum et Spes* (the Pastoral Constitution on the Church in the Modern World) by St. Pope Paul VI and the Vatican Council II under St. Pope John XXIII.

Brother Willy was well informed of these documents, and his progressive consciousness ran alongside the mind of these two pontiffs. He was also rubbing elbows with the liberal members of the religious and clergy. At that time, most religious orders and academic institutions were relatively slow in implementing the precepts covered under the concepts of the Church in the modern world. Most congregations did not allow their members to join the parliament of the street. They were taking the safe side and remained conservatives. This was not to the liking of Brother Willy. He decided to involve himself with the grassroots in their conscientization[28] and active involvement in the local Church.

He became a social worker in the parish, working with the youth of Bula – this to the consternation of the religious superiors. He was marginalized by the Congregation but was much appreciated by the parishes where he was involved. For several years, he worked with the local community but not within the framework of the apostolate of the Marist Brothers. This opened the doors for his involvement with the Socio-Pastoral Institute based in Davao City. He worked with this organization for some years. But the Congregation thought he had stayed outside for enough years. He was given an ultimatum: to return to the community or apply for dispensation from his vows. At first, I thought that he would leave the Congregation. But he didn't easily give up. He requested that his work be considered part of the apostolate of the Marist Brothers to continue working with SPI much longer. It was to no avail. So, being an obedient Brother, he ended his stint with SPI and came back to join the community.

One of the best decisions Brother Willy did in his life was to go out of the Congregation for a while. He applied for a one-year leave plus a two-year exclaustration[29] from the Congregation. He tried to see more of what was happening outside the highly structured religious world. When he worked at a non-government organization [SPI] in Davao City, he experienced more struggles as he was basically on his own. He had to scrimp for food every day because of his meager salary. But he felt freer. He felt more at peace with himself. Perhaps it was his introspection that made him understand himself better, that made him find strength in the seemingly hardest point in his life.

After three years of self-discernment and introspection, he returned to the Marist Congregation with much-renewed fervor and passion.

* * * * *

Brother Willy celebrated his 25th year as a Marist Brother in 1997. He was honored at the NDDC auditorium along with the late Brother Jose Torrecampo and Brother Paterno Corpus (the current President of Notre Dame of Marbel University). Brother Willy had just accepted the Presidency of NDDC two years before. On the occasion of his Silver Jubilee, my co-author Briccio wrote a tribute to honor Brother Willy.[30] It was published in the *Marist News Bits,* a newsletter of the Marist Brothers of East Asia Province. This article encapsulates most eloquently the man with a mission. Briccio delivered the tribute

One of the most significant contributions that Brother Willie shared with the Marist Brothers in the Philippines, a gift which up to this very day few of the Brothers have known and appreciated, was his social and political awareness at the time when most religious men and women were still seriously discussing what clothes to wear and what kind of prayers to recite. He was, to my mind, one of the very few who understood the real significance of the mystery of the incarnation as it relates to the life of the Church and its implications to religious life and formation.

It is with fond memories – fraught with bittersweet and nostalgic moments – that I remember the days some ten to fifteen years back. A small group of Brothers would gather late in the evening up to the wee hours of the morning and discuss the "events" of the day (during assemblies and retreats) and the "signs of the times" (during holidays when the Brothers could meet each other in a more relaxing way). We held endless sharing and discussions. This prompted some Brothers to christen our group as a bunch of "gabbers", not knowing that the term was used, wittingly or unwittingly but nevertheless good-naturedly, by the "members" themselves as its unofficial title. Unknown to most of the Brothers, serious matters were discussed, and, generally, issues and concerns were tackled. During those times, the group already discussed words and terms such as re-founding, solidarity, mass-based consultations, concern for the least favored, and ecology. At their consternation, the Province was relatively "slow" in its consideration and implementation of such matters.

One staunch member of this "group" was Brother Willie. He was not the most vocal, but he was undoubtedly one of the group's most inspiring and influential members. As if piece-by-piece, he introduced some fascinating tenets into the jigsaw puzzle of the life of the Brothers. Gradually, some articulate members articulated Brother Willie's thoughts and feelings as if patiently fitting the pieces together. Later, we created a picture, albeit hazy at first but nonetheless true to form. It was the beginning of an unfinished vision when, sometime in the future, it would evolve into a clear and distinguishable image, not of an impossible dream but a dream come true.

One may ask what brought about the enlightened thoughts, which Brother Willie was able to share with the group. Suppose I have to offer one answer to this question. In that case, I have to say that it was because of the gradual unfolding of his gift of awareness brought about by the unique experiences, which only he can fully explain up to this very day. Who can actually realize and understand what he went through during the times when he was grappling with the concepts of institutionalized Church while at the same time struggling to organize the basic ecclesial communities? What were the thoughts in his mind as he worked to organize the youth sector of Bula, most of whom were the poorest of the poor? What untold struggles did he have to undergo as he worked with the leaders and members of the Church? What depths of challenges did he have to cope with as he worked for three years with the Socio-Pastoral institute (SPI)? The litany of questions can be endless.

Brother Willie went through the transition in his life that was filled with tumultuous personal search. The burden was such that a weaker breed could have just chosen to give up; but not Brother Willie. He stuck to his guns and ended up the victor and a better person. It was a struggle spanning almost ten years of questioning and looking for answers that were as elusive as daydreams in most cases. But the search goes on – the horizon becoming more expansive and the miles ahead stretching to a far distant destination. The beat of the drums signals the rhythm one must follow. Brother Willie is listening to something else – to the beat of some distant drums that he hears within himself – and that he must follow.

It is very difficult to fathom the depths of a person's inner thoughts and feelings and his struggles and difficulties. But one thing is sure – somehow, somewhere throughout his life's journey, Brother Willie has become stronger in the end. We see in him a man tried by fire. He has used his hardships and challenges as stepping-stones to make himself more mature, firm, and stable. They have become of him the very wellspring of his patience, understanding, and concern for others. In them, he has learned to value hard work and dedication. Through them, he will be able to reach the heights of success.

Now as Brother Willie commences a new chapter in his religious life more challenges are coming his way. New inspirations will present themselves as he finds new strength in facing them with renewed vigor and hope. Brother Willie will have to meet them in his own uniqueness and in his own special way. He cannot fit himself in a master mold, with which others expect him to conform. He must try to see himself as his own person. He must endeavor to understand his own personality and be willing to discover how he can harness it to fulfill his dreams. As everyone else must do, he will have to find his strength in his trust, faith, and hope in God, who will help him continue his life journey.

On this special occasion, it is our wish that Brother Willie continues to grow in wisdom and in love. May he achieve peace and serenity as he continues to face and carry the heavy burden of responsibility given to him as an administrator. May our Mother Mary keep him in her loving embrace.

Brother Ted Fernandez added his own impressions to remind us of a man who championed the poor, just like St. Marcellin Champagnat.

> I see in Willy through so many years that unending desire to go to the poor, help them in their plight, and even sacrificed his vocation to be with them. He took a leave of absence and left his comfort zone just to appease them. Being tagged as a leftist and at one with the communists did not faze him. The Brothers dared not criticize him because he was fighting for a cause. He was way ahead for most of us. The "rebel in him" indeed prompted him to take the road not taken. He came back to us filled with the Christian ideology of what it means for us to be a religious in this day and age.
>
> Finally, as he was inevitably given the role of leader of our tertiary institutions, he carried with him that vision. He made the schools models of growing trees and flowers to invite the birds to come to the city. Instead, it was us who started dwelling and admiring in this forestation. He saw many of these students deprived of tertiary education at another stance. His point of interest was the *Lumads* [Cebuano word for Indigenous People], who we rank among the poorest in our society. He took many more initiatives for

> others, especially our young Brothers, to continue and hone this interest to serve the poor.

Brother Robert Teoh of Malaysia, the former Provincial Superior of the Province of East Asia, said this of him during his tribute, Brother Willy was a champion of “the lost, the last and the least!”

The President, the Administrator 1995-2021 10

""Effective leadership for me is one which is characterized by a lot of common sense, hard work, dedication, and good relationships."

~Willy Lubrico, FMS interview by Dr. Joan Palma~

Brother Willy indeed went back to the Marist Congregation a new man. He was forty-three and in the prime of his life. For the next twenty-six years, he vigorously applied his experiences and skillsets with great success across all facets of the academia, in the local as well as national government units, non-governmental and international organizations. He was comfortable with his success without pretentions and pulled others up the ladder of advancements in the process. It was a singular talent that Brother Willy was able to do, making his legacy too important and encompassing to fully encapsulate in words.

But he also paid his dues starting as a community worker. People judged him at first glance and assumed his value by appearance. He did not take offense; he knew his worth in salt – he was competent, deserving, worthwhile, etc. In fact, I sometimes believe he actually relished in the misconceptions and find unsettling enjoyment when he told stories about being mistaken for a gardener or janitor on campus, or a longshoreman on the ship dock.

Brother Willy was the Director of Community Extension Service from 1990 to 1995 at Notre Dame of Kidapawan College in North Cotabato. It was there where he got the phone call that would change the trajectory of his life forever.

He recalled that particular day during the 2020 pandemic lockdown and recorded it in his journal in vivid details.

January 2, 1995:

Brother Renato Cruz called. He was then Provincial of the Marist Brothers residing in Cotabato City. He wanted to see me. I took the bus from Kidapawan to Cotabato City the next day. Brother Rey, as we fondly called him, informed me that the Board of Trustees of Notre Dame of Dadiangas College (NDDC) appointed me as the next President of the College starting June, in six months! I was shocked. Fear and anxieties were real to me then. With no administrative experience, I hesitated to accept the appointment. I bargained with Brother Rey if he could give me two months to reflect on the offer. He informed me that I should not give him any difficulty, for he was on his way to the United States for a bone marrow transplant for his life-threatening leukemia.[31] He was leaving the next month.

After two weeks, I read in our community Bulletin Board the Brothers' assignments for June. I heard nothing at all from the Brothers about my shocking assignment. I kept it to myself. I didn't mention it to anyone. I brought my things to NDDC in General Santos City slowly in the span of three months. But I kept my next assignment a secret.

June 1995:

A personnel assembly was scheduled at NDDC where I will be introduced to the faculty and staff. An hour before going to the venue, I received letters of resignation from the three top Administrators. I felt total dismay. I took it as a sign of their not accepting me. I had a short meeting with them almost begging them to give me a chance since I felt I wouldn't last long in the position anyway. But all I got was the look of lack of trust and a half smile of "why you?"

Brother Bob McGovern gave me a book about the life of a President of Notre Dame University in South Bend, Indiana that same week. A Jesuit priest, he wrote about his challenges, failures, successes, and joys as the head of the renowned institution. He would go on to serve as the University President for twenty-two years!

I never expected that I would outlast him and be President for 26 years of two Notre Dame Universities.

* * * * *

Brother Willy's recipe for his twenty-six years of success as a President of not one but two universities and his countless accomplishments, is best described by his friend Briccio:

One of the things I admired most about Brother Willy was his persistence and determination. When he puts his mind into a project, he sets his focus into it, plans it, and makes sure that it gets accomplished.

One day, we were into one of our regular sharing of experiences and ideas. He was excitedly narrating the updates of his ongoing projects. (For anyone who does not know him, it would seem that he doesn't get excited at all. He exudes this stoical façade that could sometimes be misconstrued as arrogance or apathy.) When he finished, I told him how I envied him. When I was president of Notre Dame of Dadiangas College (NDDC), I thought I had so many good projects and plans but I always encountered rejections and refusals from the Board. But with him, it seemed to me that he got everything he wanted or planned. He then told me that it wasn't true at all. He, too, got so many rejections and refusals. But he was more persistent.

When the Board told him that there was no budget, he would find ways to produce the budget – make loan plans and ask for donors. When the Board told him that the plan or project needed more preparation and explanation, he would go back to the drawing board and improved it until the Board got satisfied. When the Board told him that the contractor had questionable track record, he would get someone else whom they trusted or respected. He was that persistent! Both NDDU and NDMU benefitted from his vision, which he persistently transformed into a formidable mission, which he shared with his constituents.

*****

This narrator observed how his Facebook wall is a study of his self-effacing personality and wry humor. His Facebook followers find it so endearing that he engaged with them, taking the time to randomly respond to their comments. As busy as he was, he used social media vociferously especially during the pandemic. He played along with his Facebook friends on the online games apps.[32] One of these apps purportedly examines your personality using algorithms and the result of this game he posted on his Facebook account. For good measure, he also forwarded it to me and to many of his friends through Messenger's personal messaging system.

The app asks: "What do people fear most about you? Tap on your birth icicle to find out."

Result: Willy - October. YOUR STUBBORNNESS. Willy is a force of nature, all passion, and strength with a heart made of gold. He can be as stubborn as a bull, but that side only comes out when he is standing up for someone or something that he really believes in. Willy feels everything deeply and is an incredible friend or partner to have because once he has given someone his heart; he loves with every fibre [U.K. spelling of fiber] of his being.

My co-author Briccio didn't need the algorithm to figure out his friend Willy. Briccio had already shared with me his uncanny observations long before I received the result of the app. He wrote,

I guess one of the most obvious characteristics of Brother Willy is his "bull-headedness". When he puts his mind into something, he will never leave a single stone unturned until he achieves what he has planned to do. Time is not of the essence for him. Even if it takes forever, he will still pursue his dreams until he succeeds.

Brother Willy made use of his "bull-headedness" to his excellent advantage. He was able to do this because of his superb judgment. He has a cunning way of calculating what will work and what won't. Actually, his decisions do not just come out of the blue but are consistently thought out and well planned.

I wrote my dissertation on the cultural model of achieving excellent performance in an educational organization. Specifically, I wrote on the "Conceptualization of a Model on the Interrelationship of Culture and Performance in a School System".

My thesis was based on the concept that the school has its own culture, a set of assumptions, beliefs, and norms shared among its members. It may be consciously created, or it may have simply evolved across time. My study tried to essay on one crucial aspect – that there is a direct relationship between the organizational culture and the organizational performance of a school or an organization. The more excellent the culture of an organization is, the greater the level of its performance will become.

The Marist Congregation gave me a one-year and one-summer study leave to write my dissertation. I flew to Manila to enroll in dissertation Writing at the University of Santo Tomas. I was assigned to Dr. Emily Tan as my adviser. She was very strict, but I appreciated her for it. I spent a couple of months doing the related literature review and taking notes. I remember how Dr. Tan specifically "ordered" me to visit all the libraries of the prominent universities in Manila and the libraries of the major embassies there. It took another month to write my dissertation proposal. When I was through with the proposal, I showed it to several people for comments, suggestions, and recommendations. The list included Brother James Adams, Brother Paul Meuten, Brother Manny de Leon, Brother Robert McGovern, Brother Paterno Corpus, and Brother Willy Lubrico.

Everyone gave me very satisfactory compliments except Brother Willy. Being a man of few words, Brother Willy just managed to say, "Good, Brix".

That proposal enumerates the expected cultural practices, symbols, and norms that would help spell out the desired Marist organizational performance. Brother Willy planned to implement these cultural practices, symbols, and norms in NDDU unbeknownst to me. Within a span of one semester, he transformed it into an institution rich in cultural significance and symbolism. Overnight, NDDU became a Marist architectural showcase and ecological landscape!

Even before I got to defend my dissertation proposal, Brother Willy was already on his way towards the transformation of NDDU to showcase what a Marist institution should be culturally. Brother Willy, from then on, would become a champion of advocating the cultural transformation of the institutions and programs assigned to his care. He would leave his "blueprint" in all his endeavors.

Another thing that I admire most about Brother Willy was his unconditional acceptance of the Brothers assigned to the community where he belongs and the school he heads. To my knowledge, he has never refused any Brother assigned by the superior to become members of the community under his care and supervision. The truth is there are "difficult" Brothers, and they come in varying degrees of difficulty. Sometimes the most difficult ones are assigned in his community where every member lives under the same roof 24-7. He takes them all in stride but never for granted. He is never the one who would nag them. Instead, he gives them enough rope to hang themselves. If they decide to hang themselves, they would soon learn their lesson, and ultimately they would either shape up or ship out. One time I asked whether these "difficult" Brothers bother him. He replied: "No, because sooner or later, they will realize the consequences of their actions and have to decide for themselves. I cannot do it for them." Tough love!

* * * * *

What was it like working for and with Brother Willy you might ask? When I first conceptualized this book, I thought finding the answer to this question would be the hardest thing to do. But, on the contrary, there was no shortage of volunteers willing to share their interactions with him. Some of them knew him from when he was a young boy, others as a teacher, colleague, Boss, confrere, and a friend.

Dr. Joan Palma is the current Vice President of Academic Affairs at Notre Dame of Marbel University. He interviewed the President for a book project to celebrate the 200th Marist Anniversary in January 2017. (I personally met Joan when Brother Willy, his friend Editha Plecis, and another university dean Lynou Zacal visited my family in Rhode Island during the July 4th weekend 2016. They were on their way to attend the 7th Assembly of the Marist International Network of Institutions of Higher Education (MINIHE) at the Marist College in Poughkeepsie, New York). Joan's interview is revealing:

> Like any other young boy, he wanted to try something new, something different. He was studying then at Notre Dame of Surallah, an innocent, unassuming young boy who didn't know much about the world. His friends took the exam and joined the workshop for the Marist Congregation and he, not wanting to be left out, also joined in. Looking back, it was more of fate that led Brother Willy to become a Marist Brother and then the rest is history, so to say.
>
> But he did not have it easy. Brother Willy traversed a path covered with difficulties and beset with sweat and tears. He recalled that in some ways, he had a sort of love-hate relationship with his fellow Brothers and even with his superiors during his younger days. However, personal differences are not uncommon in any structured organization where occasional disagreements happen because of differing opinions and perspectives. But perhaps, those experiences are what made him a formidable force in the Marist Congregation.
>
> Brother Willy was not one to talk about his accomplishments in life. He did not really want public acknowledgments for his successes. He was a silent worker, one who did not flaunt what he had achieved for the entire world to see. But undeniably, he was a man of many

accomplishments. His presidency was marked by a clear vision and creativity, which opened doors for the inception of numerous programs that impacted the institutions under his leadership and all the other Marist institutions and the community in general. Among those initiatives included the following:

- the Marist Education Commission, which primarily aims to provide a forum for the different Marist schools in enhancing the Marist education ministry;
- the Marist Formation Program, which caters to the development of neophyte school administrators;
- the Green University Program, which advocates environmental care;
- the Women Advocacy Program, which caters to issues and concerns of women;
- the "Abante Lumad Scholarship Program" which raises funds to financially support the college education of the poor but deserving indigenous college students in South Cotabato;
- and the school museums, which allow us to revisit the Marist history and revel in its beautiful memories.
- the latest project he established is the Marist Hope Center for Justice and Good Governance, an arm of the NDMU College of Law. The Center aims to increase access to justice to the marginalized sectors of our society and intensely advocate good governance.

Indeed, when he was still alive, some young Brothers would call him a living legend. They looked upon him as a leader with Midas touch in that wherever he was assigned; the place was beautifully transformed by the touch of his magic hands.

By being entrusted with key positions, Willy had also been recognized by outside agencies and institutions. Among those key offices include the following:

- President, Notre Dame Educational Association (NDEA) from 2014 to 2020;
- Board Member, Catholic Educational Association of the Philippines (CEAP) from 2013 to 2020;
- But perhaps, one of the most significant acknowledgments of Brother Willy's selfless dedication and service were when he was awarded the Pontifical Distinction Cross *Pro-Ecclesia et Pontifice* in July 2015. This award, known as the "Cross of Honor", is the highest award given by the Roman Catholic Church with the approval of the Pope to a layman or clergy for his outstanding and selfless service to the Church and humanity.

When asked about his formula for effective leadership, Brother Willy had this to say: *"Effective leadership for me is one which is characterized by a lot of common sense, hard work, dedication, and good relationship."* According to him, an effective leader should have a strong determination to achieve the goals he set out to do, a leader with a vigorous political will. He further noted that placing a premium on his relationship with people was where he succeeded the most. Some might have perceived him as quite stern or stoic, but honestly, he was a compassionate, tenderhearted individual.

Brother Willy had been in the Marist Congregation for fifty-two years. At 68, he had experienced a lot of ups and downs. He had moments of joy and times of sorrow, small defeats, and significant triumphs. These experiences had put him in a position to better understand the world and see it from a much broader perspective. Indeed, Brother Willy was one leader, one Marist Brother who had given much in the service of humanity.

Brother Willy was the President of the Marist International Network of Institutions of Higher Education (MINIHE) in 2012-2014. This association has members all around the globe that meet once every two years. In 2010, the international conference was held in Mexico. Brother Willy attended and sent me a photo of him and his colleagues posing with the Mexican Dancers that performed at the event. In November 2014, the Notre Dame of Marbel University successfully hosted the five-day MINIHE international conference. Not to be outdone, the university dance troupe presented a medley of Philippine dances, including a T'boli dance. He sent me a copy of the picture of Philippine dancers too. Both photos are included at the end of this chapter.

Brother Willy was a strong advocate of the visual and performing arts. A friend named Yumi (Michael Angelo Yambok) narrated that when he was studying at NDMU for his Master's Degree in Community Development he hesitantly visited the President in his office. He had heard Brother Willy was strict and tough. A member of the Indigenous people called T'boli, Yumi was the leader of the Helobung T'boli Dance Troupe that had performed at the Philippine Cultural Center and traveled to UK, Russia, USA, Australia, and many other Asian countries. Yumi wanted to present a proposal for his group to perform at the university. He was totally surprised when Brother Willy engaged him in a lengthy and profound conversation. Yumi found a friendly person who genuinely appreciated his T'boli culture and showed interest in him as a person. He wrote, "Brother Willy told me that as a young T'boli leader, I am in an excellent position to protect my culture and guard my ancestral domain. He not only approved our performance at NDMU but he also instilled in me the inspiration to be a good leader."

This year Yumi, who has racked up national and international awards as a Community Organizer and performer, is running for Councilor of Lake Sebu, his ancestral home. He credits Brother Willy for believing in him.

* * * * *

Dr. Estrella T. Golingay, his high school classmate who became his colleague at the Notre Dame of Marbel University for eighteen years taught literature and languages at NDMU and NDS High school. She spent most of those years sharing her knowledge in creative writing with her students. She attended national writing workshops in poetry and fiction genres. She has numerous poems and fiction published in the national and local magazines and journals and won in literary competitions. Her written collections appear in her blog site at starsie54.wordpess. She wrote this about Brother Willy:

> I came to NDMU like a feather. So light, at the right time and place, flitting between studying for my Masters and teaching loads that started in 1996. Brother Crispin Betita, F.M.S. was my President for half of my career. In the last half, I worked with Brother Willy when he became the President of NDMU in 2006.
>
> It wasn't the first time we were reunited because we've been active in our class reunions as members of the Notre Dame of Surala Batch 1971 since the 1990s. But it was a 360 degrees pivot in the academe. Brother Willy became my big Boss, and me, the employee when I was with the College of Arts and Sciences teaching language and literature. But when I finished my Ph.D. in Language Education at NDDU in 2012, we would meet at the conference room discussing policies and academic matters. I was then assigned as the Language Department Head.
>
> What was it like having him as a president? I'd say no exact words to put him in his niche. His dedication, expertise, and passion translated into excellent outputs, placing the school on the national educational map.
>
> So I retired in 2014, with a full mind and heart knowing that a batchmate in high school, a *barkada*, has carved a name in the academe and related leading organizations. He made us – his high school classmates - all proud!

*****

Mr. Albert Anino, CPA, MBA, joined the Notre Dame of Marbel University in 2014. He is now the current NDMU Comptroller hired to oversee the university's financial wellbeing after the retirement of the former comptroller (Andres Magallanes). Brother Willy was wearing shorts with striped shirt and a cowboy hat the first time they met in 2013, Kenneth recalled. He wrote, "At first, I thought Brother Willy was just an ordinary staff of a small company until my boss introduced me to the President of Notre Dame of Marbel University".

A year later they met again when Kenneth applied for a job at NDMU. Talking in a well-modulated but authoritative voice during the final interview, Kenneth admitted being nervous and felt so intimidated by his interviewer's presence. But his first impressions changed soon enough when he started working with the President of the university. He appreciated the quiet style and hands-off kind of leadership, and genuine interest in his new hire. "He asked me about my future plans and the factors that will make me stay at NDMU."

According to Kenneth, Brother Willy would conceptualize several projects every year, find the funds for them, and complete them - without publicity except for the months before he died. He posted on his Facebook news feed the landmarks, buildings, and structures of NDMU when he was already in Manila for his surgery. As far back as 2017, he discussed with Kenneth his future plans and offered him the Administrative Position at the university. Kenneth recalled the accompanying advice, "Provided that I grow in maturity, learn to make sound decisions, familiarize myself with the policies of the university, and build my image as a good administrator. In short, I need to do better". In his tribute, Kenneth quoted Brother Willy speaking in Tagalog (one of many dialects of which he was conversant). The authors retained some of the shorter quoted lines but for brevity, we included only the English translations of the longer versions.

Like others before him, Kenneth shared that Brother Willy even pressured him to finish his master's degree, constantly nudging him:

> ...to be the best version of myself. And Brother Willy always ensured that the employees at the university achieved the minimum required qualification or better. This is the reason why everyone under his care, particularly the administrators, continuously improved and aspired for a better NDMU. Thus, the ISO (International Organization for Standardization) became our common goal for two years. As a result, NDMU received the ISO certification last March 2020 prior to the lockdown. To me, the ISO was one of the secret plans of Brother Willy before he left us. ISO defines

a standard as a document, "established by consensus and approved by a recognized body that provides, for common and repeated use, rules, guidelines, or characteristics for activities or their results, aimed at the achievement of the optimum degree of order in a given context. In simpler terms, standards provide world-class specifications for products, services, and systems to ensure product and service quality, safety, and efficiency. Standards are likewise means of facilitating trade among nations."[33]

Brother Willy's goal to hold NDMU to the highest standards was the height of his dream. Mr. Joan Palma, Vice President for Academic Affairs, confirms Kenneth's belief:

> The ISO certification of NDMU is really one of the significant legacies of Brother Willy. He pushed for the university's certification despite the initial hesitancy of everyone at the school to go for it. When an institution is ISO certified, it has met all the standardization and quality assurance requirements on a global scale.

Therefore, getting the "stamp of approval" with an ISO certification was huge. ISO standards are a vital part of our society to ensure quality and safety in both products and services in international trade. Kenneth continued:

> Furthermore Brother Willy facilitated the Marist Administrator's Formation Program. This one-week training program allows attendees to forge friendships and connections with other fellow administrators across the Marist Institutions in the Philippines. It deepens their understanding of the Marist way of leadership and management that Brother Willy wants us to adapt, give due consideration and appreciation. It may seem daunting to implement this in one year or in one term of office but not to Brother Willy. He spent more than thirty years of his life in this Marist academic landscape and learned it from his own actual experience.

Brother Willy tasked me in 2020 to create a study on aquatic center complete with a swimming pool facility. He cited it as a curriculum requirement from elementary to Grade 12 and the college department. He pointed the necessity of training the students on basic survival swimming skills and the benefits of having this facility. He convinced me to create the study.

He said, "Kenneth, someday it would be difficult for us to compete with the State Universities in Surallah and Gen. Santos City. A well-known Catholic University [University of Sto. Tomas] from Manila is being built as we speak with excellent facilities. We should not just concentrate on curriculum improvement because we'd possibly see our graduates and personnel pirated by these universities. So we should be proactive - we should offer what they don't have."

Brother Willy even shared with me his vision of setting the brand that NDMU and other Marist Institutions may consider. "I have long proposed that we should have one system for NDDU, NDMU, and other sister schools. When others hear about us, they think we are owned by different entities with different system and quality. We should emulate Ateneo. So when folks hear the name they know right away that the Marist Brothers own the school".

Brother Willy's vision illustrates his genuine love and concern for NDMU, including all the Marist education institutions.

*****

Ms. Dalia Mesias had been the Executive Secretary to the Administrative Vice President of NDMU from November 1984 until she was re-assigned to the President's Office in 2001. Dalia was not only a secretary to Brother Willy. She was also a confidante, a *barkada* with whom he could share light moments outside office hours along with other friends. She is the current secretary to the new President of NDMU, Brother Pat Corpus who took over the helm when Brother Willy died. Dalia agreed to stay on during the transition. Her daily interaction with Brother Willy gave her the best vantage view:

This is my tribute to my Boss, whom I have worked for fifteen years. I did not expect to do this. I expected him to give a testimony on my retirement being his secretary.

I started working with Brother Willy in 2006 when he became the President of NDMU. I have met him before on many occasions during Marist events. My first impression of him was that he was *suplado* (stuck-up), very strict, unapproachable, *kakurulba* (intimidating). He was very serious-looking and rarely smiled. I think many have had the same first impressions of him. *Amo gid ina ang dating ni Brother Willy sa mga tawo nga wala pa naka kilala sa iya.* (That's what he appears like to those who don't know him yet).

When he came to the office in the early days, I'd greet him good morning or good afternoon, as the case may be. But he would just pass by *nga daw wala lang nakabati.* (Like he did not hear me). Then, finally, I got used to it. I no longer waited to be acknowledged. I just continued my usual greetings *sa iya bisan wala sia nagasabat.* (Even if he does not respond). Eventually, though, he would respond to my greetings, *na* influence *ko na sya.*

As we worked together, I discovered that my first impression of Brother Willy was unfounded. I found him to be witty and fun to be around. He liked to tease his close friends; he'd pull their leg especially if they buy his story. *Abi nila tuod, gali gina tinuntuhan niya lang sila.* He'd constantly banter with folks he liked to "bully" in a teasing way. *Malingaw ka gid sang ila estorya.* (One would be entertained with their antics).

Brother Willy also loved to tell us his funny experiences and how he enjoyed a good laugh. Once, he went to Iloilo on vacation onboard a boat from General Santos City. A well-meaning friend learned about it, and *nagpadala ba naman sang* (sent) a whole tuna fish. Brother Willy arrived late at night in Iloilo. He carried the frozen tuna on his shoulder. *Daw kargador lang kuno sya.* (He felt like a longshoreman). Embarrassed, he covered his face with a face towel. *Sang pag-istorya nia sini sa amon perti man kadlaw nia.* (While he narrated this incident to us, he laughed so hard at his own story).

Once I got to know him, I found Brother Willy to be kind-hearted, compassionate, and had great concern for people. I have witnessed how he would personally deal with the parents *nga nagapila* (lining up) during examination periods for a promissory note *para sa balayran sang ila anak* (for money owed for their children). As President, he did this to meet the parents and personally know their financial situation and otherwise. He gets miffed if the exams have already started when parents ask for a promissory note. He'd tell them that procrastinating could cause the students (their children) needless worry about studying for their exams and the uncertainty of their being able to take them.

As President of NDMU, my Boss was a man of vision and action. He improved the school facilities and pushed for excellence in the delivery of services and quality of education of the different sectors in the University. Furthermore, he highly encouraged the faculty to engage in research, publication, and work on their professional advancements. And despite his busy schedule, he took time to randomly observe classes himself, as he wanted to know firsthand how instruction is being conducted and delivered in the classroom.

Brother Willy has a profound sense of history. In institutional events, we always have commemorative projects. For example, during the 65th Anniversary of NDMU in 2011, the Abante Lumad Scholarship for Indigenous Peoples was started through fundraising.

He launched the Diamond jubilee projects in 2019 to commemorate NDMU's 73rd Anniversary. Such as Fund Raising for the IBED Chapel, Marist Hope Center for Justice and Good Governance by the College of Law, Gender and Human Development – a program for female and male students, Skillfest Caravan for the Out of School Youth of the Diocese of Marbel, and the Alumni Legacy Project where all graduating students from elementary to Graduate School are required to plant a tree as part of their graduation requirements. Participants to the Alumni Legacy Project planted trees and built markers ahead of time to commemorate the various events.

On October 3, 2021, NDMU celebrated its Diamond Jubilee without Brother Willy. But his presence was palpable. He started hanging the diamond jubilee streamer in 2019 to give the University and the community something to look forward to and remind them of the approaching milestone. In addition, he arranged to install diamond jubilee markers on the two campuses. He readied them for us two years in advance.

Brother Willy was conscious of his health. He had regular check-ups and lab tests as prescribed by his doctor. His lab work was often better than the younger Brothers in his community. *Indi sila magpati, basi daw gina baydan ni Brother Willy ang laboratory staff.* (Others didn't believe his lab results, they said, perhaps Brother Willy paid the laboratory staff).

I will miss a great boss because of his many projects and programs. He kept me very busy, but the trust and confidence he put in my ability to facilitate things for him made me grow professionally and personally. He was a boss, mentor, big Brother, and *barkada* rolled into one. He would always introduce me to his friends, becoming an extended friend. He was a builder of lasting and sincere relationships. According to one of his fellow Marist Brothers, he has charisma with people he meets. He never considered it beneath his being a President to participate in school activities organized by students or personnel; when asked to sing and he'd do it, he'd dance too although he has two left feet, and once he dressed up for the "Ati-Atihan" presentation. Always *game na game gid siya.*

Our law school administrator recently informed me that Brother Willy planned to come home on January 25, 2021, after his medical treatment for his prostate cancer in Manila. Then I remember he mentioned that after his surgery on January 15, he would stay for ten more days in Manila for recovery and follow-up check-ups. So, true enough, he scheduled his coming home to his Creator on January 25.

So may ara sang kanta nga (there is a song) "Tie A Yellow Ribbon" by the country singer Kenny Rogers the first line of which runs like this, *"I'm coming home I've done my time."* According to his B.F.F., Ma'am Prima, the song applies to Brother Willy. She messaged me and suggested that yellow ribbons be tied on trees on campus and cars as he was being met at the airport. So we did!

Farewell, Brother Willy. We will continue praying for you and being inspired by your legacies. Pray for the whole NDMU community and us, too.

* * * * *

Alma S. Hordista, a Marist lay partner, served the Notre Dame of Dadiangas College in 1983 as a teacher and administrator. She was the Principal of the elementary department from 1992-2002, Director/Principal of the Integrated Basic Education Department from 2002-2012, Director of the VoTech Programs 2012-2017. Currently, she teaches part-time in the Graduate School and is in charge of the Secretariat of the Marist Education System. She offers,

> I was in my 4th year as principal of the Elementary Department when Brother Wilfredo Lubrico, FMS, was appointed president of Notre Dame of Dadiangas College (now University) in 1995. He was my boss for 11 years. I was so motivated to do my best because of his all-out support in the programs and activities of the Elementary School and later with the Integrated Basic Education Department. He brought out the best in me as a Marist educator. Therefore, I would like to share how I see him as a school leader.
>
> Brother Willy, as we fondly call him, is a man of vision. He shared his vision with us because he believed that this vision would only be attained by the total involvement of both the Marist Brothers and lay personnel.
>
> A good listener, he initiates consultations and dialogues before proceeding with the implementation of a program. He

created different committees to handle planning, execution, and evaluation. He was a master at delegating work putting his trust in his ability to find the right people for the job.

The personnel looked back with gratitude to him for recognizing their role in the achievements of the University. The Golden Jubilee benefit package was one of his meaningful initiatives approved by the Board of Trustees during his presidency. The Golden Jubilee package is a benefit granted to NDDU personnel during the 50th anniversary of the university. This includes rice allowance, free uniforms, accelerated ranking, and summer vacation leave to college faculty who has completed twenty-three years of service. The personnel are still enjoying this benefit granted on the occasion of the 50th anniversary of NDDU.

Brother Willy had a heart for the less privileged. A four-hectare lot at Espina Estate was donated to NDDU through Brother Robert McGovern. The intent of the donation is to open a Catholic school in that area of the city. Brother Bob was able to get financial assistance for the building of the classrooms. Brother Willy, the president then, saw this as an opportunity to bring quality Catholic education to the less privileged sector. After a series of consultations, benchmarking, and a feasibility study, the school, opened for Grades 1 to 3 in 1996. The school is named Notre Dame Of Dadiangas University Integrated Basic Education Department Espina Campus. This school followed the socialized tuition scheme, wherein the tuition fees are based on the family income.

The whole school community feels Brother Willy's presence, at all levels from kindergarten to the doctoral program. He was always present in activities: academic, non-academic, small gatherings of personnel, and even students' simple gatherings to research forums. He has mastered the pedagogy of presence.

Brother Willy touched many lives. He encouraged the teachers to obtain higher degrees through the development program. But, it was his encouragement that motivated the teachers. Training, exposure trips, benchmarking, and immersion activities helped teachers gain confidence.

As we look back to his years with NDDU, we thank him for being a part of our journey. Remembering Brother Willy and the moments shared with him makes me smile; it brightens my day now that I am retired. I pray that he will continue to pray for us wherever he may be.

He was not only a boss to me but a friend as well.

* * * * *

Brother Willy influenced so many lives as all the testimonies can attest. One cannot fully measure his impact on the lives of thousands, notably of students who reside on six continents today, continents that he too had visited. According to his friend Estrella Golingay, he was a “parent to thousands”. I call him the Rolodex man as he kept an extensive address list of alumni all over the world and when the occasion presents he would contact them and let them know when he’s in their area. On his way to and from his international workshops, he’d take a day or two to spend time with former students. I would by chance meet alumni in far away places only to pleasantly discover we have a common friend in Brother Willy.

Concrete examples present themselves when least expected, like this incident that happened fourteen years ago. I have encountered countless alumni who shared their unique stories about the goodness and kindness that Brother Willy exemplifies. But, the following anecdote stands out among the best.

I vividly recall this singular incident that happened one night in October 2007. My husband Al and I had just finished dinner. I put away the leftovers while he rinsed the dishes by the sink. Then, the landline phone rang, and I picked up.

“Hello Prim,” said Brother Willy. “Change of plans. I want to notify you that I will be visiting you in Florida but later like end of this month. I want to see Juliet Nagnal in Georgia first. Then she and Glenn will drive me down to your house. I am in San Francisco right now visiting some alumni in the area.”

“Al just confirmed that your plan is okay with us,” I replied after I conferred with my husband.

"Good. But may *problema ako*. Northwest Airlines won't allow me to change my itinerary without penalty five hundred dollars daw. Can you please help?" He then proceeded to give me the details.

I called the Northwest Airlines (N.W.A.) number that Brother Willy provided as soon as he hung up the phone. A pleasant lady responded, her English impeccable with a trace of accent.

"Good evening," I said.

"How may I help you, Ma'am?"

"I am calling from Florida on behalf of a friend. He is travelling using his frequent flyer mileage reward. He wants to change his flight from San Francisco to Georgia instead of Florida. But what must he do to waive the five hundred dollars penalty?"

"Can you please give me the full name of the passenger, Ma'am?"

"Brother Wilfredo Engane Lubrico," I said.

"O.M.G.! Really? Ma'am, that's the name of the President of the school from where I graduated. May I have your full name, please?"

"Prima Guipo Hower", I complied.

"How are you related to Miss Susan Guipo? She was my teacher in Economics!"

"We're sisters."

My husband, who was busy loading the dishwasher, paused to listen to the animated conversation.

"Wow, wow, wow." the Northwest lady just couldn't believe what she was hearing. Nor could my husband and I.

The N.W.A. lady put me on hold while explaining the matter to her Boss. She delivered the good news when she returned online.

"You're all set Ma'am."

Before she hung up the phone, the Northwest Lady's parting words were etched indelibly on my brain. "Brother Willy signed many promissory notes from my parents when money was scarce and my parents could not pay my tuition fees. The notes allowed me to take my exams and graduate from Notre Dame of Dadiangas College. He is the reason why I got my degree to qualify for this job at Northwest Airlines. I live in Missouri now. Please extend my thank you to Brother Willy".

Brother Willy got his ticket without penalty. He too was incredulous at the turn of events. And a week later, we celebrated his 55th birthday at my house in Florida with Juliet Nagnal and her husband, Glenn Laughter.

Bobby Borromeo commented when I posted this story on Facebook recently. “There indeed are no events that happen by chance, everything comes in confluence at the right place and time. This is the essence of synchronicity, the good that one does, always comes back in an unexpected way”.

Signing of the ISO Certification March 2020
L-R: Mr. Arnold Z. David, NDMU ISO Consultant, Dr. Andres Magallanes, Jr., NDMU Administrative Vice President, Brother Willy and ISO Evaluators from TUV Rheinland, a globally recognized company that is accredited to give ISO Certification.

Members of NDMU Administration & Staff with ISO Evaluators

Top: Notre Dame of Marbel University hosted the Marist International Network of Institutions of Higher Education (MINIHE). Thirteen countries were represented during Brother Willy Presidency.
Bottom left: Brother Willy posed with dancers at the Marist MINIHE in Mexico in 2010
Bottom right: NDMU showcased its folk dancers (including T'boli dance) at the MINIHE event November 9-13, 2014.

The Quintessential Gardener 11

"There were many more initiatives he took on for others."

~Brother Ted Fernandez~

Brother Willy's indomitable spirit and laser focused drive to achieve embody this quote from Mario Andretti, the famous racecar driver from Nazareth, Pennsylvania:

> Desire is the key to motivation, but it's determination and commitment to an unrelenting pursuit of your goal - a commitment to excellence - that will enable you to attain the success you seek.[34]

Brother Willy was definitely self-motivated and committed to "an unrelenting pursuit of his goal – a commitment to excellence". Every initiative he is known to have tackled, Brother Willy came out winning the race. Oh I am sure there were some I don't know that turned out to be duds too.

Once he texted on Messenger an update on writing his memoir.

"I started last lockdown, in the area of my vocation, administration, relationships, success and failures".

I would have loved to read about the failures that he was referring to so we might learn lessons from it. Alas, we will never find out. But for sure, whatever they were, are outweighed by his successes.

Let me illustrate the wide breadth of his success in an area we both love and of which I am most familiar – gardening.

He was the quintessential gardener in the literal sense of the word – a person who cultivated plants and tended to them with great care. The green spaces are his indelible mark at the campus of Notre Dame of

Dadiangas University and the Notre Dame of Marbel University. Like an artist, he turned the campus of NDMU into his canvass to paint his vision of a green university with manicured topiaries, bougainvilleas bursting in a rainbow of colors, stately pine trees, mahoganies, and evergreens rendering the place conducive to learning. He also carved spaces with symbolism at every turn – a Dedication Wall to honor the retirees, a corner to imbue the NDMU Goals: build Character, develop Competence, and integrate Culture, and many more.

Being a gardener was also a metaphor of his life, an inventory of his public persona. "You reap what you sow". When a person plans to have a garden, he must have a clear vision of what that garden will look like. Then he must become the faithful caretaker to provide for the needs of his plants – good soil, water, proper exposure to the sun, and supply the nutrients the plant needs. It is labor-intensive that requires year round chores - planting, weeding, pruning, deadheading, and dedication to ensuring the plant thrives. A gardener possesses a combination of traits – patience, persistence, appreciation that nature is unpredictable so he needs resilience to changes and willingness to accept failures. He is generous and when his plants bear fruits he proudly share their bounty with others. Brother Willy's lasting legacies as President of two Notre Dame universities include the Green University Program, "planting" as a creative tool to educate the young "to care and protect the environment and humanity".

So what else did he plant? He "planted" the seeds to grow the alumni associations. He "planted" the idea to formally create the group of former Marist Brothers to become Marist Mission lay partners, and as a dream maker he "planted" the idea of creating children's libraries. These are probably his least known initiatives but the impact is widely felt in the Philippines and abroad benefiting thousands.

ALUMNI AFFAIRS: Brother Bernard Curtin, FMS, the former Director of Notre Dame of Dadiangas College (NDDC) gave me a copy of an unpublished history of the Marist Brothers in the Philippines that he wrote in the early 1980s.[35] He considered the Notre Dame Educational Association (NDEA) as the best-known regional association of schools in the Philippines. He wrote:

> The beginnings were poor and humble, like a violet planted in the wilds of Moroland. The dawn of Catholic Education in south Mindanao took place in the latter half of the 19th century. In 1874, the Jesuit Fathers and the Religious of the Virgin Mary (RVM) attempted to found a mission and a school in the Muslim town of Tamontaka, about six kilometers south of Cotabato City. They were forced to withdraw a few years later but the blood of the martyrs would enrich the soil of Mindanao to produce a fabulous harvest in the next 100 years.

Brother Bernard referred to the Alumni as the "fabulous harvest" ~ the thousands of Notre Dame graduates scattered in six continents. Brother Willy, cognizant of the significant role that alumni can play, harnessed this untapped group as a mission partner. He made it one of his priorities. Both universities of which he was President benefited immensely from the partnership from local alumni as well as those living abroad.

In 1995, Brother Willy became the President of Notre Dame of Dadiangas College, my alma mater. A fledgling Alumni Affairs Office was already in operation when he arrived. NDDC started sponsoring Annual Homecoming Events to encourage the alumni to "come home" to their beloved Notre Dame School as early as 1983. In 1987, I went home from the USA and met Brother Crispin Betita who was then the President of NDDC. Brother Crispin introduced me to Virgie Abrea, who worked at NDDC from 1983-1995 and took on the task of an alumni coordinator. Ms. Esther Lacson took over after Virgie migrated to Canada. Brother Willy hired Ms. Susan Guipo, former chair of the Economics Department at the University of Santo Tomas, to take Esther's place in 1996, and when Susan retired, her assistant, Ruben Tugari, became the current coordinator.

In June 1993, thirty-five Notre Dame Alumni in the United States got together in San Diego, California to form an alumni association. It was registered as Notre Dame of General Santos City Alumni Association, USA (NDGSCAA, USA) under a 501-c7 non-profit organization umbrella. Later, USA was changed to International for inclusivity as members from Canada, Europe, Middle East, and the Philippines joined. Its goal:

1. To promote closer ties among the alumni of Notre Dame Schools of General Santos City now residing in North America.
2. To extend moral support to its members and material aid to its Alma Mater.

Engagement between Alma Mater and Alumni Association abroad was slow in coming but Brother Willy accelerated it. A National Reunion occurred every other year, starting from San Diego, Las Vegas, and many other cities after that. I was voted as the President of NDGSCAA, USA in 1997 when the reunion was held in San Francisco, California. That year, we established a Sponsor-A-Mentor Program whereby the association sponsored their mentor in elementary, high school, and college. Brother Henry Joseph Ruiz suggested that we invite Brother Willy Lubrico as our guest speaker for the 1997 reunion in San Francisco. Brother Willy declined due to his workload but finally in 1999, he joined us on the fourth National Reunion in New Jersey/New York.

In 2003, our alumni association in the United States voted for our reunion to be held at the NDDC campus. Unfortunately, SARS hit that year and Las Vegas, Nevada became an alternative venue for those who were concerned about travelling home to the Philippines. Still, fifty-five members of our association attended the reunion in the Philippines spearheaded by Brother Willy. Two months later, he also came to the reunion in Las Vegas as our Guest Speaker. Brother Willy attended a total of eight of these NDGSCAA, USA biennial reunions in the U.S. and one in the Philippines in 2013.

* * * * *

Brother Willy also planted the seed to grow the alumni association of Notre Dame of Marbel University (NDMU). He became the president of NDMU in 2006. Two years later in 2008 an NDMU alumni association was conceived. The late Jing Ang-Ureta, who was then NDMU Alumni Coordinator, visited friends and alumni of NDMU residing in Sacramento, CA. The first international reunion was organized and held in Las Vegas, Nevada in August 2009. Brother Willy Lubrico attended along with Jing Ureta, and forty-nine

NDMU alumni and their families. It was there that the Notre Dame of Marbel International Alumni Association was formally organized with Don Donaire as its first president.

The main purpose of the organization was to connect NDMU alumni from all over the world whether they graduated from Notre Dame of Marbel elementary, high school, college departments or even if they just spent a few educational years at NDMU. The objective was to reunite, rekindle, and reminisce about their school days at NDMU. Thereafter, biennial reunions have been held in different cities in the United States such as Atlantic City (2011), Chicago (2013), Los Angeles (2015), Houston (2017), which were attended by alumni from the USA, Philippines, Canada, Saudi Arabia, and Australia. Local Alumni Chapters hosted each reunion and the attendance increased yearly. Part of the funds raised during these events was earmarked for a scholarship project for NDMU students. Thanks to the former President of NDMU Alumni Association International, Frances Mariam Morales-Estela for sharing the history and updates of NDMU Alumni Association. She added:

> The last reunion was held in Marbel in January 2019. It was a grandiose two-day affair hosted by the local alumni with the full support of Brother Willy. It was truly a wonderful and memorable homecoming for most of us coming from abroad.
>
> The next reunion was planned for March 2021 in Melbourne, Australia but due to the pandemic, it was cancelled. Brother Willy's untimely passing sadly halted our scholarship program. Brother Pat Corpus, the current NDMU president, is now guiding us in the process of accepting applications and soon NDMU Alumni Association will award our first scholar.
>
> To date, we are able to reach out to over 1000 alumni through our Facebook group and keep them informed of news about our alma mater and other matters that are relevant to the group. When things get back to normal, we hope to plan and resume our international reunions.

Sadly, Jing Ang Ureta died in 2011 before the second international reunion. Brother Willy and Jing had reached out to me to encourage the two alumni associations to collaborate. NDDU alumni Association extended invitations to NDMU alumni and six of them joined at our 12th Biennial reunion in Washington, DC in June 2011 with Brother Willy. In return, a few of us returned the favor and attended NDMU's reunion in Atlantic City one month later.

Thus continued an enduring relationship between alumni and alma mater. For NDDU it resulted to many alumni sponsored projects: Covered Court at ND Lagao Boys Department campus, a Wall Legacy at ND Lagao Girls Department campus, an Alumni Walk, Alumni Wall, and Professor's Chair at NDDC and the establishment of Children's Library in three Notre Dame campuses.

Brother Willy's initiative at the Notre Dame of Marbel University Alumni Association is the Scholarship Program.

* * * * *

Forging friendships is the most significant fruit of this alumni collaboration that was inspired by Brother Willy. He relished connecting people and so the circles of friendship widens. He also inspired individuals to "give back" to their alma mater, in "big things or small" as our school hymn espouses. There are countless such individuals that it will be impossible to list all. But it would be remiss of me not to mention the ones Brother Willy called to my attention just months before his death. Some of them I knew very well, others I did not. It was as if Brother Willy wanted to send thanks to them for the last time.

Rayland Rogan, NDL1964, was the President of NDGSC Alumni Association in 1997- 1999. He sponsored Brother Willy so he could be at our 3rd Biennial National in the New York/New Jersey. I had introduced the two gentlemen, and they bonded. (Brother Willy and Rayland's younger brother Henry Rogan were classmates at Notre Dame of Lagao Class 1971). Rayland donated the Alumni Hall at the university and spearheaded the sponsorship of the Covered Court in the NDDU Lagao Campus. He donated a large sum of money himself, which the next NDGSCAA President Angel Boloico matched during his tenure in 2001.

Brother Willy also singled out Anastacio M. Hoyumpa, M.D., NDL1954, for introducing the concept of Professor Chairs Project at NDDU. According to Ruben Tugare, NDDU Alumni Coordinator, the university has currently seven professorial chairs: The Fevi Velasquez Chair in Business, The Tomas Falgui Chair in Mathematics, The Adriano Golingan Sr Chair in Business Education, Brother Renato Cruz Chair in Science, Brother Leonard Sonza Chair in Social Science, and Brother Henry Joseph Ruiz Chair in Religious Education.

Dr. Hoyumpa sponsored the creation of the seventh Professorial Chair for Biological Sciences named after his parents Anastacio Hoyumpa Sr. and Lamberta Maningo Hoyumpa. Dr. Hoyumpa also donated a Nursing Scholarship in the name of his wife Joan Hoyumpa at NDMU.

I never imagined that my friends on Facebook would increase exponentially. At least 200 or so that Facebook added to my Friends List after he died are his relatives and friends from Notre Dame of Marbel University. It's like his gift of friendship keeps on giving.

One of these new FB friends is an NDMU alumnus I dubbed the Mystery Man. I first "met" him through Brother Willy, who one day in early 2019, was so excited he just had to text me:

"Good news! I ran into an alumnus I hear about but occasionally meet on campus. He wanted to donate a substantial amount of money. Confidential", he wrote.

Shortly after, he followed it with a picture of himself and this imposing man in nondescript blue shorts and shirt, handing Brother Willy a brown envelope.

"Is this your mystery man?" I asked. He did not respond.

Brother Willy mentioned, much later on September 8, 2020, that they held a blessing ceremony for the Cafeteria and a Function Hall donated by this anonymous mystery man. So, like Alice in Wonderland, I got "curiouser and curiouser".

Fast-forward to January 2021, during the memorial services honoring Brother Willy. Imagine my immense surprise when I listened to an Engineer Orlando "Orly" Batallones, NDMHS1979, as he delivered his tribute. Only then was it revealed to me that he was the Mystery Man. Engineer Batallones is the General Manager & Head of Operations at Bio-Life Sciences Solutions Co., studied applied Statistics at the University of the Philippines Diliman, and received his Chemical Engineering degree from Ateneo de Davao University.

Now Orly and I are friends on Facebook. Orly added that Brother Willy had shared with him the idea of creating the Professorial Chair Project at Notre Dame of Marbel University. A Professorial Chair is a recognition given to a faculty member of a University for his/her meritorious performance in the fields of teaching and research in accordance with the mission/vision of the university.

This Professorial Chair project is under consideration at Notre Dame of Marbel University.

THE DREAM MAKER: Who can fully quantify the number of students and friends within Brother Willy's orbit whose dream came true because he turned out to be the ultimate "dream maker"? How many out there could relate to my story in some level and truly appreciate how lucky they are that some one came along to make their impossible dream possible. I know how it felt to cherish a dream for five decades that your heart aches at the possibility that it will never come true in your lifetime. Then someone waved his wand as effortlessly, magically - then *voila*! Your childhood dream becomes a reality.

I went home for a visit to my birthplace Gen. Santos City in 1996. Brother Willy was in the second year of his presidency. He showed me this room at the Notre Dame of Dadiangas Elementary Department, a 20'x30' classroom converted into a semblance of a library. Scattered all over the room were piles of unopened Balikbayan boxes full of books donated by his friends from the United States, Chris and Lanie Gammon, Edna Aquino Balili, and some boxes that my husband had sent. He apologized that the new building that was being constructed at the ND Lagao campus called IBED (Integrated Basic Education Department) is still unfinished. It will house a state-of-the art library, he said. Unfortunately, in the mean time, he was running out of room to place more cabinets. Some of the books were displayed neatly in cubed shelves painted in primary colors about three feet tall "so the children could easily reach them" he explained. On one side of the room is a Children's Play Corner with a bright red plastic slide and a wooden obstacle course that little bodies could go in and out, integrating he said, "a full mind and body experience" inside the library.

I teased, *"Ano man ining library mo Brother daw bodega."*

(What kind of library is this, Brother? It's like a storage room).

He replied, *"Amo gani nga gindala ta ikaw diri."*

(That is why I brought you here.)

That was the beginning of our partnership to build Children's libraries, a lifelong dream of mine. In 2004, with the support of the Notre Dame Alumni USA, friends and colleagues, my family created the Hower-Bates Library Network (HBL Network). We established the first Children's Library at NDDU IBED Lagao, with the generous donation from our son Lee and his wife, Heather – The Trinidad and Doroteo Guipo Learning Center. Its long-time librarian, Belle Avila told us that the accreditors from the Philippine Accrediting Association of Schools, Colleges, and Universities (PAASCU) recognized it as one of the best children's libraries in the Philippines.

In its eighteenth year, the HBL Network has established a total of five Children's Libraries, at NDDU IBED Lagao campus, ND-Sienna College Lagao campus, ND Marbel University IBED, the Dilangalen Children's Library in Midsayap for the Maguindanao. A fifth library, The Tboli Community Library & Culture Hub (TLC), was built in Lake Sebu during the pandemic and opened on March 27, 2021 serving the T'boli Community and other Indigenous People in the area managed by a T'boli leader named Yumi (Michael Angelo Yambok). A Reading Center was also opened at the Iram Elementary School near Olongapo in Luzon for the Aetas Community displaced by the eruption of Mt. Pinatubo on June 15, 1991.

The Hower-Bates Library Network has shipped more than 75,000 books as of January 2022 to these five libraries and reading center plus fifty-one other libraries in public schools, barrios, and cities of Luzon, Visayas, and Mindanao. In addition, we just agreed to partner with the congresswoman of our Province of South Cotabato (my birthplace). Congresswoman Shirlyn Banas-Nograles started the initiative to build "*Tahanan ng Libro*" (House of Books) in the far-flung underserved barrios. We pledged to supply these barrio libraries with books.

Thank you, Brother Willy. Your love of books and reading benefits countless children and you made us all believers in our dreams. I am so grateful that you made these passions we shared a part of the centerpieces of your legacy – alumni affairs, libraries and garden.

Alma Hordista shared this anecdote when she was the Principal at NDDU for eleven years when Brother Willy was the President. His "simplicity is worth mentioning," she said.

> Brother Willy periodically trimmed the trees and bougainvillea flowers around the campus during the early mornings. He would be in his farmer attire.
>
> There was a parent who came early one day. She saw a man she believed was the janitor or the gardener. She asked, "*Manong, saan ang office ni* Brother President?"
>
> (Sir, where is the office of the President?).
>
> Brother Willy gave her the direction.
>
> Imagine her surprise upon finding out the true identity of the "janitor"!

Every time an alumnus or alumna in the U.S. who we know mutually goes home to the Philippines, they'd ask me what to bring Brother Willy as *"pasalubong"* (gift). In 2018, Lulut Palacios Chan, current President of NDGSC Alumni Association, and his classmate in high school went home to the Philippines. She asked, "What would Brother Willy like?"

I relayed the message to Brother Willy and our conversation went something like this. "Wow! Just in time. But Prim I'm asking a huge favor. You live in Rhode Island," he replied.

I didn't quite know what to make of his "big favor" bit.

His next text read, "Can you please buy me a tree pruner, Fiskars brand, send it to Lulut in Virginia to bring home?"

I proceeded to send him a screen shot of said pruner. My idea of a "huge favor" just did not quite mesh with his idea. I was thinking of thousands of dollars fund raising project, he was thinking $8 gadget for his garden.

The gardener asked for a huge favor indeed.

I sent two with Lulut and three more via Balikbayan box along with the children's books for his NDMU IBED library because a gardener can never have too many pruners!

GREEN UNIVERSITY PROGRAM

Brother Willy placed a premium on the Green University Program at the NDMU campus. In fifteen years, he transformed the campus into state of the art place of learning. On December 13, 2020, he posted on his Facebook wall "NDMU Goals: build Character, develop Competence and integrate Culture".

Brother Willy with his classmates in junior and senior years from NDLagao & NDDadiangas Batch 1971 that won the Most Attendees Award at the 25 NDGSCAA International Reunion in Seattle, Washington. L-R: Jean Lim Saygan, Rose Cababat Jackson, Remedios Concha, Susan Tan Kuchman, Virginia Quinol, Brother Willy, Marinela Tan, Nenita Bauer, Lulut Palacios Chan, Arsenia Acharon Bumgardner, Mazee Zabala.

Marist Mentors with NDGSCAA Officers (l-r): Art Henares, Bro. Alfred Ouellette, Ding Mateo, Bro. Kevin O'Neill (RIP), Bro. Paul Mueten, Bro. Bob McGovern (RIP), Bro. James Adams, Bro. Willy, Rayland Rogan, Nena Guipo Adonay (RIP), Jess Mendoza

Brother Willy was also a member of the NDSurala Batch 1971 (freshman and sophomore years). His classmates gathered in his office at NDMU for a “Send Off Party” before he left for Manila Jan. 3, 2021. Estrella Golingay notified me that they too postponed their 50th Reunion due to Covid-19.
L-R seated: Seated L-R: Vilma Pareja Damariñas, Estrella Timones Tañalas, Sonia Garcia Demaraye, Cecilia Biare Alluden, Sylvia Azuela, Brother Willy, Dr. Madeline Guay Bendita, Lolita Lorenzana Espeleta, Rosie Bigot Asong, Candelaria de los Reyes Clavesillas, Cecilia Hisolana Pobre, 2nd row L-R: Oliva Badayos Hechanova, Zenda Crespo, Cecilia Pangilinan Belaza, Estrella Tano Golingay, Norman Blancaflor, Hernando Celino, Ernie Mallorca, Flora Templonuevo Arangali, Ely Arellano
Back Standing L-R: Freddie Daylusan, Rodney Santoyo

The Notre Dame of Gen. Santos City Alumni Association (NDGSCAA) International, national reunion in Las Vegas, Nevada 2017. The association was founded in June 1993 at San Diego, California. Brother Willy, an alumnus NDL 1971 (9th from right back row) was the guest speaker.

Homecoming January 2019 at Notre Dame of Marbel University International Alumni Association based in the USA celebrated their 6th Biennial Reunion at the campus of their alma mater hosted by Brother Willy and the local chapter of the NDMIAA.

Notre Dame of Marbel University Alumni International Reunion & Homecoming in the Philippines, January 2019. Bro. Willy with ND Marbel alumni taken at the NDMIAA (f. 2009) reunion in Koronadal City in January 2019 L-R: Congressman Dinan Hernandez, June Morales Mercado, Beng Morales Lucido, Frances Morales Estela, His Eminence Reverend Cardinal Orlando Quevedo, DDS, Anne Morales Reinoso, Tessie Paez-Morales, Brother Willy, Lourraine Morales UySison

One of the members of NDDGSC Alumni captioned this photo "Brother Willy's Angels" at the Seattle Alumni Reunion in Seattle, Washington 2019. Some of these friends helped him cross off his bucket list to visit Alaska. Photo by Fatima Pinto second from right (front).

THE CHILDREN'S LIBRARIES

NDMU Children's Library

Library for Indigenous People, Lake Sebu photo by Michael Yambok.

Taken during the Blessing and Ribbon Cutting for the NDMU IBED Children's Library. Photo by Editha Plecis. Top: The new Children's Library at NDMU IBED Bottom: Photo of donors & Notre Dame of Lagao Batch 1967 and friends. L-R seated: Lanie Zerrudo Gammon, Celia Parica Esma, and Herlina Sogon Castanares.
L-R Standing: Angelina Senas, Eulita Lumasag, Esperanza Perez Maramara, Rose Datoy Reyes, Pacita Derit Estorque, Evelyn Corazon Rivera Saranillo, Diosa Jagna, Michael Guipo, Chris Gammon, Merlita Guipo, Brother Willy, Angelo Guipo

The Marist Experience (Marex) 12

"Yes, a chapter for MAREX, a worthy project, and one closest to his heart!"

~ Briccio Baynosa~

On January 14, 2021, at 9:41 pm eastern standard time in the United States, I initiated a conversation on Messenger with Brother Willy. I sent him a photo taken at our house in Warren, Rhode Island, when he visited in 2016. Everyone was gathered around our dining table for a July 4th celebration, and we were all raising our glasses.

"Thinking of you today, and praying all is well. Cheers to your health. So you can come visit us again. Hugs...By the way, a friend of yours Mr. Rodolfo Regacho Mapada, bought Al's book. He saw it on your posting, I believe. He told me he is an ex-Marist".

"Yes, he is one of my best friends during our days in Lagao", he texted back.

Until then, I had never heard of the MAREX. But, I learned from Rudy all about this Marist Brotherhood. In the process, it expanded my network of friends by introducing me to Filipino Marist Brothers I had not met before. Brother Willy put into motion this chance meeting with Rudy by advertising my husband's newly published book *No Greater Service* on his Facebook news feed. It also reconnected me to former Marist Brothers I knew in high school and college.

I mentioned in this book's Introduction that I almost abandoned the idea of writing about Brother Willy. While research is one of my strong suits, with him gone, I doubted my ability to gather enough information that would be believable to the readers. My knowledge about the Marist religious congregation is severely lacking. Enter my co-author Briccio Baynosa, who I still call Brother Brix, because until we reconnected on Facebook after Brother Willy died; I was unsure if he was still a Marist Brother. I knew him as a youngster because we graduated from the same high school; he was only four years ahead of me. In fact, his younger brother Hector was my classmate.

When Brother Willy died, an article Briccio wrote about his friend and my own tribute to Brother Willy appeared in the Marist Newsletter, *Marist News Bits.* I reached out to him to ask his permission to include the article in this book. I had other ideas though – I asked him to help me write the book. He readily said yes to the first request, but convincing him to co-write the book with me took a lot of cajoling. First, he offered to be my resource person instead, but he too was self-effacing, so much like Brother Willy; said he did not want to "steal my thunder". However, he finally acquiesced, and I am totally convinced that Brother Willy would have hand picked him for this role.

I couldn't have found a more articulate and brilliant writer than my co-author; at the same time he embodies the MAREX mystique. From the beginning, I wanted to add this chapter to the book, but I felt so inadequate to write about it. The first time I heard about the group MAREX, I felt an air of secrecy, the subject I found impressive or too baffling without "inside" knowledge.

Often I feel Brother Willy's guiding hands in finding the right persons to tell his story, like Briccio who narrated,

A religious vocation is truly a mystery, something that defies reason and understanding – easy to appreciate but difficult to explain. For those who have joined a congregation and later on decided to leave, the worn-out quotation "Many are called but few are chosen", could be an easy cop-out explanation. Personally, I believe that the mystery shrouds itself more deeply in the life of the consecrated person as he lives his vocation day by day. He perseveres only through God's infinite goodness. In ways that only God could truly fathom, we bow in awe to which direction He leads us and humbly accept the life in store for each of us. For us, who experienced the gift of once belonging to a community with a vision and mission can only utter words of gratitude for having been part of a great design. But we have to execute our grand exit because our role has ended in the script and never to appear on the stage again.

Part of you remains with me even after I go (adapted from the song popularized by Southern Sons entitled You Were There). This line poetically symbolizes my sentiments when I decided to cut off ties with the congregation I was a part of for more or less fifty years.

For most of us, ex-Marists, two significant sources of connectivity and association remain unbroken after we decided to part ways with the congregation that has become a considerable part of our formation. These are MARIST SPIRIT and BROTHERHOOD. As espoused by Saint Marcellin Champagnat, the Marist Spirit mysteriously engulfs the recipient with a pervading life force born out of the virtues of an extraordinary woman dearly called by the Marists as the "Good Mother". She exemplifies what Marists should be – loving, compassionate, understanding, and caring. Brotherhood, born out of friendship, is another significant spirit among Marists with all the clichés attributed to it – heart beating as one, marching to the same rhythm, a shoulder to lean on, etc. This friendship remains even after each has gone his own way to pursue another destiny.

I believe that Brother Willy had in mind these two things when he decided to formally assist in organizing the MAREX (Marist Experience Brotherhood). He extended his personal time, energy, and creativity to perpetuate the Marist Spirit and the essence of Brotherhood bound by common experiences in formation, mission, and vision.

* * * * *

As the stand-in author for the one who died, this narrator feel so privileged that Briccio accepted the task to bring into fruition Brother Willy's biography. We all can appreciate the might of his eloquent pen. Through him and the other ex-Marists who helped me with this project, namely Joe Sevilla, Norberto Barsal, Saturnino Bayona, Rudy Mapada, and my high school classmate Angelito Sonico, we come to a better understanding of their life at the Marist Formation Center and after Marist.

My consecrated friends shared that in the 1970s and 1980s, there was a significant exodus of religious men and women from their congregations. The Marist Brothers Community in the Philippines was not immune. A case in point is Brother Willy's cohort. Out of the eighteen in his original Marist Novice group, only five stayed; three had died, and the rest left the Marist Family.

In 2009, Brother Willy bridged the gap between these former Marist Brothers "outside" and the Marist Brothers "inside", as one ex-Marist Brother put it. Angelito Sonico, an ex-Marist himself, shared:

> The ex-Marist Brothers themselves planted the seed, which eventually led to the development of the MAREX Brotherhood, in different areas (Luzon, Visayas, Mindanao, and abroad). Brother Willy watered, nurtured, and provided the proper environment for its accelerated growth, so much like the gardener that he was. He opened the doors literally for the MAREX to have access to the school facilities, like the classrooms, function rooms, library, chapel, the boardroom, and the convent. He would allow MAREX members to join the Marist Brothers community meals, including accommodations. We were not strangers to him – we were brothers who took a different path to serve Jesus thru Mary.
>
> Brother Willy, I believe, is the significant enabler, a visionary, and an inspirational Leader of the MAREX Marist Brotherhood Inc. No other Marist Brother initiated this kind and generous treatment. But, unfortunately, his motives were questioned, and he was even misconstrued by some of the Brothers.
>
> Without him, we would still be at the infant stage. Perhaps the Lay Marists sprouting all over the world inspired him. Marbel is a natural base. All MAREX passed through the Scholasticate formation either as Aspirants or Scholastics then to Notre Dame of Marbel University for their degrees.
>
> A Mission-Vision statement of the MAREX created on December 19, 2011, at NDMU states:
>
> **Vision:** To become a reliable service provider, specifically amongst the former Marist Brothers, their families, and friends on a journey to fulfill God's mission through the Marist spirituality.
>
> **Mission:** The MAREX is committed to caring, serve and extending assistance to former Marist Brothers, their families, and friends and in line with the FMS Spirit, to educate the underprivileged sector of the community, we the MAREX, give our unwavering support and assistance to the mission of the Marist Brothers.

The Marist Experience (MAREX) is a gathering or reunion of those who, at one time in their life, experienced being a Marist Brother, imbued with the spirit of St. Marcellin Champagnat. This is legally incorporated and registered at the Philippines Security Exchange Commission.

The primary purpose of this reunion is to continue deepening the "Marist life experience" with friendship and support for one another and their family members.

Hence, it is envisioned that the reunion activities will eventually focus on "journeying together" as extended family members of the Marist Brothers. A project is conceived to make this organization stronger.

History:

In 2006, in the wake of the late Leonardo Genota in Tacurong City, a group of former Marist Brothers met. An instant "small" reunion happened. Rarely seeing each other, exchanging pleasantries, and recalling experiences were spent over a few cases of beer. The dream of a reunion started. The same objective was further discussed at the Santos Cardos' wake in 2007. At the wedding of Rudy Mapada in Pigcawayan, a group of former Brothers or those who underwent Marist formation spent overnight at the house of Sergio Jorolan in Midsayap, Cotabato.

In 2008, the first formal reunion was held at the former Scholasticate at the Notre Dame of Marbel University now called the Marist Formation Center. [The old Scholasticate building was demolished since it was a fire hazard). There were twenty-eight attendees, including five spouses and friends. Alumni residing in Marbel donated food and drinks. In addition, Willy Basilio invited the group for lunch at his restaurant and provided more food in the evening.

After a short evening prayer and introduction, the rest of the night was spent eating and telling stories of the individual attendee and their family, career, and past experiences as a Marist Brother.

In 2009, the second reunion happened again at NDMU with forty-four members, including two from outside the country: Teofilo Cantos from the USA and Salvador Dionisio from Brunei. Six came from Manila and the rest from Malaybalay, Cotabato, Kidapawan, General Santos, Tacurong, and Marbel. Reno Velasco donated a lechon for supper while Winnie Javier, through his local connection, generously donated soft drinks and other Christmas giveaways. Boxes of delicious durian from Rene Ochia's orchard were served before midnight. Some donated food, drinks, and cash. The highlight of the reunion was the group sharing facilitated by Angel Sonico, which lasted for almost 2 hours.

In 2011, thirty-eight MAREX members with twelve Marist Brothers blessed the gathering with notable attendance of Brother Paul Meuten from the USA and two retired Brothers – Brothers Gabe and Pop. Romy Roda from New York joined the group for the first time. A thorough discussion was done on what MAREX is all about in that gathering. It was also an opportunity to discuss the dreams for the MAREX. A core group of officers was elected.

* * * * *

In the years leading to the 50th Anniversary of this narrator's high school graduation from Notre Dame of Lagao (Class 1967) in 2017, I was reconnected with an ex-Marist Angel Sonico through our mutual friend Bing Hoyumpa. We communicated regularly on Facebook and now we are partnering in raising funds for our shared advocacy, providing solar lights to the T'boli and Ubo Indigenous People of Lake Sebu where electricity is absent. I requested Angel to share his life story as a MAREX. On February 10, 2021 he texted:

> I would like to share our ex-Marist experience here in the Manila area. This is my own perspective, and my fellow former Marist Brothers can fill in their own stories. Each one of us has a unique story to share. Our coming to Manila was not a conspiracy or an invitation from someone with the same experience. Meeting an ex-Marist in Manila was pure coincidence or part of God's plan. There was no prior communication.
>
> To meet an ex-Marist Brother in Manila was an opportunity to gather and reminisce happy days and provide

support for the guy financially and/or in-kind like board and lodging or just someone to talk to. It was very natural and spontaneous. We were really brothers helping one another.

We came to Manila as strangers, searching for work and with no close relatives; we were strangers even to our relatives, but not among the ex Brothers. So we could share relatable stories all night.

We were already closely knit during the early stage of our professional life outside of the Marist Community. As for myself, I had the opportunity to stay with Joe and Alma Sevilla, and the kids for some time. The family treated me as a brother on a journey, not a stranger. I also slept at Armando Aquino's place. Reno Velasco, Andy Versoza, and I believe Sonny Javier were together in a small apartment. Together with Teo Cantos, we managed to live a joyful life. We shoot basketball hoops on weekends and play bridge on certain nights.

We had religious retreats to nourish our Spiritual life and discussed topics based on Marist discipline. We brought our prayer books for the morning, afternoon, and evening prayers. We had one retreat in Tagaytay and another one in Baguio. Once Brother George Ouellette was invited as our Spiritual Retreat Master. We were spiritually and socially nourished. In one of our retreats, the Cabrera family, Gus, Marjorie, and Kids came all the way from Mindanao to join us. There was also an instance when the family of Sid and Suzette Saranillo and kids traveled all the way from South Cotabato by land and joined us in one of our gatherings.

Like all the ex-Marist Brothers, we are all indebted to the Marist Brothers for giving us the discipline, knowledge, and skills to survive and become financially independent. The training with the Marist is holistic. It greatly influenced our mental, social, physical, and, most importantly, spiritual lives. We had our own ex-Marist "culture" that our wives at the beginning could not fully comprehend but later on accepted and adjusted to it.

To end my share of our story, we did not have any organization to speak of. The support and care for one another were natural, like a family. We are all alarmed with

Nem Blanco's condition. We are saddened that we could not connect with Sonny Javier and his family. We are happy that Saturnino Bayona is one of us. We constantly pray for one another, Nem Blanco, Andy Versoza, Benny Braganza, Teo and his family, Joe and family, Expedito and family, and the rest of the ex Marist now experiencing challenges in life.

When I joined the ex-Marist in Mindanao, I experienced the same enthusiasm and zeal to be connected with everyone. I felt then and more so now that sense of Brotherhood with everyone. Bert, Lucio, Erning, Ruel, Tony, Serge, Rudy, Caloy, Archie, Rene, Cris, Ely, Ex, and the rest are very inspiring. This is now our opportunity to work hand in hand with the Marist Brothers as lay partners, given our broad life experiences and charisma.

Our differences in ideas, perspectives, personalities, and even expressions could destroy us or fuel us to move forward and achieve our vision and mission. Let us be inspired by the courage of St. Joseph. He guided Mother Mary and Jesus.

Even Brother Willy was not exempted from the challenges within the congregation like every one of us based on our stories. Still, he persevered and died as a Marist. It was his choice to stay. We also made a choice to leave and never to return. So now we have a singular opportunity to reunite and pursue that Marist brotherhood and work as partners with the Marist Brothers to bring souls to Jesus through Mary.

I hope that we will nurture, cherish, and pursue that Mission and Vision of the MAREX Marist Brotherhood. And the way to do this is to be guided by our values. So let us be guided by our Values to build our "culture" of Brotherhood. We are doing this for Jesus thru Mary.

* * * * *

Brother Willy is the "founder" of the MAREX as far as its members is concerned. He kept in touch with many of them on a regular basis. In good times and bad times, he was there with them and for them.

When the late Santos Cardos was going through his devastating health challenges, Brother Willy did his best to provide moral support and kept the MAREX members updated with his situation. When Rudy Mapada's first wife died of cancer, Brother Willy steadfastly stood by him and when Rudy remarried ten years later, he was there to stand as the couple's *ninong* (godfather). He also was the baptismal *ninong* of Rudy's eldest son. When Norberto Barsal was looking for an apartment in Marbel and in need of a place to stay, Brother Willy invited him to live at the Marist Convent for two weeks. And the list of good deeds and recipients go on and on!

These are not earthshaking heroic deeds but rather, sustained and significant random acts of kindness that is so ingrained in the man. It just came naturally to Brother Willy reminding me of the song we used to sing at church during communion. The song embodies his Christ like essence. The American Roman Catholic Priest, teacher, playwright, folk-composer, and author Willard F. Jabusch (1930-2018)[36] wrote this "social justice" theme song.

Whatsover you do to the least of my people,
That you do unto me.
When I was hungry, you gave me to eat;
When I was thirsty, you gave me to drink.
When I was homeless, you opened your door;
When I was naked, you gave me your coat.
When I was weary, you helped me find rest;
When I was anxious, you calmed all my fears.
When in a prison, you came to my cell;
When on a sickbed, you cared for my needs.
When I was laughed at, you stood by my side;
When I was happy, you shared in my joy.
Now enter into the home of my Father.

For all these, we pray Brother Willy entered into the home of his Father.

Brother Willy and Brother Pop Armendez with the former Marist Brothers who are now Lay Mission Partners of the Marist Notre Dame Schools

Left: Wedding of Rudy Mapada and Analou Serot. Brother Willy was the Ninong (godfather)
Right: MAREX Board Members with Brothers Willy and Theo, former Marist Provincial Superior.

Friendships 13

"His favorite song was You've Got A Friend"

~ Rodolfo Regacho Mapada ~

Most if not everyone reading this book must know the song "You've Got a Friend", by songwriter and singer Carole King. During my interview with Rudy Mapada, I told him I couldn't thank him enough for his help. He said, "Just make sure you mention Brother Willy's favorite song. That evens the score."

Brother Willy was in senior high school when Ms. King released the song in her 1971 album *Tapestry*. It became one of the all-time favorites of Brother Willy. Rodolfo Regacho Mapada, his friend of fifty years, told me that Brother Willy lived by the lyrics of the song, that come hell or high waters even in the darkest of night, when a friend is in need, they could count on Brother Willy. He will be there.

It is no wonder to this narrator therefore that in his outline; Brother Willy dedicated a chapter to Friendships. One cannot even begin to speculate how he would have gone about choosing which friends to invite as contributors to his book, there are so many of them.

The "sharers" in this book painted different versions of the man they called a friend. It reminds me of the Parable of the Blind Men and the Elephant. The parable has several variations, but it is believed that the earliest versions trace its origin from Buddhist, Hindu, and Jain texts "as they discuss the limits of perception and the importance of complete context".[37] As the story goes, there was a group of blind men who heard about a strange animal that just came into town. No one knew of its shape or form. They decided to inspect the creature by touch, the only way they could determine. The first blind person groped the tail and stated it must be a snake. Another touched the ear and declared it a fan; the one who touched the leg said it was tree-trunk, and so on. "The parable has been used to illustrate a range of truths and fallacies; broadly, the parable implies that one's subjective experience can be true, but that such experience is inherently limited by its failure to account for other truths or a totality of truth... the parable has provided insight into...the need for deeper understanding, and respect for different perspectives on the same object of observation."[38]

"Who is Brother Willy to all his friends?" one might ask. Like the parable, we each have seen a different version of the same elephant. This book will reveal some side of him that will help us glean a new and deeper understanding of the man we thought we knew so well. Seen from different sets of eyes, we then discover his complex personality unfold as we have never seen it before.

It's now January 25, 2022, his first death anniversary. A year ago, I had sent a text to Brother Willy.

"What time is your MRI?"

He replied "9 pm".

It was dated January 22, 2021. That was the last I heard from Brother Willy. In the Philippines, and I imagine other parts of the globe, others may have received their last text from him between January 9 and January 23 when he was in Manila waiting for his surgery.

I know for sure there were four people who received the same message that his nephew Macky sent announcing his demise in real time. His niece Pia Baysa who was one of the nieces who took care of him in Manila texted "*Tita*, there are four people that Brother Willy listed to notify in case of emergency - Brother Allan, Satur [Bayona], Orman [Manansala], and you."

Was it all a premonition? That Brother Willy composed letters on his laptop what seemed like goodbye letters to his family and friends while waiting for his surgery in Manila? That he offered his treasured mug collection to his classmates and visiting friends from Australia weeks before he died? That he insisted on his Lubrico family getting together during the 2020 Christmas holiday and ensured that photos were taken at these occasions? Portents all?

His niece Cecille sent photos of the happy Christmas Holiday reunions. She wrote, "Last family bonding *namin* with T'yoy Brother was at Susan Beach, Glan on December 28-29, 2020. Our family living in Naci *ginlagaw man niya* to tour Lake Sebu in two vans *sila* sponsored by cousins so they could enjoy the resort with him. And for the first time he took us to the celebration *sang* personnel *sang* iya nga birthday in October 2021 held at NDMU IBED for lunch and *merienda* at the Main campus. Happy *gid tanan*!" (The personnel knew that Bro. Willy was not fond of drawing attention to himself like celebrating his birthday at school. So, as a tradition every year, the staff purportedly celebrated the culmination of the month of the Holy Rosary on his birthday, a double celebration).

In retrospect, many of his friends did notice his more than usual posts on his Facebook wall. Anyone who visits his wall today would see the prolific posts two months before and while he was already in Manila for his medical procedure. It was as if he was highlighting what he deemed important to leave as his "footprints on the sands of time". I took his cue and chose many of the same photos included in this book. His few last texts to this narrator were concerning but I chucked it to just a normal reaction for one who just found out something more ominous than his prostate cancer – a suspicious lump in his liver.

It is heartwarming to note however that Brother Willy may have been in pre-operative isolation due to the pandemic in Manila two weeks before he died; but he was not alone. Many of his friends kept in touch with him virtually until the day he died. Joe Sevilla, a former Marist himself now living in Canada, shared his last text that showed the seventeen-minute phone call with Brother Willy made on January 17, 2021. Dr. Madeline Guay Bendita, a classmate in high school, called him everyday to check on his symptoms. Her son Dr. Jesson, a cardiologist from St. Luke Hospital in Manila extended his professional advice as well. Two of his nieces Pia Samonte Baysa and Dolly Lubrico Fenis were his in-house caregivers. The Lubrico nephews, nieces, and grandkids took him to mass at a church in Baclaran and visited him as often as their work schedules would allow. So did his best friend Saturnino Bayona and his family. Around the world alumni mobilized the prayer brigade.

Three of his friends shared their experiences days leading to his trip to Manila. Estrella Golingay who introduced us to the boy named Bargas in Chapter 3 remembers her last meeting with Brother Willy,

> On January 3, 2021 our Notre Dame of Surala High School Class 1971 met with Brother Willy. It was the most significant get-together with Brother Willy. He offered for the second time, his office and conference room for our use at the Notre Dame of Marbel University. It was meant to be a small send-off gathering five days before he left for Manila for his medical treatment. Still, the attendees just kept on coming until the number ballooned to more than thirty.
>
> Recalling the preparations still amuses me. We planned for a potluck party, and Brother Willy insisted on hosting his own, but I said, "No, just relax and wait for us".
>
> "Then I'll just offer my cutlery," he said.
>
> "And drinking water please!" I added.
>
> Upon arrival at his office, we saw the collection of imported ceramic cups and mugs on top of a table by the window, his memorabilia from different places in six continents that he visited. He told us to choose one. Just one, he said, at the same time musing aloud how to get rid of all those memorabilia when he retires.
>
> "Can we have more then?" We said in jest to solve his dilemma.
>
> "No, leave some for others, too."
>
> I chose a slender cup from London.
>
> Remembering that gathering, I still feel some shivers recalling the short talk by Nanding Celino about Brother Willy's early life; they were elementary school buddies. It just sounded like a testimony for a memorial service. The messages by Dr. Madeline and others were capped by his personal views on his life, especially his medical condition. It came off as a complete recipe for a real send-off for his last journey, of which we never had any inkling.
>
> I thought he had one too many sharing that he didn't typically give in our past reunions. That was surprising. He even suggested to another batchmate, Cecilia Pobre, to hold

a monthly gathering for our batch NDSurala '71 to keep abreast with each other. He said a dish of *kamote* (sweet potato), banana, or any native food would be a sumptuous fare. Dr. Madeline remembers the date he mentioned was February 17, 2021. After that gathering, he could still go up and down the university stairs, walk us to our cars, and pose with us for the numerous picture taking.

Our first organized reunion with Brother Willy was in May 2012 at Rose Ariola's eatery and function hall. He donated one whole lechon and joined the parlor games and the dancing. I recall vividly how Cecilia Pobre jokingly insisted on dancing with him; he obliged to the group's delight.

In 2013, the batch went to Tagum City, the turf of Alma Lim Uy, another batch member. She was among the campus personalities then and now as the better half of the Governor. Brother Willy came all geared up for the long ride from Koronadal to Davao del Sur.

In 2015, Brother Willy offered the Marist EcoPark at Paraiso, City of Koronadal for free as venue for the batch reunion. The event was meaningful with added activities such as the visit to St. Lawrence Orphanage and the Allah Valley Hospital where the better half of Dr. Madeline Bendita – a batch member was being treated, and lastly the University tour that revealed to the batch his accomplishments as the University President.

We met again in 2016 at Mt. Zion, Gen. Santos City that offered a breathtaking view of the whole city below, all clothed with a haze of light. Although Brother Willy came late, he inspired the event as he stayed and joined the fun.

During the 50th foundation of our alma mater Notre Dame of Surala (NDS), in 2017, our batch dominated the affair, being the inaugural freshmen students in 1967. Brother Willy gathered the group after the school program, all of us still in our formal attires. Then, he extended the never-ending storytelling at a local Hotel & Café over glasses of wine and bottles of beer.

In the intervening years, we would meet for birthdays and, yes, for burials of classmates. In December 2020, we were at the necrological service of one of our batch mates, Nestor Espinosa. Brother Willy gave an extraordinary and inspiring prayer, his last.

Afterward, during our lunch at Migz Restaurant, he mentioned his fondness for some of its menu, fresh seafood chop suey, and yes! Fish head! He ate well, and between bites, he reminisced about his career, projects, the NDMU University IBED gym, and swimming pool. "World class!" he proudly said and told us to attend the blessing.

I wondered why in such urgency, he incessantly stuffed us with his struggles and achievements above the noise of the Video Karaoke, highlighting something here and there. There were things that he said which may not find space on this page but can only be indelible parts of his memory.

Before he left for Manila for medical treatment, Brother Willy asked his sister Deding to cook his favorite dish of Misua and tinapa again. She obliged, unknowing it would be his last request.

Our group never stopped seeing each other even during the pandemic, stubborn ones-these seniors!

This year, 2021, we are facing the most awaited time of our batch, to celebrate our 50th anniversary minus him.

What would it be like without Brother Willy? One can only guess.

* * * * *

My co-author Briccio Baynosa recalled vividly his last encounter with his friend:

Brother Willy was one of the very few Brothers who made serious efforts to contact me and ask how I was doing after I left the Congregation. Before the pandemic, whenever he was in the General Santos City area, he would regularly call me or message me through Messenger. Brother Willy would invite me for a meal in one of the malls in the city. While enjoying our meal, he would ask how I was coping with life and about me in general.

Our routine stopped because of the restrictions imposed by the pandemic. For us senior citizens, travel was restricted. I was locked down in the Malapatan area, thirty kilometers outside the city limits. It took almost a year before I was able to meet with my relatives in General Santos City again.

Ruel Tuble (also a former Marist Brother) gave me the opportunity to visit General Santos City again. He invited me to give a seminar-workshop for the Department of the Interior and Local Government (DILG) on the topic "Workplace Communication and Documentation". Ruel is presently connected with DILG Region XII. When they were planning this seminar-workshop, he thought of me being the right person to facilitate it. So he invited me and I accepted. The venue was in Marbel. This event gave way to my in-person visit with Brother Willy.

The seminar-workshop for the first batch was on the first week of November 2020. I arrived late afternoon in Marbel and settled down in my hotel room. I announced my arrival by texting Brother Willy. Immediately, he dropped everything he was doing and told me that he was picking me up for dinner.

Several minutes later, he arrived. I was waiting in the hotel's restaurant. When he came in, I noticed that he had difficulty walking. I thought then that he had grown much older. He wasn't as perky as the last time we met.

He told me that the hotel serves good food, so we decided to have dinner there. I ordered sweet and sour fish fillet, one cup of rice, and orange juice. He followed suit.

While we were eating, he asked me how I was doing. So, I told him that I was well and good. I was living a very simple lifestyle - especially now that I was affected by the pandemic. I lost my teaching job because of travel restrictions. I have to contend with my measly monthly allowance of Pesos 3,700 [$73]. I also had to stop all my maintenance medicine because I just couldn't afford them anymore. I turned to a healthy diet – vegetables and affordable fruits like banana and papaya. I regularly commune with nature to absorb divine energy. I climb hills and mountains, ford streams and rivers, swim in the ocean for negative ions, and do the needed physical exercise to keep the body fit and healthy. His reply: You can still do that? You're healthy!

I turned the conversation towards him. I asked him who was assigned where. For about six years, I lost contact with the Brothers.

All I knew about them was what I read on Facebook. I get to chat on Messenger with some of them but not too often. He filled me up with those whom I know.

I asked him how the schools were coping with the pandemic. He said that the institutions are suffering financially due to the drop in enrolment. He talked about the challenges of online learning. Nevertheless, he said that the schools are managing pretty well. He noted that the Congregation is the one severely affected because of the lesser subsidy coming from the schools.

I then asked him how he was doing. He first talked about what he had accomplished since I left Notre Dame of Marbel University as his administrative assistant. He spoke about his ongoing projects, particularly the IBED gymnasium, and mentioned opening the Law curriculum and other new academic offerings. He was delighted to share all these things with me.

Finally, I asked him how he was. His very words were: "Brix, I'm already very tired. I want to retire." The board of Trustees told him that 2020-2021 would be his last year in NDMU. He will not be given another term or extension. So, I asked him what his plans were. He said that he would request a sabbatical.

Usually, sabbaticals are granted a religious person a year for rest, further studies, or ongoing formation. He said he wanted to stay and spend time with his family, specifically with his sister Teresa who lives alone. He wanted to give her his companionship, care, and attention. He also wanted to spend more quality time with his nephews and nieces and their children.

I told him that he has to plan his sabbatical well because one year is short, especially if he plans to visit friends abroad. He agreed with me and promised that he would really plan it to maximize the one-year allowable.

During our conversation, never did he mention his health issues. It did not cross my mind to inquire because I know that the Congregation always takes care of the health concerns of the individual Brothers. So at that time, there was never any hint of foreboding. On the contrary, I thought everything was all right.

The waitresses were getting fidgety because we were the only customers left, and I thought they wanted to retire and rest. Hinting my observations to him, Brother Willy paid the bill, and as he placed the payment inside the cash pad, he pulled another P1000 bill and gave it to me. *"O, ara ang* Christmas gift *ko sa imo"*, he said with a smile.

We stood up, and I walked him to the parking lot. I thanked him for the evening. He said that I should just notify him if I wanted a university tour, and he would gladly oblige.

My seminar-workshop in Marbel for the second batch of DILG participants was scheduled for December 9-11, 2020. Accordingly, I was picked up at about 3 pm at my residence in Lun Padidu, Malapatan, Sarangani Province the day before - the feast of the Immaculate Conception of Mama Mary.

The trip going to Marbel took approximately an hour. I arrived at the hotel at about 4:30 PM and immediately checked in. I had a reserved room, so I was settled down in no time. I placed my things in order in my room and I texted Brother Willy. I asked if he was still willing to give me a tour of the NDM University campus as he promised. He texted back that he was presently out of town to attend a gathering at the Notre Dame of Kidapawan College for religious and personnel. He would be coming back to Marbel very late in the evening. So, he suggested that he pick me up at 5:30 AM the next day and give me the promised tour and breakfast afterward.

The next day, December 9, 2020, was the start of my seminar workshop. It would start at 9:00 AM, so we had enough time to go around and have breakfast later. He arrived at the parking lot at precisely 5:30 AM. I was already having coffee in the hotel's restaurant and had a good view of the parking area. When I saw him, I dropped everything and rushed out to meet him. He didn't anymore alight from the car when he saw me coming out of the restaurant.

After the greetings, I immediately apologized for bothering him at such an early hour. He said not to worry because he actually sleeps late and wakes up early, sometimes as early as 4:00 AM.

It was a beautiful and sunny day. Cool. I requested him to do away with the air-conditioning in the car, and he gladly obliged. The gentle breeze was so soothing to my face.

I would inject a question, and he would fill me in. He did most of the talking. So, I gave a listening ear and allowed him to dominate the conversation.

We started at the NDMU IBED [Integrated Basic Education Department]. There were many new structures built. The Senior High School (SHS) dominated the adjacent lot of the original IBED campus. The new covered walk along the wall wasn't there the last time I visited the area. There was a new Science building, the renovated student center; the greeneries; the gymnasium's ongoing construction, the soon-to-be-constructed chapel; the swimming pool, etc. He was full of plans and dreams!

He talked about people who supported him financially. Donations were not wanting. Some donated what amount they could afford, and some gave big-time [many from alumni]. These people, he said, gave him the impetus to provide only the best for the students and other stakeholders. He was proud and happy to share all these things with me. I can say this because I firmly believe that I was someone whose approval and affirmation he truly appreciates and looks forward to. I guess this was one reason that when I left the Congregation, he would call me up for a meal or coffee. He needed a sounding board, and he found it in me.

Off we went to the main campus. Again I observed so many changes – the well-manicured lawn and landscape. It was green all over, giving credence to the success of his clean and green campus advocacy. Some structures were already in the can, some were ongoing, and others were still a dream. I told him that I was happy for him. He knew that I was sincere and genuinely appreciative of what he had accomplished. Still, his humility just got the better of him. Nonchalantly, he said, it was part of the job.

After the campus tour, he told me that someone was aching to see me – Brother Rene Reyes, his bosom friend and a very dear friend of mine. Actually, the feeling is mutual because Brother Rene was also one person I really wanted to meet since we hadn't seen each other for ages. I really had a grand time meeting again with Brother Rene. Brother Willy just let us be for a long while as Brother Rene and I laughed ourselves silly, reminiscing about the good old days.

It was time for breakfast, and we had to leave Brother Rene behind. Brother Rene said that it's good that we talked by ourselves. He didn't join us for breakfast. I guess he had inkling that Brother Willy was going to share something private. Brother Willy took me to this *carenderia* (eatery) that he claimed served a delicious Filipino menu, and he was right. We ordered fish, fried *talong* [eggplant], and coffee.

Our breakfast conversation was earnest. We talked of retirement and death. He reiterated his plans for the sabbatical.

He asked me about myself, so I told him that I was well and good. But, because of financial constraints, I had to stop all my maintenance medicine. I lived a very simple and money challenging lifestyle, but it was both a choice and a necessity. I turned into a healthy diet, which enabled me to spend less on food consumption. My wants and needs are few. I live alone and have conquered all my fears of being so. Before, I would be afraid that if something happened to me, no one would ever know. I told him that now I leave everything to God. I'm ready for death anytime. After I celebrated my 70th birthday, I thanked God for the gift of life; and from then on, I considered everything a bonus for me. I lived a good life, and that is all that matters. My only prayer was that if God decided to take me away, He would do it quick. So that I would not be a burden to my family members who themselves have to eke out a living to survive.

He said that he felt the same way. He was ready to go anytime. In fact, he said, he feels so tired already. The sabbatical is something to which he looks forward.

There was a long pause towards the end of our breakfast. I wanted to have some time to prepare for the start of my seminar. So, I told Brother Willy I had to go.

He took me back to the hotel. Just before alighting from the car, I told him if we could have some more time together after my seminar with Brother Rene. He committed to attending a beach picnic with college batch '86 in Gumasa, Glan in Sarangani Province, so he declined.

I finished my seminar-workshop on the afternoon of December 11, 2021. While I was in my room, I was putting things in order. I couldn't find my camera. I texted him if he saw my camera in his car because I couldn't find it. He texted back that he didn't find any camera in his car. He was in Glan then with college batch '86.

That was my last communication with Brother Willy: December 11, 2020, 3:15 PM, according to my text messages record.

* * * * *

Orman Ortega Manansala, who wrote about his class being Brother Willy's "happy pills", shared the last days he spent with his beloved mentor:

> Brother Willy told me on December 26, 2020 that he was diagnosed with Stage 2 prostate cancer. I told him that he would surely overcome this. However, my friend never let on his health concerns. He mentioned it to some of our close friends but not to me. I respected that.
>
> Brother Willy informed me about the findings on his liver on January 15, 2021 while he was in Manila for a prostate robotic surgery. He asked for prayers. Despite his not wanting people to know about his health issues, many started prayer brigades not mentioning his name per his request. From January 18 to 20, I constantly communicated with him; he gave me updates on his condition. He was waiting for the results of his MRI.
>
> I could have been more expressive about how much I loved and cared for him, but that's just so like Brother Willy. He was never expressive and will always leave you second-guessing regarding his real feelings. I knew he cared for me for those many years of our friendship. He was there when I lost both my parents. He was there when my love life was either blossoming or in turmoil. But we never really hugged. I remember hugging him once, and I just felt he was uncomfortable with the show of affection. So a warm handshake was our only means of passing the love between us as friends.
>
> When I sent him a text on January 23, it was his nephew Macky who answered.
>
> January 23 - 8:25 PM
>
> Hi this is his nephew. He is in bad condition and more prayers needed.
>
> January 25 - 3:47 AM
>
> No pulse and heart rate *na po* 20 minutes ago. We are waiting for the doctor to confirm it officially.
>
> He died peacefully.

Brother Willy has joined his creator at exactly 3:52 AM today, January 25, 2021.

That's the last text I got from the cell phone of Brother Willy.

Just like that, I lost a mentor, a confidante, and a friend.

* * * * *

When he was in Manila waiting for his surgery, his lab test revealed, "*may bukol*" (lump) in his liver, as he put it. I posted on two occasions on Facebook a call for prayers per his request, but he won't let me mention his name. So instead, he said, "Just say your BFF needs prayers. God knows *naman* you mean me".

A mutual friend had read my post. Her two brothers died of prostate cancer she told me. So she was quite familiar with what Brother Willy was going through. She offered to introduce Brother Willy to a friend for a second opinion. He is the top urologist in the Philippines, she said. This urologist had helped her brother when he was diagnosed with the disease and prolonged his life for ten years. I relayed the well meaning and what I thought promising offer to Brother Willy.

He texted back, "Please thank her for the offer. My primary doctor found me a urologist here in Manila. *Baka ma insulto*". (He might get insulted).

Baka mainsulto. So just like Brother Willy. He undoubtedly was the fiercest champion I know for the causes of the downtrodden, the weak, the marginalized, the sick, "the least of his brothers".

But when it comes to himself, he was a poor advocate. Not a self-promoter even when his life depended on it. Self-effacing Brother Willy, always and to the end.

JANUARY 10, SUNDAY, BACLARAN DAY
The National Shrine of Our Lady of Perpetual Help

I asked you about your plans that day and you just simply said, "Nothing". And so I said, "Let's attend mass in Baclaran". Excited you replied, "Tara! Haven't been there in a long time." It was around 8 AM, and the mass started in 30 minutes. God may have cleared the way for us, as it has never been possible to reach Baclaran from Mandaluyong in a short span of time.

You went inside the church and looked for empty seats. We stayed outside. We let you pray in peace and have your solemn conversation with the Lord.

Right after mass, we walked towards the parking lot and you said,

"Let's take a photo of the church. *Bilis, habang walang dumadaan*!"

(Quick, while no one's around). So we did.

We will never know what your prayers were but I am happy that you were able to pray for yourself and had that conversation with Him – able, peaceful, personal.

Today, February 2, 2021, we lay your earthly remains to rest.

May it also lay our sorrows, and pains of losing you behind us.

Your memories, however, please let hold on to them forever.

Thus, our unending farewell, T'yoy.

~Macky Lubrico~

Tributes 14

"Brother Willy was very much like my grandfather, General Paulino Santos. They both touched so many lives and accomplished so much for the short time that they were here on earth."

~ Soledad Santos Cuenco ~

There are events in our lives that stand out in our memory. Take the assassination of President John F. Kennedy. It happened fifty-eight years ago when I was thirteen, yet I can vividly recall being on our porch with my sisters Susan and Josie taking a break. We were in the middle of weeding the Bermuda grass lawn that surrounds the perimeter of our house in Lagao, General Santos City. It was mid-morning. We were enjoying our *merienda*, a bottle of coke, and a plateful of boiled Saba bananas. Music was wafting from our adjacent living room from the 18 inches by 24 inches RCA radio tuned in to the local DXGS station. They were playing our 60s favorites. It was November 23, 1963, at 9 a.m. in the Philippines. Then the music abruptly stopped, and a radio announcer came on. *"Ladies and gentlemen, we just received the tragic news from Voice of America that President John F. Kennedy was fatally shot this morning of November 22."*

Similarly, if we asked his friends, "Where were you when you heard Brother Willy died?" I would hazard a guess many could paint a vivid picture of their circumstances.

As his friend Sol Santos Cuenco wrote in the quote, relative to his mother and father who lived to be 96 and 90 respectively, Brother Willy died too young at 68 – more than twenty years younger than his parents.

The first memorial service for Brother Willy was live-streamed from Metro Manila for two days in coordination with Marist Marikina. (Appendix E – Memorial in Marikina). His body was then flown to General Santos City International Airport, from whence it was transported to Notre Dame of Marbel University. The streets on campus lined with palm trees tied with yellow ribbons welcomed him along with teary-eyed university personnel and students. NDMU held nightly memorial services at the gymnasium in his honor for seven days. The events live-streamed on Facebook, YouTube, and Zoom are now archived at NDMU Facebook Live Website.

The chart below indicates the number of people who "viewed" or attended virtually from every continent except Antarctica. As I watched remotely, I could see a line of in-person mourners paying homage to their fallen President from morning till midnight. Everyone observed COVID-19 protocols in the strictest sense. Everyone seated socially distant wore a mask, except for the speakers who stood on a stage more than twenty feet away from the closest person in the seats. It was an event never before witnessed and would be difficult to replicate in the future. Perhaps, his Marist Family would have preferred a simple, low-key funeral service given the pandemic. But the two universities that he loved and its populace would have none of that. His final burial services would befit their beloved President. In the word of Orman, "*Bonga*!" (Grand!)

His response to my suggestion to write a memoir still haunts me. "That's impossible. First, I am not a good writer. Second question, who would be interested to read?" Wanting to prove to him that he was a good writer and that people would be interested, I collated statistics from the live stream video as tracked by Facebook using an algorithm. To write this book as "comprehensively" as he'd wished, I spent a few days watching again the LIVE streamed videos of his memorial service. The chart paints an impressive picture.

To put the chart in perspective, Facebook Live counts the number of views differently than other platforms like YouTube, Zoom, etc. The standard number of views for both Facebook and Facebook Live is the number of times someone watched your video for three seconds or more. However, Facebook tracks several video view metrics...and average watch time.

ATTENDANCE: BRO. WILLY'S MEMORIAL CELEBRATION
FACEBOOK LIVE

Zoom Meetings not included

Date 2021	Event	Reactions -Emojis	Comments	Views	Note
January 26	First night Marikina, MetroManila	no data	no data	no data	Laid in repose Mass & Evening Prayer Service
January 27	Send-off Marikina to NDMU	354	45	6.9k	Evening Prayer Service & Tributes
January 27	Arrival-Notre Dame Marbel U	724	231	19K	Meeting BW at GSC airport & NDMU "homecoming"
January 28	Mass – NDMU Gym	279	67	9.2k	Mass & Tributes
January 29	Prayer Service - Tributes	251	19	5.5k	Prayers & Tributes
January 30	Prayer Service – Tributes	207	49	4k	
January 31	Prayer Service – Tributes				
February 1	Send-off NDMU to Tamontaka	437	106	10K	Leaving NDMU for final resting place in Tamontaka
February 1	Arrival – Tamontaka	272	92	6.1k	
February 1	Memorial Tribute	380	124	11k	
February 2	Funeral Mass	552	205	13k	Archbishop with priests
February 2	Prayer Service	149	44	2.8k	
February 2	Burial	367	143	6.7k	
Total		3972	1125	94.2k	Total
January 27 *	Arrival-Gen. Santos City Airport	256	68	14.K	Posted on Facebook, was shared 231 times

Chart of Attendees as Recorded on Facebook Live

> Despite the ambiguity around views, video usage on social media is on the rise and has been for years. 81% of businesses use video, as a marketing tool in 2018, up 18% from 2017 so social media video is important. And when you look at your video view metrics, you need to know what you're seeing...55% of people watch videos in their entirety, and 43% want more marketing videos.[39]

A clearer picture emerges when emoticons or emojis and comments support the number of views and are added to the equation. Viewers are engaged. During the Facebook Live stream on the Notre Dame of Marbel University website, for example, a total of almost 95,000 views were registered during his memorial services in seven days. Of these viewers, 3972 sent Emojis, and 1125 commented in real time for a total of 5097. That's 95K views and 5K engagements from all over the world. These statistics do not include the audience viewing on Zoom and YouTube. In-person attendance at the NDMU gym was high, too, considering the pandemic. As the Thursday, January 28, 2021, Prayer Vigil shows (see photo), viewing at the NDMU gymnasium started at 11 a.m. through midnight. To observe the COVID-19 Protocol, groups had to register to attend, and the mourners were staggered during the day. And a sophisticated digital contact tracing was closely monitored through cell phones.

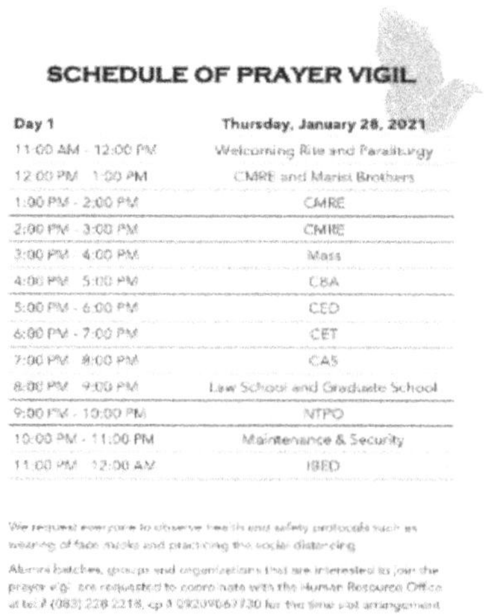

SCHEDULE OF PRAYER VIGIL

Day 1	Thursday, January 28, 2021
11:00 AM - 12:00 PM	Welcoming Rite and Paraliturgy
12:00 PM - 1:00 PM	CMRE and Marist Brothers
1:00 PM - 2:00 PM	CMRE
2:00 PM - 3:00 PM	CMRE
3:00 PM - 4:00 PM	Mass
4:00 PM - 5:00 PM	CBA
5:00 PM - 6:00 PM	CED
6:00 PM - 7:00 PM	CET
7:00 PM - 8:00 PM	CAS
8:00 PM - 9:00 PM	Law School and Graduate School
9:00 PM - 10:00 PM	NTPO
10:00 PM - 11:00 PM	Maintenance & Security
11:00 PM - 12:00 AM	IBED

We request everyone to observe health and safety protocols such as wearing of face masks and practicing the social distancing.

Alumni batches, groups and organizations that are interested to join the prayer vigil are requested to coordinate with the Human Resource Office at tel # (083) 228 2218, cp # 09209067730 for the time slot arrangement.

Schedule of Memorial Services for Brother Willy

During the seven-day memorial service, four to six speakers were invited each night to share their memories of Brother Willy. A mass and evening Holy Rosary preceded each Tribute by "sharers". We selected a few representative views from people very close to Brother Willy.

Dr. Evelyn V. Dollete worked with Brother Willy. She is the Executive Director of Notre Dame Educational Association (NDEA), Regional Program Coordinator Region 12, and BARMM-Private Education Assistance Committee (PEAC). She is now residing in Tacurong City, Philippines. She earned her Master's degree in Educational Administration and Supervision from Sydney, Australia, her Ph.D. from the Notre Dame University of Cotabato City. In addition, she worked as a volunteer at the Ministry of Education and Vocational Training in Zanzibar, East Africa.

> Helen Keller once said, "The best and most beautiful things in the world cannot be seen or even touched — they must be felt with the heart."
>
> This is how I described my relationship with Brother Willy. I cannot remember exactly where this kind of bond between us developed. In September of 2016, I had just returned to the country from my one-year volunteering work in Tanzania, East Africa, with VSO [Voluntary Service Organization based in London][40] when the former NDEA Executive Director retired. Brother Willy was the President of NDEA. I applied for the job as an Executive Director and there were many applicants. When I asked him, "Brother, were there any other applicants to this position?" He said yes and continued to say, "but I did not entertain them anymore." I must be lucky then because from among the many, I was handpicked.
>
> Going down memory lane, my first association with Brother Willy was when I was with Notre Dame of Cotabato. It was in the late 80s. [Brother Willy taught at the Notre Dame of Cotabato High School for Boys in 1987-1988]. I was an ordinary classroom teacher. Brother Willy's career blossomed through the years, and so did mine. Brother

Willy became President of Notre Dame of Dadiangas University (1995-2006) and later of NDMU (Notre Dame of Marbel University 2006-present). In like manner, I also climbed the ladder of success through hard work, dedication, commitment, and passion. Silently, I believe Brother Willy followed my career path, and perhaps, this was his reference for choosing me.

Brother Willy was my number one "bully" [in this context, bully means one who teases playfully] whether face to face or through social media. And I loved him for that. I never took offense to his brand of "bullying". He never took offense either when I returned the favor. I have no Facebook post that, Brother Willy missed commenting. Because of these, without us knowing it, we've developed followers. One mutual friend of ours said, "Every time you post on Facebook, I would scroll and look for a comment from Brother Willy'". Another said that she went to sleep laughing because of our lighthearted exchange. When I fired back at him, I would send a follow-up saying, "Peace Brother Willy love you mwah". This is how comfy we are with each other.

Let me cite one instance when we were in Taiwan in 2018. This was a gift from PEAC (Private Education Assistance Committee) for turning 50. Brother Willy convinced me to take a pose because he loved to play the photographer. I told him bluntly NO, Brother Willy, no way! But Brother Willy was so persistent, "Go, pose because the background is perfect". Finally, I gave in. I posed like an awkward model, and I could hear the click click click on his cellphone camera. Later, I found out that he posted said photo on his Facebook wall with all the pictures he took of me with the caption, "*The trying hard and frustrated model of Baguer, a small and quiet barangay of North Cotabato.*" At the bottom, he added a PS: With a smile emoticon, *"She forced me to be her photographer."* In fairness, he posted nice photos of mine with much preferred flattering poses. And I thanked him.

I am saddened to say this, but today, I see Brother Willy at every corner, grounds, and façade of NDMU. At the moment, I don't relish stepping again into the campus because Brother

Willy is no longer here. At the moment, I say that NDMU is never the same without Brother Willy. I have no more liberty of taking away or stealing his plants. Every time I took away his plants, of course, in his absence, I would choose the nicest ones, but later, I would show him the plants I took from his garden. He would say in Ilonggo, "*Amo lang na ginkawat mo kadamu didto buhi na. Kamanol sa imo!*"[41] (Is that all you stole? How miserly of you!) I burst with laughter. And Brother Willy would join me demurely with a smile.

It pains me to say these words, Brother Willy, now that you are gone go in peace, rest with the Lord. You spent a well-lived life. Many love you. I, for one, love you for so many reasons but most especially because of your simplicity and humility. Your memories will stay forever in our hearts. I will miss you dearly. We shared so many memories of laughter and fun.

I lost a dear friend, a Brother so down to earth worthy of emulation (except for being a "bully" to me).

Goodbye for now Brother Wilfredo E. Lubrico, FMS.

* * * * *

Dr. Noemi Basco Silva is currently a part-time professor at Notre Dame of Marbel University, a researcher, and HR consultant for projects funded by national and international agencies. She held numerous positions for forty years from administrator both in graduate and undergraduate levels, teaching, and director of various programs. An editor of the NDMU Research Journal, she also handled the university publications. Many who contributed to this book may not realize this. Brother Willy loved poems and once dabbled in it when he was at the Marist Formation Center, according to his Novice Master Brother Ted Fernandez. It is so fitting therefore that the tributes from his friends includes poems. Dr. Silva represents the Faculty Retiree as she delivered her message,

My favorite poet Henry Wadsworth Longfellow wrote an unforgettable poem entitled *The Psalm of Life*. I particularly love the seventh stanza, and I quote:

Lives of great men all remind us
We can make our lives sublime,
And, departing, leave behind us
Footprints on the sands of time;

Brother Willy Lubrico, FMS, was a person worthy of accolades for his life not only because he was the President of Notre Dame of Marbel University (NDMU) and Notre Dame of Dadiangas University (NDDU) for decades. Not because of the many positions he held in prestigious organizations but because he touched many lives and made a significant difference.

It took a long time for me to process the news of his death because I had known that he would always come back in his many travels and simply resume his responsibilities in the university. However, it never occurred to me that that was his last trip.

Upon reflection, I realized that Brother Willy unknowingly taught me several lessons:

First lesson. Pursue your passion. Go where your heart is. My passion is in teaching, and since 2010 when I left the administration; I have found my fulfillment and happiness in teaching. Thank you, Brother Willy, for making me realize that there are more important things in life than the pursuit of success.

Second Lesson. Confront your own fears and take risks. As one door closes, more doors of opportunity can be opened. Thank you, Brother Willy, for allowing me to utilize my competencies that I did not realize I possess.

Third Lesson. Agree to disagree but remain friends. Brother Willy and I did not see each other very often, but when we do, we simply pick up where we left off. I can still hear his voice, saying, "*Kamusta ka na Noems (*How are you Noems?*) Ano ang gina busyhan mo* (What keeps you busy)*?* The easy banter starts as if we meet daily. Thank you, Brother Willy, for your simplicity, presence, and friendship with other people you come in contact and me.

Fourth lesson. Maintain good relations and recognize the value of a person. Brother Willy made sure that retirees of NDMU are still welcome to the institution through invitations to attend important events at the university. Retirees look forward to joining the personnel Christmas party not because of the cash gift and giveaways but the opportunity of rekindling friendships with former colleagues. Many thanks, Brother Willy. We will always remember your concern and genuine appreciation for those who have served the institution until they retire.

I would like to remember Brother Willy not only as a towering figure of power and achievement. I see him:

- as a person with vision for NDMU and worked to achieve it;
- as a person who stood up to the challenges that he met;
- as a person who tried to correct his weaknesses and made amends;
- and as a person who made a difference.

For your dedication and commitment to your mission as a Marist Brother, thank you very much, Brother Willy. You can now rest with our Creator and have eternal joy in His Kingdom.

* * * * *

Lina Mondejar, a retired personnel represents the NDMU Staff. She finished a BS Degree in Commerce major in Accounting (1978), then later a Master's Degree in Education major in Mathematics (1983), from Notre Dame of Marbel College. After graduation she started working at her Alma Mater, first as a Research Staff then later as College Instructor, Mathematics Department Head, and Graduate School faculty member at different points of her career. Up to her retirement in 2011, she worked as the Research Director of NDMU since 1998. Lina also holds a Doctor of Philosophy in Education degree in Research and Evaluation (1999) from the University of the Philippines (Diliman). Lina shared,

Brother Willy's stern look and sometimes seemingly harsh words would offend those who don't know him very well, but not me. Perhaps the close affinity with him helped me see beyond his "brutish" words.

I worked with him on the Marist Provincial Committee. Later, he became my boss when I was the Research Director at NDMU. He also spent some years in the high school from where I graduated. I often drop by the office adjacent to his, belonging to my close friend Dalia (Mesias), his secretary. Dalia would offer me some food from the lot served in an ongoing meeting or conference. He'd tease, "*Daw wala ka man naimbita diri*". (It seems that you were not invited here). I'd just laugh because I knew he was joking, as he would later admit.

Brother Willy was more than just a boss. He was also a *barkada.* He, Brother Rene (Reyes), Dalia, and I are close friends. On their birthdays, the four of us would go out for a meal or coffee to celebrate. However, when the celebrant is busy due to some important commitments, we postpone our date and give a rain check to the celebrant. When Brother Willy died; I still owed him for his 2020 and 2021 birthdays. Bro Willy, *indi mo ako pagsukton kon sa diin ka man karon ha*?

(Brother Willy, please don't ask for a rain check wherever you are, okay?).

Every year, my birthday gifts to him are items like shoes or slippers or shirts from "*ukay-ukay*". [*Ukay-ukay* literally translates to "sort-sort" and refers to items being sold at thrift shops.] He seemed to like them more than the gifts I get from a fancy department store. Speaking of *ukay-ukay*, he also enjoyed going to the *talipapa* [stalls] to check out things. I would caution him to be mindful of who might see him there as employees, teachers, and students might run into him in these places. Well, he seemed not to mind being seen by anyone buying *ukay-ukay*, part of his staying true to his vow of poverty by living a simple and unpretentious life.

Brother Willy, despite exuding the impression of being suplado (unfriendly, aloof, distant), is a magnet to people. He inspired loyalty. I had seen his former students and old colleagues who, given an opportunity, would drop by wherever he was assigned to say hello or hang out with him for a while. Perhaps because of his simplicity and unassuming personality, people felt very comfortable with him. He was so relatable.

But I am more inclined to say it's because he was a model of thoughtfulness and demonstrated a fiercely sincere love for his friends.

* * * * *

Brother Dionesio (Jong) D. Acosta, Jr., FMS joined the Marist Brothers Congregation in 2007. He finished his Bachelor's Degree in Secondary Education major in Religious Education. He is currently doing his Masters in Educational Management. He was assigned in Marbel Community in 2013-2015 with Br. Willy while teaching at NDMU-IBED. He also volunteered at the La Valla 200 Project of the Marist Brothers Congregation as a part of an International Community and was assigned for two years in Cuba. Presently, he is assigned in Marbel Community working at the Senior High School Department. His tribute:

> Much has been said and shared about the achievements and accomplishments of Brother Willy. His success is evident everywhere - in the academe, the Church, and society in general. Therefore, I would like to speak more of my personal encounter with him as a fellow Marist Brother and a friend.
>
> I would like to begin with the phrase in Ilonggo, *"Daw Manol Ka"*, a form of expression that I will always attribute to him. I supposed this was true not just for me but also for many other people who had become close to him.
>
> *"Daw manol ka!"*
>
> [*Manol* is a Hiligaynon word used in this context as a bumpkin, naiveté, see endnotes for full explanation].
>
> He says this phrase both in the literal sense and as an expression to show the measure of his affection, friendship, or degree of closeness to someone. I believe he could use the phrase because I know his rich personal and professional experiences and accomplishments. I know I could learn many lessons and pointers from him about life itself.

Looking back, that phrase now becomes a reminder for me to always be open to learning new things and aspire to be better in whatever endeavor I pursue in life, a reminder neither to settle for less nor to be satisfied with the status quo. Brother Willy's life is a testament to that, a life, which speaks of how great a visionary he was.

Brother Willy is also *manol* despite his lofty accomplishments, *manol* especially regarding information and technology. Whenever I had the chance to throw back the phrase at him, I always did. He'd just then look at me, as if saying, wait for my turn. But mind you, he is a fast learner. He never lets on that he already knows more than you do - posting more photos and updates on social media, sending quotes, emojis, gifs, memes through messenger, and using mobile apps that I haven't even heard of. This only speaks of his humility to continue growing, learning despite his position and his achievements in life.

Speaking of personal and professional development, he also encouraged me to begin my graduate studies when I was in Marbel. When I returned to the country in November from two years in Cuba, his first question was about my studies. This solidified my plans to pursue my graduate studies. This month, I have enrolled again.

In the first years of my apostolic life as a Marist Brother, I lived in the same community under the same roof 24/7 in Marbel from 2013-2015 with Brother Willy. But I first met him when I was a college student here at NDMU in 2006. Like everyone else, I only knew him then as the school President who sometimes signs my promissory note with an intimidating look. [A promissory note allows a student to take his exams with the promise to pay his school fees when able and before he graduates.]

I got to know him better when I joined and started my formation with the Marist Brothers, especially in the Novitiate, where he frequently visited because of his best friend, Brother Rene Reyes, our Community Superior at that time.

When I moved to Marbel, Brother Willy started a tradition. As our Community Superior, he suggested an initiative to invite our Lay partners to join us in our community prayers and meals twice a month.[42] This is to show them that our Marist home is always open and welcomes those who want to know more about the Brothers' life and how we live in the community setting. This has also opened the eyes of many of our lay partners, especially the new ones. They got to see the other side of Brother Willy: a kind, gentle, generous, and humble person with a sense of humor who knew how to laugh.

Last December, he asked me when would I visit him in Marbel. I told him that I would be around on Christmas day. He said, "See you at dinner". Period. No more questions asked. However, because I attended a celebration at my parents' house, I went to sleep and almost forgot about it. I texted Brother Aljon and asked if Brother Willy is around. He told me that Brother Willy put dinner on hold, waiting for me. That is how patient Brother Willy was. So, I hurried to Marbel and joined him for dinner.

The following day, as we all know how he loves to listen and be listened to, he shared his feelings health-wise and his scheduled medical trip to Manila. I did not know that that was the last time I would have a long and meaningful conversation with him.

Will, thank you for your witness and for giving your heart in living the Marist life, especially for your love and dedication to education. Your memories will surely live on. Not only because of your accomplishments. But more so because of the life you have beautifully lived and shared among and with all of us.

While this narrator listened to Brother Jong's tribute during the memorial service, I could not help but chuckle. One of Brother Willy's endearing traits was his capacity to laugh at himself. In June 15, 2013, he posted on Facebook his picture captioned, exactly that - *Daw manol!*

I could almost hear him say it. This particular post shows him doing a "Jump" in the middle of Dubai desert. I urge you to look for this post. It's hilarious. To find it on your desktop or laptop, just go to his Facebook page "Willy Lubrico". Directly below his name there is a header. Go to the extreme right after "Message". Click on the three dots ... for the drop down button. Choose "Search Profile" from the drop down. A pop up will ask you, *"Looking for something?"* Above it, type *"Daw Manol!"*

You'll find him. I promise it will make you smile. If you want a good laugh, scroll through the forty-seven comments. You'll appreciate his quick wit and sense of humor.

Roland Manansala Gingatan: *gi* hold *up ka ninong*?

Joe Jun Sevilla: Leaving "footprints in the sand"...

Rey Patilan Maglente: Hello Bro Willy, *naano natabo dah hehehe. Nadula ka sa disyerto?* You need compass or GPS? (What happened? Are you lost in the desert?)

Willy Lubrico: Nice to get lost once in a while in yourself. Too crowded with bad spirits LOL.

Prima Guipo Hower: We are entitled to one *manol* moment Brother W. One only ha? We can tell how much rapport you have with alumni. You can go all over the world and find an alum friend who will be so happy to host you. Very low maintenance guest ka, *tapos ga panilhig pa kag mag* garden. (Guest who sweeps the floor...)

Willy Lubrico: Blessings. I don't know how to thank God.

* * * * *

Sol Santos Cuenco graduated from Notre Dame of Lagao High School Class 1974. She was the Past President of Notre Dame of General Santos City Alumni Association International (2003-2005), and a proud alumna of Notre Dame of Marbel University (ETEEAP). She is the granddaughter of Gen. Paulino Santos, after whom the City of General Santos was named.

> Brother Willy came into our lives when our son, Ramon Paul (RP), was about ten years old; he is now thirty-three. Brother Willy made a side trip to San Francisco, California on his way to some international event. We invited him to stay

with us in Concord, about thirty miles east of San Francisco. He wanted to tour San Francisco, the city by the Bay. My husband, Ramon, and I were working full-time and could not take off from work, so RP was volunteered as personal tourist guide for Brother Willy. They took the Hop-On, Hop-Off bus and explored the city.

We kept in touch all through the years. We made every effort to see Brother Willy whenever we visit General Santos City and later Marbel.

Brother Willy cared deeply for an individual's development. When he found out that my sister, Eli, and I were not able to pursue a four-year degree, he encouraged us to enroll in the Expanded Tertiary Education Equivalency & Accreditation Program (ETEEAP) at the Notre Dame of Marbel University. This is how I became an alumna of both Notre Dame of Lagao (high school) and Notre Dame of Marbel University (ETEEAP).

Brother Willy adopted my four children in his own special way. Knowing him, I know he included them in his daily prayers. In our conversations, he never failed to ask about their whereabouts. "*Saan na* si Yvette, Joan, RP, Isabella?"

My family and I are incredibly thankful for one of Brother Willy's numerous initiatives. He spearheaded the efforts in conceptualizing and establishing the General Paulino Santos Museum (GPS Museum) at the Notre Dame of Dadiangas University to house my grandfather's memorabilia. Brother Willy personally approached my aunt, Atty. Rosa Santos Munda (Tita Rosky), who was residing in Davao City at that time. [They met for the first time at the Notre Dame of General Santos City Alumni USA reunion in New Jersey in 1999 when Tita Rosky was the guest speaker]. Brother Willy informed me later that he and Tita Rosky connected well and were both excited about establishing the GPS Museum. I told him, "*Siyempre,* you're both academicians. You share the same mission – the desire to encourage, to develop young minds, and always to educate."

Brother Willy's most significant legacy for me is establishing the General Paulino Santos Museum at Notre

Dame of Dadiangas University. Future generations will benefit from the Museum.

Brother Willy was very much like my grandfather, General Paulino Santos. They both touched so many lives and accomplished so much for the short time that they were here on earth.

*****

This narrator observed that as accomplished as he was, Brother Willy was not one to claim attention to his person, so he went about life quietly without fanfare or complaint. His self-effacing nature sometimes can be a plus or a minus depending on your point of view.

He visited my family in July 2016 on July 4th weekend. He was on his way to attend the Marist International Network Institute seminar at the Marist College, Poughkeepsie, New York, with Deans Lynou Zacal and Joan Palma. With his wry brand of humor, he amused us by conferring an honorary title to their driver Dr. Editha Plecis and declared her "Director of Ways and Means". Edith lives in New Rochelle, New York, an alumna of Notre Dame of Marbel, and drove the trio on a round trip four-hour one-way trek to Warren, Rhode Island. We all played along with Brother Willy and had fun with it. We figured she was deserving of the title.

Our Guest Book was rather filled up that summer. Brother Willy's group arrived just two days after a set of guests had left. I quickly made the beds for his foursome. When they left five days later, I hurriedly stripped the beds again to prepare for the next batch of guests.

I went to the room that Brother Willy had occupied. It looked like the bed was never slept on. The bedspread was laid out very neatly. When I peeled it off, I realized to my utter dismay, my President had been sleeping on an unmade bed, on top of the course mattress cover! In my haste I did not prepare the bed properly. Luckily, I had changed the pillowcases.

I dialed Bro Willy's cell phone right away. The seminar was about to start. I said, "Brother, why did you not tell me that your bed has no fitted nor flat sheets? That mattress cover is as rough as a sandpaper!"

"Don't fret over it Prim", he said. "I did not mention it because I did not want to embarrass you. I had slept before on bamboo benches without pillows or sheets even on a hard, wet uneven ground under the sky no roof over my head. No big deal".

He had an uncanny way of turning an embarrassment into feeling okay. But, it took me a while to get over that "no big deal" incident because I kept wondering if he told anyone about it! Did he momentarily think I was *"Daw manol?"*

Brothers Jong, Allan de Castro, Rene Reyes, Roy Deita, and Willy sharing a meal with lay partners.

The five-day "Endurance Workshop" in Warren, Rhode Island 2016
L-R: Bro Willy, author, Lynou Zacal, Joan Palma, Edith Plecis

Reflections 15

"He was a natural leader with his vision, his life witness, his harmony with God and his attention to the needs of children and young people and those who worked with them."

~Brother Joao Carlos do Prado, FMS ~
Rome, Italy

Brother Willy held leadership roles on local, national, and international stages, both religious and secular organizations. His impact was immense. Yet, he stayed humble through it all. Therefore, it was no surprise that when he died, an outpouring of love and profound sympathies exploded on his social media.

One of the chapters he listed in his original outline was titled "Reflections". Sadly, he only finished writing eight paragraphs about "the highlights of my life" before he died.

This chapter is not about his own reflections, as he intended it to be. Instead, it is the reflections of many about him. As I am fond of saying, he was prescient in his remark when he wrote on his outline, "we can ask the opinions of my friends from long, long ago (many of them) and my students".

Here then are those "opinions" he couldn't have imagined. They are coming from leaders: the Marist Councilor General in Rome, a university President, a Superior General of a Religious order, and government officials. They came from all walks of life and different parts of the world.

*****

Brother Joao Carlos do Prado is the Councilor General for the Province of South Central Brazil who lives in Rome, Italy. He was born on January 15, 1971, in Jabora, Santa Catarina, Brazil. He made his first profession as a Marist Brother in 1992 and his perpetual vow in 1999. He has a Master's degree in Education from the *Pontifica Universidad Catolica* (PUC) of Parana (2009), a Bachelor's degree in Religious Studies (1994), a Bachelor's degree in Letters, and a specialization in Psychology of human development. From 2011 to 2016, he was director of the Secretariat of Mission of the Institute. Since 2017 he has been a member of the General Council. He began:

> Greetings from Rome, also from Brother Ernesto Sánchez and all the members of the General Council.
>
> Today we are all gathered to pay our respects to our beloved friend, a Brother, a leader, Brother Willy Lubrico. Each of us carried in our hearts and minds the testimony of Brother Willy's life and dedication to youth and how much he loved being a Marist Brother. I personally had a great friendship and admiration for Brother Willy.
>
> During the time I was working here in Rome at the Mission Secretariat, I had the opportunity to participate with him in the Marist International Network of Institutions of Higher Education. From 2012 to 2013, he was the President of this network. Together, we planned the Network's Assembly, which took place in Koronadal City, in the Philippines in 2014.
>
> What I express of admiration for Brother Willy also reflects the feelings of many friends he has made worldwide, both Brothers and laypeople. Brother Willy was a visionary. He was able to discern the signs of the times. However, he was very connected with the local reality. We all know his accomplishments and how much he contributed to the evangelization and education of youth. Allowing thousands of young people to realize their life projects.
>
> He was a natural leader with his vision, life witness, harmony with God, and attention to the needs of children and young people and those who worked with them. I always admired the affection with which he treated the Marist

Brothers and the lay people around him. Many messages and images translate this reciprocity of affection and friendship today on his Facebook.

Brother Willy was someone who loved his vocation as a Marist Brother and vibrated for it. At the same time, he felt supported by each of you in God's call to him and in the mission that had been entrusted to him.

So today, we say thank you very much, Brother Willy, for your life witness, for your joy, and friendship. Thank you for helping us look at the world and the people with another eye. Thank you for helping us to believe more and more in human beings. Thank you for being the simple and inspiring presence of God in our midst. Now, with Mary and Marcellin Champagnat, intercede to God for us, especially for the Church and Marist mission in the Philippines.

*****

Fred Gaspar and Brother Willy worked together at Socio Pastoral Institute Mindanao (SPI) during the late 1980s. He then joined the Philippine International Forum, a network of foreign volunteers, missionaries, and laypeople in solidarity with people's struggles in the Philippines. Together with three other long-time community development workers, he co-founded *Kinaiyahan* Foundation, a non-governmental environmental agency in Mindanao. Fred and his wife Helen Harrington-Gaspar moved to Nova Scotia, Canada, in 1990. They have two adult girls, Inna based in London, UK, and Julia in New York City. Fred finished his Master's degree at the Maritime School of Social Work, Dalhousie University. For twenty-eight years, he worked for the Metropolitan Regional Public Housing and the Nova Scotia Health Authority's community mental health services. He is now retired and enjoys volunteering, walking, reading, painting, and gardening. From Canada he paid his tribute:

> I would like to share a reflection on Brother Willy. I worked with him at the Socio Pastoral Institute Mindanao (SPI). It was in the late 1980s [1986-1988]. SPI is a "training and service institution through a systematic socio-pastoral

education program for church peoples involved in the integral social change and total human development". It promotes a "biblically-rooted view of Jesus from the poor and the oppressed" perspective. SPI provided workshops, retreats, trainings, and other resource information to church people in Mindanao. SPI had a closed network with other church organizations like BCC-CO (Basic Christian Community, Community Organizing), EANCHOR (Ecumenical Alliance of Nationalist Church Organization), PCPR (Philippine Promotion of Church Peoples' Response), SAMIN (Sisters Association of Mindanao), International Forum, and other social development agencies.

Sr. Genevieve Damaso, OND (nicknamed Bebang), Brother Willy, and I were collectively working together in SPI's Education program. Our Executive Director then was Nonoy Cabazares. Our focus was directed to the emerging historical model of the church, the Church of the Poor. This church is geared towards preferential love and option for poor people. The SPI's education program we provided promotes "spirituality of stewardship", which is a springboard in shaping our local churches and communities to adopt this model that is at the service of the poor and the oppressed.

Brother Willy and our team believed that human liberation and development are at the heart of all faith-inspired work. We promoted a "development for peace based on justice using spirituality and the common ground found between faiths" as a basis for collaboration, networking, and alliances. Both Brother Willy and Sr. Bebang took charge of SPI's Formation program, which looked after the continuing development of community church leaders in Mindanao. These church people took the initiative on community development projects that embraced the dimensions of their communities' socio-economic, political, cultural, and spiritual context.

Coming from Brother Willy's experience in Cotabato areas, I saw the passion and dedication of Brother Willy in the integration of interfaith setting where there is a sharing of social beliefs and Islamic faith. This was a very important issue to Brother Willy, since it is the key to working together to address the pressing socio-economic, political, and spiritual issues that overwhelmed these disheartened communities.

My other former colleagues mentioned that Brother Willy opted to work outside the confines of his convent and schools, even during his sabbatical leaves. He totally immersed himself in the realities and struggles of the poor, understood their situation, and shared his hopes and aspirations with them. Brother Willy lived very simply. In fact, he's comfortable wearing t-shirts, sandals, and *tsinelas* (slippers or flip-flops). He was very friendly, brotherly, and fatherly. He's quiet but willing to listen and share his thoughts.

Others reflected that Brother Willy touched many people's lives because he was kind and understanding. *Mahigalaon sya sa mga tao nga iyang makauban, usa ka determinado nga tao ug isog siyang modawat og mga gimbuhaton nga ihatag kaniya.* (He was friendly and determined to the people he worked with and always ready to accept any tasks assigned to him). He was open, willing to learn, and adaptable to change. Brother Willy had no problems talking to the basic sectors of our society despite his status as a professional Marist Brother. He's genuinely an agent of change. *Usa gayud siya ka buhing ehemplo nga nagdala og kabag-ohan kung asa man siya mahimutang.* (He is a living example in bringing change in whatever situation with which he is involved). His style of leadership is infectious – firm but yet clear in purpose.

Brother Willy and I got reconnected through Facebook in July 2019. I was so happy that we did, and he thanked me for keeping in touch and said that he's active on social media. For the last twenty-six years, he informed me of his position as President of not only one but also two of Notre Dame universities in Marbel and General Santos City. I responded and appreciated his efforts on the ever-challenging job as President. I told him that I am happily retired as a Social Worker in our Community Mental Health Services. His response then was he wished he could also retire. However, he further said, "life is okay with me too." I would like to end my reflection with a poem by Kevin McCormack [who wrote this piece in 2020 during the height of the pandemic]:

Today, we mourned you differently – not in the way we would have liked to or felt you deserved. A restricted celebration, not enough to even begin to pay tribute to the life you've lived.

Today, we mourned you differently. The pageantry was sparse, we had no singer to sing your songs, and the shoulders of the fine men you reared were bare – they would have gladly, though sadly taken your weight with pride, and carried you to where you now sleep.

Today, we mourned you differently – your [friends, teachers, students lined the church or in the gym] – a noble gesture, but a poor substitute for the squeeze of a shoulder, an embrace, and the vice-grip handshakes full of grief, solidarity and questions.

Today, we mourned you differently, but this much is true – you are gone, but not without a trace, as you are in every face you leave behind, in every imprint of your foot on the path you so diligently wore from the garden to your kitchen door.

Today, we mourned you, Brother Willy differently.

* * * * *

Jerwin Tampe and Lester Lubrico Tugade hosted Brother Willy's Memorial services on February 2, 2021. They introduced the "sharers" who paid their tributes to Brother Willy. Listed on the program were his sister Teresa Lubrico Golveo, Margie Silva (a parent), and other luminaries including the Mayor of the City of Koronadal, Engineer Eliordo Ogena. He was on his way to pick-up groceries for his wife, he said, when he got a call to memorialize Brother Willy. He dropped everything, because the next day Brother Willy would be taken to his final resting place in Tamontaka. He went directly to NDMU Gymnasium, apologized for not being dressed up for the occasion, and delivered his moving speech. A year later, Mayor Ogena would honor Brother Willy for his significant contribution in the greening of the city with *The Wilfredo E. Lubrico, FMS Award for the Cleanest and Best Landscaped Barangay (Urban Category),* the prize in the amount of P150,000.00 for the winner.

Dr. Allan Farnazo, the Director of Regional 12 Department of Education, was one of the speakers on this night. He delivered his profound condolences to the family and friends of Brother Willy, the Notre Dame community, and the Marist Brothers. He also relayed the personal sympathies from the Philippine Secretary of Education Leonor Matolis Briones.

> "Who is Bro Willy to the Department of Education?" Allan asked.
>
> You may not know this but Brother Willy facilitated many great engagements with Department of Education (DePeD). First is providing an educational home to the Masters in Cultural Education Scholarship Program of DePeD. Hence a lot of our teachers in culture, arts, music, and other kinds of arts expressions are studying at NDMU. Second: Brother Willy is also providing a home equivalent to a graduate studies program for the distance learning Southeast Asian Ministry of Education Organization. Brother Willy was a very active online tutor in fact of their programs including many other professors of NDMU. The third is his very prominent engagement in the Department of the Regional Director of PEAC (Private Education Assistance Committee). There are three of us in this committee, he as the Director and Dr. Evelyn Dollete as the Secretariat. This committee is very active in the implementation of the Senior High School (SHS) Voucher Program. Brother Willy even visited distant areas of BARRM (Bangsamoro Autonomous Region in the Muslim Mindanao). This committee provides assistance, guidance, and subsidy in the operation of the SHS program. He does validation for Private schools other than Notre Dame institutions.
>
> He provided the guidelines and directions to the national Committee of PEAC where we almost always meet every month. I was personally instructed by the Secretary of Education of the Philippines, Dr. Leonor Magtolis Briones to extend her sincerest condolences to the Lubrico family.

I first met BW in 1992 when I was still a high school teacher at NDDU IBED Lagao. He was the convener for the CMRE (Campus Ministry Religion Education). I was then with the campus ministry at Lagao campus. Members of CMRE were Religion teachers, some of us ex seminarians, ex sisters, and laypeople. Brother Willy took the initiative as Convener of Marist Schools of the Philippines to prepare us to be competent to hold the job. He did not limit these services to the Marist schools but expanded to other private schools. I was one of the first graduates in Masters in Religious Education of NDMU.

Our second personal encounter was when NDDC (now a university) was pursuing the PAASCU accreditation. Brother Willy was doing an inventory of the teachers – who finished PHD, who are candidates, etc. I was one of those caught sleeping on "my job" for a long time. After finishing my Comprehensive Masters Exam, for four years, I haven't taken any action to write my thesis. Brother Willy prodded me. By that time, I have lost my drive. I could not find inspiration or reason to get to the finish line.

"Brother, *pangita ka na lang sang iban kay mango mango gid ako"*, I implored. (Please find someone else because I feel so stupid). I thought that was the easiest way to keep him off my back. His response was stern, "Allan, you have to finish".

I had no choice. He sweetened the deal with a six months leave with pay.

I struggled the first two months trying to find the drive to get started. I could not sleep. I did not know what to do. On the third month, my fear of failing Brother Willy motivated me to start writing vowing to finish. What I have not finished in four years I finished in three months.

Without Brother Willy, I don't know where I'd be. Brother Willy was sent by the Lord to push me. Brother, you made me. I would never have been where I am today if not because of you.

Our personal bond flourished. He was our ninong at our wedding. He became a part of my family including naming my oldest son. My wife still teaches at NDDU IBED Lagao. Several times I invited her to join me at DePeD and leave Notre Dame High School. But, she stayed. All our children are free at this school courtesy of my wife's employment at NDDU as part of her benefits.

In 1998, being married for two years, I realized I had to be the breadwinner to my growing family. I decided to leave NDDU and pursue a political post in our municipality. I have never planned or dreamed to be a politician. It was something for which I was not prepared. Brother Willy was very worried. He told me one day, "Allan, even if you are already running for a political career, I will leave your teaching position open so you have an option to come back in case things don't work out".

I know I am not the only one he offered such privileges. There are many of us who were influenced, helped, and nurtured by Brother Willy.

He also warned me, "Allan be careful about pirating my teachers".

I replied, "I am 'raiding' your teachers because you are producing good ones. I would like to claim that I am your best contribution to DepEd". He just smiled.

Speaking in a necrological service is not my territory. It took a lot of courage to stand here before you.

But we are privileged to share this night together in honor of my godfather who has been a part of every event in my life.

He is not dead. He lives in us. He is present in us.

* * * * *

Sr. Erlinda Hisug, OND is the Superior General of the Sisters of Oblates of Notre Dame, Cotabato City, Philippines. She shared:

When Sr. Pat Babiera, OND, asked me to pay the last tribute to Brother Willy as a mission partner I readily said yes. I did not wish to miss the opportunity to share with his Marist Community and his family how grateful and how appreciative we are for what Brother Willy has been to us, the

Oblates of Notre Dame. We learned of Brother Willy's demise on the third day of our congregation's own bereavement for the death of Sr. Diana Fe Gillesania, OND, Directress of the Notre Dame of Bongao in Tawi-Tawi. Most of the sisters were shaken when condolences and messages stormed Facebook. Brother Willy and Sr. Diane were colleagues in the education ministry and attended many conferences convened by CEAP or NDEA together.

I used to confer with Brother Willy when he was the President of the Notre Dame of Dadiangas College, and later at NDMU. I wish to share his exemplary values and qualities with you, at least three that impressed me most.

First is his availability. Every official appointment I had with Brother Willy was both business and pleasure. I would request his secretary, Ms. Dalia Mesias, or the OND Sister for an appointment. If he were just on campus, he would always make himself available. We'd schedule our business conference for about fifteen minutes. The next hour shall revolve around his current projects, dreams, and plans for the university. He would show the ongoing construction or those that had been completed. He'd talk without haste. It was as if a volume of work did not await him. If he were not on campus, like once when he was on vacation, he allowed that we converse over the phone if only to respond to the OND's concerns. Once, I heard the sound of strong waves hitting the shore and distant laughter from the background, and we needed to speak louder to be heard. I learned that he was in Siargao. It was always a pleasure because we'd talk about other things while we shared whatever Dalia served us for a snack. Almost always, I would leave with a clearly established agreement and take home a bunch of key chains and magnets, precious tokens from his travels.

The second is his imagination. Pandemics and other clear present social issues often create new attitudes, needs and behaviors, and interventions we need to anticipate. Brother Willy's accomplishments at NDDU and NDMU are powerful witnesses of the imagination with which he was gifted. He was optimistic in sharing his plans. His excitement was contagious. He talked about building the (NDMU) library, and the wing for the President's office would be renovated. Years ago, he invited me to attend the Marist School Congress as an observer so I would be given a glimpse of the dynamics of the Marist Education. And while there, he would ask what my impressions were. Once he took me to the Marist House to show the renovations. On another occasion, he invited us to dine at the Café Marista. Imagination! The capacity to create, evolve, and exploit mental models of things or situations that do not exist yet is crucial in vetting in and creating new opportunities and finding new paths to growth. Brother Willy is one imaginative Marist Brother. He has left us testimonies to his unwavering commitment to quench the thirst of the young and old alike; for relevant and culture-changing Education that the Marist Education advocates.

The third is as a consecrated person. My visits had always been about the projection or evaluation of the participation of the OND sisters in the ministry. However, our conversation would always include a sharing of reflection on our life as consecrated persons. He would affirm the need for fidelity to our commitment to community life, to the challenge to live in simplicity, and to create or allow opportunities for spiritual growth for community members. He supported the OND's scheduled spiritual exercises such as monthly recollections, annual retreats, and the occasional gathering of the Sisters for the district or congregational activities. He was always open to the change of the assignment of the sisters. He was cognizant that as missionaries, we are ready to be uprooted anytime and to go where we are sent as participants and stewards of God's mission. His concern for the sisters' wellbeing was most concrete when he caused the major renovation of the house for the ONDs. He even assisted in organizing the garden. I learned that he either visited the sisters or invited them to the Marist House for a leisurely chat or simple celebrations of life. I sensed that what Brother Willy affirmed in us were also among those that he valued as a Marist Brother. As the scripture says, "for where your treasure is, there your heart will also be" (Mt.6:21)

We often say that the hour of death cannot be far-fetched. We imagine this hour would be in the distant future when we say this. We often thought that the thief we called death, who arrives without prior notice, would take someone else, not the person nearest to us, like Brother Willy.

Brother Willy, we do not mourn you. Instead, we celebrate you because you have been a real gift to the Oblates of Notre Dame, the Marist Community, the church, and the world. Our sadness of your passing is tempered by the memories of your availability, your imagination, and your life as a consecrated person, a Marist, a long-time friend to many ONDs. Jesus' resurrection guarantees life beyond the grave. In the resurrection, we find there is hope in our despair, joy beyond belief.

Dear Brother Willy, you were steadfast and always excelled in the Lord's work. We trust that your labor in the Lord is not in vain. Therefore, do rest in the bosom of the Lord. He has initially called you to be a missionary disciple, following the Marist way. May you encounter the Blessed Virgin Mary, welcoming you home in God's dwelling place with the affection of a mother for her beloved son. Amen.

* * * * *

Brother Manuel de Leon is the current President of Notre Dame of Dadiangas University. He took over the presidency when Brother Pat Corpus was transferred to Notre Dame of Marbel University to fill the void that Brother Willy left when he died.

Countless were shocked and overcome with grief when we found out that Brother Willy had died. We couldn't easily reconcile how someone could be posting beautiful images on Facebook one day and is dead the next. Very few of us knew about his health issues, so the lingering question floats around, "What happened?"

I hope that someday soon, we will have processed our loss to a point where life could be lived in such a way that only the happy memories of Brother Willy stay. Such as the shared reminisces by many, including that of Brother Manny. As a narrator, I appreciated his willingness to share his personal thoughts on Brother Willy's significant legacy and the clinical explanation regarding the cause of his death. Brother Manny wrote on his Facebook news feed:

> These are my personal thoughts and feelings. I tried to be factual and objective as far as possible. I want to share with people I believe deserve to know more about Brother Willy, as I have known him. And I consider these thoughts and feelings sacred.
>
> As I sit outside the patio of our residence in Lagao, I look at the beautiful moon, thinking of our departed Brother Willy, now back in his beloved Notre Dame of Marbel University [lying in state] in the company of people he served, befriended, and loved. He had touched thousands of lives directly and indirectly as a classroom teacher, Director of Student Affairs, Campus Ministry Director, Director of Community Extension Services, Pastoral Worker, College and University President, NDEA President, Superior of the Community of Brothers, member of the Provincial Council, President of the International Network of Marist Universities and Institutions of Higher Learning, a caring family member, etc.
>
> Like the moon, no matter how bright and brilliant, it derives its light not from its own but from the sun, and so is the life of Brother Willy. He could not have accomplished all these without God's grace and the help of many people who were there at his side supporting him. And the reflections, either with shades of darkness or with the freshness of the new moon or resplendent on a full moon, depended on how Brother Willy made himself open to God's grace and the generosity and goodness of the people around him.
>
> Brother Willy will be remembered for being a "builder": building structures, building a reputation of academic excellence, building bridges by reaching out to different sectors of society, and building deep and lasting personal relationships. I have not lived with him in a [Marist House] community nor worked in the same ministry together. Our encounters were always in formal meetings or gatherings. Or, if I had to deal with him, it was always in an official

capacity. I was his Provincial for ten and a half years. I was the Chairman of the Board of Trustees of NDDC and NDMU when he was President of these institutions. Reversal of roles, he was the Chairman of the Board of Notre Dame of Kidapawan College when I was President. At the Board Room, I was a personal witness on how he presented his plans, defended them, and eventually got them approved. And some of those meetings were contentious and difficult meetings that he had to go through. Often times I injected humor and became facetious to lower the temperature. And so, I have been called a "trouble maker".

Brother Willy has a vast network of friends with whom he felt more comfortable and with whom he had shared his joys, hopes, dreams, difficulties, disappointments, and hurts. But as to his health condition, he would rather keep it to himself and not burden others. I suspect he was in great pain all these months, considering the fact that he had an advanced stage of liver cirrhosis. The irony was that he was focused on his prostate, which was only Stage One based on medical records and can be treated with surgery using the Robotic Radical Prostatectomy. The Intrahepatic Cholangio Carcinoma or cancer of the bile ducts was only discovered after an MRI was conducted [after he arrived in Manila for medical treatment]. He developed hepatic encephalopathy. The toxins were not appropriately processed due to decompensated liver cirrhosis entering the blood vessels and affecting his brain. This was why the doctors gave him a slim chance of survival when he had a cardiac arrest on the late evening of January 24. (Note: Information on the medical reports is based on the communication of Brother Provincial supplemented by my own readings.)

I quote Fr. Ron Rolheiser on FIDELITY as a way of saying farewell to a confrere, a fellow Marist Brother.

"When there is fidelity within a relationship, eventually the hurts, misunderstandings wash clean and even bitterness turns to love. We are all weak, wounded, sinful, and easily hurt. We cannot promise that we won't disappoint each other and worse still, hurt each other. However, the promise that we won't walk away because of disappointments and hurts, that's all enough as a promise".

Brother Willy may have been disappointed and hurt by us. We ask for his forgiveness if we did because of our insensitivity, selfishness, and ego or simply because of unmet expectations. He could have "walked away" when the temptations to give up were so strong to resist. But he has chosen to remain faithful. His mission on this transitory existence is over. He is going on a well-deserved rest in the company of angels and saints with his Divine Creator.

REQUIESCAT IN PACE, Brother Willy.

* * * * *

The Rio Grande de Mindanao meanders along the rolling hills just beyond a row of stately trees where a sacred burial ground exudes total solitude. A wrought iron fence, its white paint aged and stained, enclosed the burial ground. Brother Willy had meandered too around this lush ground of the Novitiate for two years during his formative years. His Novice Master Brother Ted Fernandez recalled Brother Willy and his cohorts patrolled the area during the Muslim and Christian conflict in Cotabato in the 1970s. His friend Rudy Mapada remembers catching boys stealing pili nuts. It was here that Brother Ted observed young Willy, his novice, writing his poems in the gardens that he tended. This is the patch of God's land where notable men who "Died Empty" had been laid to rest.

Let me explain.

Bing Hoyumpa, a friend of Brother Willy recently forwarded to my classmates and me a story circulated on Facebook about a book by Todd Henry, "Die Empty". The author drew his inspiration while attending a business meeting. A speaker asked the audience, "Where is the richest land in the world?" "Oil-rich Gulf States" came an answer from the audience. Another added, "Diamond mines of Africa". "No," said the speaker. "The answer is the cemetery. Yes, it is the wealthiest land in the world. Because millions of people have died and departed, who carried with them countless valuable ideas that did not come to light nor benefit others. Ideas were buried with them in the cemetery".

My favorite takeaway from the message is, "Do not go to your grave and carry inside you the best that you have. Always choose to die empty. The true meaning of this expression is to die empty of all the goodness that is within you. Deliver it to the world before you leave. If you have an idea perform it. If you have knowledge share it, if you have a goal achieve it. Love, share and distribute. Do not keep it inside".

This narrator is a big fan of Todd Henry's book. Let us all heed his call to "Die Empty" precisely like Brother Willy did.

He died empty except for those poems he once wrote as a young lad, but shared only with Brother Ted, and perhaps with the stately trees that now welcomed him under their shade.

Briccio Baynosa, my co-author, describes this patch of land.

At the farthest end of the Immaculate Conception Novitiate of the Marist Brothers Philippines, lies serene is the Marist Cemetery. This is now Brother Willy's final resting place since February 3, 2021. There is nothing more fitting a place for him to be laid to rest than this garden of peace and sanctuary. From a bird's eye view, one can see how various sturdy trees reaching the heavens surround this part of the property. The lawn is carpeted by green grass as green as the rustling leaves of the trees dancing in the sky.

Atop a big mound stands the statue of the Immaculate Conception of our Blessed Mother, hovering over the Marist Brothers, keeping her watchful eyes on her beloved departed children. They who have gone back to their Creator; who have persevered and "Died Empty" as Marist Brothers: Roger Bagares, Renato Cruz, Danilo Pamplona, Timoteo Cabangon, Jose Torrecampo, Fernando Armendez, Leonard Sonza, Regis Creegan, Herbert Daniel Dumont, Norman Roy, Michael O'Keefe, Maurus James Doherty, Felix Gilligan, Robert McGovern, Reginald Theodore, and others.

It is the belief of the Marist Brothers that for all those who have died as Marist Brothers, they are assured of eternal salvation.

This is the scene Brother Willy would have loved to see himself carried to as his final resting place – nature at its best. He, the nature lover, an advocate of the clean and green movement, harmonizer of structural design and natural beauty, and most of all, a farmer and a gardener at heart, would be smiling his most beautiful smile.

The backdrop of this beautiful place is part of the majestic Rio Grande de Mindanao, the longest river in Mindanao, and the second largest in the Philippines.

The river is wide and still but very deep, much like Brother Willy.

The End

Awarded the Pontifical Distinction Cross *Pro-Ecclesia et Pontifice* in July 2015. This award, known as the "Cross of Honor", is the highest award given by the Roman Catholic Church with the approval of the Pope to a layman or clergy for his outstanding and selfless service to the Church and humanity. Photo by Orman Ortega Manansala.

Brother Willy was honored in the memorial service held at the NDMU Gym for seven days on January 28-February 2, 2021. Photos by NDMU Website Live archive.

On February 2, 2021 his remains were taken to the Marist Cemetery in the Immaculate Conception Marist Novitiate in Tamontaka. The cemetery lies close to the Rio Grande de Mindanao. He was laid to rest on February 3, 2021.

Top: Bro. Willy visited The Breakers Mansion in Newport, Rhode Island with Edith Plecis, Lynou Zacal, and Joan Palma. Below: Bro. Willy was with Juliet Nagnal Laughter from Georgia. She and her husband Glen brought Bro. Willy to Tampa, Florida to be guest speaker at the College of Nursing, University of South Florida.

Postscript

In the End

"On a personal note, I think your tandem sparked beautiful moments to happen. The organization of the Notre Dame Alumni abroad is one of them, and the library project is another fruit of this."

~Briccio Baynosa~

(Note: This was my tribute to Brother Willy delivered during the Memorial Service Live Streamed on Zoom and Facebook Live on January 30, 2021. Some stories told in the preceding chapters may have been repeated here as this was written one-year prior and minimal paragraphs were edited out).

Let me begin this ending by paraphrasing the opening line from the novel *Love Story* by Erich Segal.

"What can you say about a 68-year-old BFF who died?"

That he loved mugs. People. Museums. Gardens. Travel. Libraries. Books. Children. He also loved Dimboy, his miniature poodle, Aning, Gab, and all his apos, his Lubrico family, and the Marist Family. And yes, not to forget, he also loves *ukay-ukay*.[43]

He just happened to have been President of two universities – Notre Dame of Marbel and Notre Dame of Dadiangas, earned a doctorate and an awardee of the highest honor from the Pope – *Pro Ecclesia et Pontifice* 2015. He never allowed such high falutin' pretentious titles or awards to go to his head as many do. He'd be the first to admit he had a radical streak. I think of him as the brave soul who marches to the beat of a different drum, his own drum! His critics are few relative to his multitude of admirers. But he didn't let his critics stop him from achieving his goals for the common good. He bore his pain with dignity and grace.

Much has been said about his academic achievements, leadership roles, social work, and many more. But I want to speak of his humanity - his shining legacy. The love stories shared by hundreds of admirers will endure long after the structures, gardens, titles, and facades are gone.

He was fond of sharing his favorite quotes on social media. The last I received read, *"The most beautiful things in life are not things. They are people and places and memories and pictures. They are feelings and moments and smiles and laughter".*

I knew of Brother Willy as an aspirant at the Marist Juniorate fifty years ago! I was then the secretary to Brother Henry Joseph Ruiz, Director of NDDC. But our friendship deepened when he became the President of NDDC in 1995, ended only by his death. I called him my "Little Brother", being two years younger than me. He visited my family for days every time he was in the U.S.

On his 2007 visit to Tampa, Florida were we lived for 32 years before we moved to Rhode Island, I introduced him to the Deans (my bosses) at the School of Nursing, University of South Florida (USF). Invited to speak at a weeklong Nursing Profession Symposium, he discussed the phenomenon "Brain Drain of Nurses" in the Philippines. He received a standing ovation and a USF Mug. I was not sure what he appreciated more, the ovation or the mug! We went home to my house, and without skipping a beat, he transformed from Guest Speaker to the cleaner of our tile floor! Fascinated by a disposable mop called Swiffer, he said, *"Bakal man ako sini para sa Marist Convento."* (I'll buy one like this for the Marist Convento).

July 3-7, 2016, was the last of his many visits with my family. Before attending the Marist International Network of Institutions of Higher Education Seminar in Poughkeepsie, New York with two of his Deans – Dr. Joan Palma and Dr. Lynou Zacal - they stopped in Rhode Island. Former Professor Edith Plecis, his friend from Notre Dame of Marbel University and now living in New York, was their Uber driver. We celebrated the Filipino-American Friendship Day on July 4th weekend, partook of a good old American fare, kayaked on the Kickemuit River, and watched the fireworks at night from the boat dock.

We toured the famous Vanderbilt Newport Mansion, The Breakers. Afterward, I made a stop to pick up some children's books at the Newport Salvation Army Thrift Store. Excited he said, *"Hala Prim may ukay ukay na dira*!"

(Hey Prim, there's a bargain sale there!)

"Yes, Brother brand new and upscale items *pa because mga millionaires ang* donors."

Brother Willy treated himself to a Ralph Lauren shirt and a designer shoe pair, all for $9.92! I know because I picked up the tab, as countless of his friends do, large and small bills, international and domestic airline tickets, hotel stays, etc. He elicited that kind of benevolence from people who just wanted to pay him back for good deeds received when they were down and out. We went home to my house and went clamming! I was working as Brown University Faculty Affairs Coordinator at that time, so of course, he got a mug from an Ivy League school.

Every time I go home to Gen. Santos City, we meet without fail. I went home in 1996. He showed me this room he called Library at the Training Department of the old campus of NDDC. Strewn all over the room were piles of unopened Balikbayan Boxes donated by his friends from the United States. I said, "Ano man ining library mo Brother daw bodega. (Brother, this library of yours looks like a storeroom). "Amo gani nga gindala ko ikaw diri". (That's why I brought you here). That was the beginning of our partnership to build Children's libraries, my secret childhood impossible dream that I have shared with him. In 2004, with the NDGSCAA alumni, personal friends, colleagues at work, and my family, we created the Hower-Bates Library Network (HBLN). Brother Willy and I established the first TD Library at NDDU IBED Lagao, dubbed by PAASCU accreditors as one of the best children's libraries in the Philippines. In its 18th year, the network has established three more children's libraries – Notre Dame-Sienna College Lagao, ND Marbel IBED while he was President there, and the Dilangalen Children's Library in Midsayap for the Maguindanao children. A fifth library, The T'boli & Culture Hub (TLC) is currently being built in Lake Sebu, opening next month. [Update: TLC is now fully operational. Our library Network has shipped more than 75,000 books to these five libraries plus 51 other libraries in public schools, barrios, and city libraries in Luzon, Visayas, and Mindanao]. Thank you, Brother

Willy. Your love of books benefits the children and inspires us to dream the impossible dream.[44]

He loved to travel as part of his Marist related leadership roles on the international stage and soaked in everything that he observed. The people oriented man that he was; he'd check his address book and visit friends in proximity along his route. His repeated refrains, *"Ay katahom sina, himoon ko man ina sa Pinas."* (Wow, that's beautiful, I'd replicate that in the Philippines). And he did. Look around you and appreciate the beauty of the gardens, the museums, the buildings, etc. They began as ideas that he picked up from his travels, carried in his head, nurtured, and spread with love in your midst to enjoy. It is sharing, a special form of caring.

Brother Willy emailed me early in 2019, how saddened and quite concerned he was that he might have to retire when his term ends. It was a challenging time for him. He turned to his trusted confidants near and far, and he poured out his struggles, doubts about his future, and even fears. But he was a man who never stayed downhearted too long. Brother Willy intimated finally in October 2020 that he has reconciled with the idea of retirement starting June 2021. He began to chart his future away from the academia that he so loved. I teased him about staying on as a gardener at NDMU; he'd be set for life.

"My family will build me a room," he said at his sister's house in Surallah. "*Ma* garden *ako*, learn to paint, cook, live simply and peacefully, write highlights of my life. Ambitious no? My niece Annie Lubrico Golingay in Ontario, Canada wants me to visit."

I told him I lived an hour away by plane. We planned to organize an NDGSC Alumni Association reunion. "Good, that will be my last journey", he said.

Brother Willy received a signed copy of the book on December 18, 2020, written by Alvin J. Hower, my husband, published by Reader's Digest. Al was a Peace Corps Volunteer who served for five and a half years in South Cotabato. He taught Economics at Notre Dame of Dadiangas College in 1969-1972 to replace two faculty members pursuing their Masters in Economics and Business Education.

"Nice book Prim, I read it right away. I like the style, simple and well organized."

On Facebook Messenger, I reprised a conversation we had in Alaska two years prior. "Brother, *kumusta na* Bucket List *mo magsulat libro*?

(Brother, how's your Bucket List to write a book?)

"*Di ba* I told you that's impossible? I am not a good writer. Second question, who will be interested to read?"

I continued to egg him and suggested that he should start a journal while he is recuperating after his surgery. "*Sige*, I promise Prim."

(Okay, I promise...).

On January 9, 2021 he informed me that he had arrived safely in Manila. His doctors canceled his surgery and sent him for an MRI test on January 23 to check his liver. On January 22, I texted him, "I had my MRI yesterday in an open machine. I was ok and will get results Monday. Thinking of you. Hugs. What time is your MRI on the 23rd?"

He replied, "9 AM", sent on January 22 at 10:33 PM. That was the last I heard from Brother Willy. He was taken to the ICU the following morning. He died two days later.

Brother Willy died at the St. Luke's Hospital in Manila on January 25, 2021. A memorial service was held at the Marist Marikina campus for two nights. His remains were flown from Manila to General Santos City International Airport on January 28 and taken to the campus of Notre Dame of Marbel University. Brother willy was honored in the memorial services held at the NDMU Gym for seven days on January 28-February 2, 2021. On February 2, 2021 his remains were taken to the Immaculate Conception Marist Cemetery in Tamontaka Marist Novitiate. The cemetery lies close to the Rio Grande de Mindanao. He was laid to rest on February 3, 2021.

Fourteen thousand (14K) viewed his "homecoming" from Marikina to General Santos City streamed Live on Facebook from Notre Dame of Marbel University. Alumni from Australia, Qatar, Malaysia, Bangladesh, Sri Lanka, Peru, Jordan, Europe, Dubai, Mexico, etc., a dozen states of the U.S., three provinces of Canada, many provinces of the Philippines and countless undisclosed locations attended the Nightly Prayer Services virtually and in person. Can you hear the soft sobs, deep sighs, and the echoing whispers from across six continents? We love you Brother Willy. Vaya con Dios.

I can go on and on about Brother Willy. Instead, let me reserve the rest of his story for his book. It will be a simple narrative about the complicated man if that is at all possible. His life lived well serves as a beacon for us all. Meanwhile, let the tears continue to fall. Someday, soon I hope, may our fond memories of him stem the flow.

*****

It is now January 25, 2022 the first anniversary of Brother Willy's death. As Briccio and I work on the finishing touches on this book, Brother Willy is being fondly remembered across the globe.

Claire Dorothy Declarador, an inner circle friend, was the first speaker to pay homage on the first day of the memorial service at NDMU. She shared Brother Willy's love of animals and stories about his pet miniature poodle Dimboy. Sadly, Dimboy escaped from the Marist House one day and was never seen again. Claire directed my attention to an event at the university that paints a picture of a pet lover and like-minded people in the community.

To celebrate the annual Season of Creation, NDMU held the Blessing of Pets on October 3, 2019, at the University Gymnasium after the Eucharistic celebration for the NDMU 73rd Foundation Anniversary. Posted on Brother Willy's Facebook News Feed, it read, "With the beloved pets of the NDMU community gathered together, the blessing ceremony is a prayer for a better quality of life and ecological balance on earth. In his homily, Fr. Ariel Destora, the university chaplain, brought attention to environmental protection as the mission of the Catholic Church. The Season of Creation is an annual commemoration in the Christian tradition starting from the Day of Prayer for Creation on September 1 through the Feast of St. Francis of Assisi on October 4. St. Francis of Assisi is the Catholic Church's patron saint of animals and the environment".

Claire also shared this heartwarming anecdote.

One day, Brother Willy was puttering in the university gardens wearing his garden clothes. A young boy asked for directions to speak to the President of the University. Brother Willy directed the boy towards the office. His curiosity piqued, Brother Willy followed the boy keeping a safe distance. Upon reaching the President's office, he let the boy inside, walked over to his table, and sat down. He then proceeded to speak with the flabbergasted young boy with contained amusement.

"He loved children very much and was playful with them," Claire wrote.

His Facebook wall exploded with tributes from friends, colleagues, students, and parents when his death was announced. Joyce Kho Mirabueno posted, "Brother Willy might be the only NDDC President so well-loved by the elementary school kids of the 1990s that when they see him walking around the campus, they flock to him and make *mano po*!" [*Mano* is a traditional Filipino greeting, a gesture of touching the back of the hand of an elder lightly on one's forehead as a sign of respect].

Teachers at the schools he was assigned as acting Principal shared that there were times when the teachers had to bring their kids to school for lack of caregivers at home. Brother Willy would take their child to his office and babysat for the kids for the duration of the classes.

His niece Pia Samonte Baysa wrote, *"Lahat kami inalagaan mga pamangkin at mga apo ni T'yoy Willy makikita talaga namin na mahal nya kami...noong sa Matina, Davao siya ng dalawang taon dinala niya mga pamangkin Emelda, Annie, Dolly, Carmen at Ronald para mag college. Dinala din niya ako noon Grade III pa ako magbisita.* Every night *at 6 pm mag* rosary *kami tapos dinner at mag* tutor *siya sa aming lahat".*

(He took care of his nephews, nieces and babysat for his grandkids so we really felt his love for us...when he was working [for SPI] for two years in Matina, Davao he took his nieces and nephews there to live with him so they could go to college. He took me there when I was in third grade to visit them. Every night at 6 pm we prayed the rosary after dinner and he tutored us all.)

His good friend, Estrella Tano Golingay wrote: I don't know what he has in him, that he attracts children's attention. Even during the University programs, when the little kids are around, just a nod of his head and they come rushing to him, never mind that he is seated in the front row or a number is being rendered on the stage. The audience's attention would of course be riveted to them. *Sige lang,* we didn't mind, kinda cute actually and *ka* charming *sa ila tan-awon.* He couldn't only tame the system of the academe, he could also tame the little kids *na makukulit*! [Rambunctious kids]. Was he even a human being? Not only that, even those supposedly antagonistic toward him, he could turn into his friends and supporters, effortlessly.

During our recent chat on Messenger, I just had to ask Briccio before we said goodbye, "What made Brother Willy so? He could walk around in his flip-flops and baggy shorts one minute and be in his spiffy barong Tagalog with luminaries the next, and not skip a beat! He could be so naïve about certain things and yet his visions and legacies belie the fact. He loved The Louvre Museum and the Versailles gardens in France, was in leadership roles at the national and international religious and secular organizations and sometimes '*daw manol man*' (bumpkin) in other matters."

Briccio simply said, "I see him as you do; a complete paradox. I think that's what makes him so endearing".

Prima Guipo Hower
January 25, 2022

"Life is adventure. Do not be afraid to try anything once."
~ Brother Willy Lubrico
Brother Willy kayaking along Kickemuit River with author Alvin Hower, Peace Corps Volunteer who taught at the Notre Dame of Dadiangas College 1969-1972, Rhode Island USA 2016. Lynou Zacal and Joan Palma in the background. Photo by Edith Plecis

"Life is a camel ride...slowly, calmly you see the horizon of your destiny."
"Man is a single dust in the desert until he makes the best of life that God wants him to be."
~ Brother Willy, Dubai Desert 2013 ~

Photo Booth, Alumni Reunion, Seattle, USA

Sister Genevieve Damaso, OND, SPI colleague

Bro.Willy with Dimboy, during The Blessing of Pets.
His friend and Dimboy's babysitter Claire Dorothy Declarador third from left.

His endearing way of being able to laugh at himself is displayed in his Facebook news feed. It is a precious legacy in itself.

THE NOTRE DAME OF LAGAO CLASS 1971

Brother Willy was a staunch supporter of alumni reunions. He attended as many of these reunions as his schedule allowed.

Thank you to all of his classmates who wholeheartedly supported his Abante Lumad Scholarship Program. The names of donors are listed under Acknowledgement.

He could comfortably "walk with kings" without "losing the common touch".
~Anastacio M. Hoyumpa, MD quote from Kipling's poem "IF"

Bro. Willy, Geraldine Rebutiaco, Liza Aliligay Lourdes Orquia, and Dalia Mesias at Christmas Party 2019.

Bro. Willy with NDAlumni based in USA Past Presidents Art Henares, Angel Boloico & Lanie Zerrudo Gammon, Seattle, Washington May 2019

Photo that Brother Willy posted on his Facebook December 22, 2017. "New OND House in Marbel"

Acknowledgement

One man plus three diverse groups of people in his orbit equals a book.

BROTHER WILLY, because you are a magnet to like-minded individuals, they came together to honor you. We thank you for being a part of our life's journey. You galvanized us to fill in the blank pages of the book of your life so others may find inspiration from your remarkable story. We just hope we make you proud.

FAMILY: First came the outpourings of tributes for Brother Willy from his friends and colleagues. These are valuable materials, the impetus for the creation of this book. But without the help of the Lubrico family, this book would not have been as meaningful. Thank you:

- Teresa Lubrico Golveo, Rodolfo Lubrico, Jaime Lubrico, Cecille Lubrico Longanilla, Macky Lubrico, and Lester Lubrico Tugade for inviting us to meet your family and opening the window to your memories so we could glimpse into Brother Willy's childhood. Your stories colored this book.
- Pia Samonte Baysa, Dolly Lubrico Fenis, Annie Lubrico Golveo, and Mhelanie Baguna Golingay for anecdotes and photos.

COLLEAGUES: Brother Willy planted enduring goodwill. From superiors to subordinates at the universities of Notre Dame of Dadiangas to Notre Dame of Marbel, to Socio-Pastoral Institute, Notre Dame Educational Association, Marist International Network of Institutions of Higher Education, to various Notre Dame Alumni Associations, the Department of Education and the Marist Council in Rome. This book would have been so thin indeed without your tributes and testimonies.

FRIENDS: To everyone else who provided us with the resources and the help we needed to create a book that encompasses the life of Brother Willy, we appreciate your gift as varied as they come. Thank you to:

- The Officers, Board Members, the Council of Past Presidents of Notre Dame of Gen. Santos City Alumni Association, Intl. and members for supporting this project project.
- Bueno Silva for the oil painting on the cover, his sons Eulalio and Patrick for technical help and Anastacio Hoyumpa, MD for your invaluable input
- Orlando Batallones, Rodolfo Regacho Mapada, Angel Sonico, Norberto Barsal, Joe Sevilla, Saturnino Bayona, Ruben Tugari, Andy Francisco, Allan Sumadic, Chris Gammon, Claire Dorothy Declarador, Michael Angelo Yambok, classmates Hernando Celino, Madeline Guay Bendita
- Sarah Turner of LifeRich Publishing and her team, and Estelle Lang for technical help
- My family, especially my husband and personal editor, Alvin J. Hower, for doing everything else so all I have to do is write a book.
- My apology to anyone I may have left off this list inadvertently.

To Bobby Borromeo, what fun collaborating on two books in 17 years! I think we're good for one or two more in our lifetime. I am truly grateful for your friendship.

To Briccio Baynosa, thank you for saying yes. I have no doubt, Brother Willy sent you to be his stand-in author. You are a lifesaver. *Salamat.*

ACKNOWLEDGEMENT

Notre Dame of General Santos City
Alumni Association, International
List of Sponsors & Kickstarter Backers*

Rhododendron Sponsors

Allan & Lulut Palacios Chan, NDL71 & Family*
Ramon & Soledad Santos Cuenco, NDL74 & Family*
Alvin & Prima Guipo Hower, NDL67 & Family*

Sampaguita Sponsors

Leroy & Eileen Gray Bacheller, NDD56 & Family
BJ & Rose Cababat Jackson, NDD74 & Family*
Paul & Bernadette Buensuceso Graham, NDL68

Waling- Waling Sponsors

Brian & Arsenia Acharon Bumgardner, NDD71 & Family*
Chris & Leilanie Zerrudo Gammon, NDL*
Andy & Elena Tingzon Gonzalez, NDL72 & Family
Rolando & Shirley Zolina Victa, NDL66 & Family

Ylang-Ylang Sponsors

Helen Biadoma, NDD67, NDDC71
Melchor, NDD68, 72 & Joyce Sambas Bonifacio, NDDC77
Nenita Narciso Ferrer, NDDC70 & Family
Marie McHone, Honorary member
Vincent & Odita Maamo Matthews, NDL Teacher
Editha Plecis, ND of Marbel University, 1965

***KICKSTARTER BACKERS**

Mario & Amy Andrade
Marilou Garcia Aponesto, NDSurala 1971
Engineer Orlando Batallones, NDMarbel 1979
Dr. Madeline Guay Bendita, NDSurala 1971
Saturnino Bayona, NDLagao 1971 & Family
Hernando Celino, NDSurala 1971
Luzviminda M. Delgado, NDSurala 1971
Estrella T. Golingay, NDSurala 1971
Lolita Lorenzana, NDSurala 1971
Orman Ortega Manansala, NDDadiangas1979
Haydee Abegail Peria, MSU
Rane Rose
Rosela Datoy Reyes, NDDU1965
Haydee Abegail Peria, MSU
Lolita Wong, NDDU

DONORS & BACKERS
FAMILY, FRIENDS & CLASSMATES
OF BROTHER WILY

Anonymous
Mitch Abajar
Merchie Lissa & Karl Jed Alabat
Johmel Alo
Rosario Bayona Aquino
Cleopatria S. Asibal
Teresa Bacor Bacalzo
Norberto & Judy Barsal & Family
BJ, Linda Hower, Zoe & Lexi Bates
Ellen & Bruce Bates
Vickny Bayona
Hanibal Bayona
Francis Bayona
Pascual Bayona
Nemesio Blanco
Salvacion G. Boncag
Herminia Cirera Butil
Marcelo A. Cabel
Ofelia Bayona Caldo
Teofilo Cantos & Family
Merlyn D. Carreon
Ma. Magdalena Cobrador
Susan E. Correos
Lyneth Bayona Crisostomo
Milagros Cruz
Conchita de Guzman
Nenito dela Cuesta
Norberto Diaz Perez
Evelyn Villaruel Dollete
Expedito Estandarte
Rosario Estrella-Ruiz
Bing Santillan Ferrariz
Carlito & Elvie Ferrariz
Evelyn Bayona Flecher
Maria Cristina Gonzalez Gadayan
Annie Lubrico Golveo Golingay
Marilyn Fuentes Gomez
Carmen Limjap Gorme & Family
Josie Grana Guipo
Angelo & Sonrisa Guipo & Family
Merlita Landero Guipo & Family
Estelle & William Lang
Virginia Tiongson Llido & Family
Rosie Madria
Araceli Mandac-Lopez & Family
Rodrigo Manzano
Analou & Rodolfo Regacho Mapada
Rodolfo C. Mapada Jr.
Rodhel C. Mapada
Dalia Mesias
Lina Mondejar
Helen Bayona Natividad
Dominica Yamson Navarro
Pura Nunez Tiamzon
Ernesto Ortiz
Antonia Martinez Paculdo & Family
Joan Palma
Ester Pundavela Pastrana
Lilia Perez, Bob & Family
Alejandro Pineda
Lourdes Purto-Orquia
Al Quillope
Alex, Janet, Alexis, & Gabriel Racela
Elma B. Rafil
James Reamon, Gilda & Family
Elizabeth Banquerigo Requieron
Rit Rivera
Josephine Bona Rosali
Roberto T. Royeca
Angelito Sonico and Family
Benita Tandog
Sylvie Blanche Tandog
Frances Cyrille Tandog
Lucina Tapucar
Teresita Pallarco Tupas
Mazee Zabala & Family

THANK YOU – KICKSTARTER SUPER BACKERS

Top Left: Bro. Willy & Engr. Orlando Batallones

Top Right: Lulut Palacios Chan & Allan Sr.

Left: Heather, Lee, & Summer Hower

Bottom: Soledad Santos Cuenco Family
RP, Isabella, Sol, Ramon, Joan & Yvette

The NDGSCAA International Officers and Board Members

EXECUTIVE OFFICERS

Front L-R: Malut Diaz-Corlett, Asst. Treas; Bernadette Buensuceso Graham, Treas; Janet Zolina Racela, Sec; Rose Cababat Jackson, VP; Lulut Palacios Chan, Pres; Marilen Zabala Masanga, Auditor, (back second from right)

BOARD MEMBERS

Back L-R: Shantal Biadoma Wig; Juliet Nagnal Laughter, Fatima Pinto, Lilia Salangsang Perez, Noh Dalid Conrad, Bing S. Ferrariz, Mazee Zabala, Orman Ortega Manansala

This book was made possible through the leadership of Lulut Palacios Chan and the generous members of the NDGSCAA, International. Lulut, the current president is a high school classmate of Brother Willy. She lives with her husband Allan and family in Virginia. In 2021, as part of her administration's project, she and the officers launched the NDGSCAA Scholarship Program named after Bro. Wilfredo Lubrico, FMS. Profits from the book will be donated to Bro. Willy's favorite initiative "Abante Lumad Scholarship" to financially support the college education of poor but deserving indigenous students in South Cotabato. The Officers meet on Messenger. Other fund raising project launched in 2021 was The Brother Joseph Damian Teston 100 Birthday Fund, the beneficiary of which was the Carmelite Nuns of Savannah, Georgia to build their convent.

THANK YOU
CONTRIBUTORS: TRIBUTES

Brother Joao Carlos do Prado, FMS
Councillor General, Rome, Italy

Bro. Ador Santiago, FMS
Provincial, Marist East Asia Province

Bro. Ted Fernandez, FMS
Bro. Willy's Novice Master, 1972

Bro. Manny de Leon, FMS
President, Notre Dame of Dadiangas University

CONTRIBUTORS: TRIBUTES

Bro. Jong Acosta

Abed Adre

Kenneth Albert Anino

Saturnino Bayona

Dr. Evelyn Dollete

Dr. Allan Farnazo

Fred Gaspar, SPI

Dr. Estrella Tano Golingay

Sr. Erlinda Hisug, OND
Superior General, Oblates of Notre Dame

CONTRIBUTORS: TRIBUTES

Dr. Alma Hordista

Macky Lubrico

Orman Ortega Manansala

Rodolfo R. Mapada –MAREX

Dr. Lina Mondejar

Dalia Mesias

Dr. Joan Palma

Angel Sonico, MAREX

Lester Tugade

Appendix A – Conversations with Brother Willy

My plans...
Enjoy the company of my brothers n sisters neices n nephews and all my apos from manila bacolod and here in mindanao
2. Explore other non school or non administrative ministry
3. Visit friends n relatives
4. Do gardening
5.write highlights of myife

Ambitious no

I started last lock down...in the area of my vocation, administration, relationships, success n failures.

I started last lock down ...in the area of my vocation, administration, relationships success n failures

Daming heartaches n turnabouts, crossroads n ups n downs

Daming heartaches n turnabouts,crossroads n ups n downs

That's right as you are doing in your writings. You write clearly n comprehensively.

Thats right as you are doing in your writings. You write clearly n comprehnsively

We could ask opinions from my long long friends (many of them) and my students.

We could ask opinions from my long long friends (many of them) and my students

OMG you are awakening my interest in writing. Sometimes too many dark shadows ang buhay ko
and I took the road less travelled by. Rebelde, emotional, etc.

OMG you are awakening my interest inwriting. Somesomes too many dark shadows lang buhay ko and i tookthe road less teavellwd by. Rebelde emotionsal , etc

Conversations with Brother Willy continued

If we could do this ...life is over for me hahaha. Everything wlbw recorded includingmy collections mugs key chains coins marist memorabilia

Hahaha.thsnks lets include my horror funny irrational stories; my insecurities,fears n drama etc

Agreeing with you.thats in my heart too ...that people would not remember the history...,the people and the turning points of the cpngregations,institutions n that gave tbeway to the present

Yes.too excited Prim.binubuhay mo ang tulog kong damdamin lol. I feel like retiring tomorrow to do this

Still looking for some pictures

Bro. Willy's Plans

Elem n high school gym. Bleachers patapos na.

E launch ko lang sa january ang university diamond jubilee...then slowly ill phase out

If ok na.i might visit america n canada.daan din ako sa mga neices ko sa dubai...kong kaya pa

Yupi have neice in toronto.thanks sa invitstion. I dont want to miss you of course

RAY had been waiting for me in Aklan
And a student in viting me to australia...but

Hehehe. Thanks i know you.will always do things for me. Ikaw pa.lets see

All will be remembered in their hearts

As soon as i see Als outline Ill forward mine to you for your comment

Appendix B – Curriculum Vitae

Name	:	**BRO. WILFREDO ENGANE LUBRICO, FMS**
Date of Birth	:	October 28, 1952
Place of Birth	:	E.B. Magalona, Negros Occidental
Present Position	:	President Notre Dame of Marbel University
Contact Address:		Notre Dame of Marbel University Koronadal City 9506 South Cotabato Philippines
Email:		welubrico@yahoo.com

EDUCATIONAL BACKGROUND

Post Graduate

Doctor of Philosophy in Education (Ph.D.) Major in Educational Management	:	Notre Dame of Marbel University City of Koronadal March 2002

Graduate

Master of Arts (MA) Major in Theological Studies	:	Loyola School of Theology Ateneo de Manila University Quezon City 1982

College

Bachelor of Science in Education Economics	:	Notre Dame of Marbel College (now Univ.) Major in Koronadal, South Cotabato 1976

WORK EXPERIENCES

2006 – present	President Notre Dame of Marbel University
2008-2009	Acting Principal Integrated Basic Education Department NDMU
2006 -2009	Director, Campus Ministry & Religious Education Notre Dame of Marbel University
1995 – 2006	President Notre Dame of Dadiangas College (now University) General Santos City
1990 – 1995	Director, Community Extension Services Notre Dame of Kidapawan College, N. Cotabato
1988 – 1990	Executive Director Socio Pastoral Institute – Mindanao, Davao City
1987 – 1988	Teacher Notre Dame of Cotabato Boys Dept. Cotabato City Parish Worker Archdiocese of Cotabato
1986 – 1987	Parish Worker Sto. Niño Parish, Bula, General Santos City
1983 – 1986	Director of Student Affairs & Dir. Campus Ministry Notre Dame of Dadiangas College General Santos City
1980 - 1983	Teacher Notre Dame of Marbel College Koronadal, South Cotabato
1979 - 1980	Teacher Notre Dame of Kidapawan College, N. Cotabato
1976 – 1979	Teacher, NDDC, General Santos City

Curriculum Vitae continued

AFFILIATIONS/OTHER ASSIGNMENTS:

	PAASCU accreditor in the areas of Students Services and Community Extension
2018-2019	Flexible Learning Tutor (Online Tutor) for Teaching and Learning Excellence in School Leadership for Southeast Asia (TEACHeXCELS) Flexible Learning course for selected school heads of DEPED Region XII implemented by Southeast Asian Ministers of Education Organization-Regional Center for Education Innovation and Technology (SEAMEO-INNOTECH)
2015-present	Chair, Board of Trustees Notre Dame of Kidapawan College
2014 - 2020	President, Notre Dame Educational Association
2014 – 2020	Member of the Board, Catholic Educational Association of the Philippines (CEAP), Regional Program Director, CEAP Region XII
2014-2020	PEAC Regional Program Director, Region XII and ARMM
2014-2019	Member, Board of Trustees Notre Dame of Dadiangas University, Gen. Santos City
Dec 2013-2016	Councilor, East Asia Provincial Council, Marist Brothers Congregation Coordinator, Philippine Sector, East Asia Province, Marist Congregation
2012-2014	President/Chair-Executive Committee, Marist International Network of Higher Education Institutions
Sep 2012	Chair, Evaluation Committee for USM President (Appointed by CHED Chairperson)
2011	Chair, Search Committee for Presidency of Cotabato City State Polytechnic College (appointed by CHED Chairperson)
2009	Online Tutor, Flexible Learning Short Course on Instructional and Curricular Excellence in School Leadership and Management for DepEd Administrators implemented by Southeast Asian Ministers of Education Organization-Regional Center for Education Innovation and Technology (SEAMEO-INNOTECH)
2008 – present	Member, Executive Board Association of Teacher Education Institutions in Mindanao, Inc (ATIEM)
2008 – present	Member, Marist International Institutions Federation
2006 – present	Member, Board of Trustees (as president of university) Notre Dame Educational Association
2006 – 2007	Member, Board of Directors Marist Development Foundation, Inc. Lagao, Gen. Santos City
2006 - 2007	Member, Provincial Council Marist Brothers Congregation of the Philippines, Gen. Santos City
2005, 2007, 2009	Project Coordinator Philippine Cities Competitiveness Ranking Project involving 3 cities in Region 12), a project of the Asian Institute of Management, Makati City
1995 – 2007	Member, Board of Trustees Notre Dame of Kidapawan College, Kidapawan City
1995 – 2006	Member, Board of Trustees Notre Dame of Marbel University, Koronadal City
1997-2006	Founder and Chairman of the Board, Gen. Paulino Santos Museum, GSC
1995-1999	Consultant, Bureau of Non-Formal Education Department of Education, Manila
1992 – 1996	Member, Board of Trustees Association of Non-Traditional Education in the Philippines Manila
AWARD:	Papal Award – Pro Ecclesia et Pontifice, 2015

Initiatives of Bro. Willy throughout his years

A. Organized the group of former members of Marist Brothers (MAREX) as Marist Mission partners.

B. Started the Green University Program of the Notre Dame of Marbel University as an answer to the Marist Educators' Congress Resolutions of 2010. One of the resolutions was the desire to find new and creative ways to educate the young and to have common advocacies which affect especially the environment and to intensify zero waste management.

The program was intensified with the creation of the Green Schools, an organization of Koronadal City schools and institutions that promotes the care and protection of the environment and humanity.

C. Initiated the Marist Administrators Formation program for the present and future administrators of the Marist institutions in 2011 with the following objectives:

I. Develop competence, integrity and accountability in administering a Marist School.

II. Learn the basic principles and pedagogies of Marist Educational leadership as well as its Marist culture, values and practices.

III. Appreciate the values and roles of Administrators as part of the mission of the Church.

A total of four batches of the program were conducted, the latest of which was in 2019.

D. Initiated the "Abante Lumad Scholarship Program," a program of NDMU that raises funds to financially support the college education of poor but deserving indigenous college students in South Cotabato.

E. Started the socialized education program in NDDU Integrated Basic Education Department in Espina campus which makes Marist Education accessible to the poor.

F. Initiated programs for Women Development (for College Female Students) and for Peace and Environment in the two Marist Universities.

All information listed was taken from
Marist Bits Special Edition Vol. 3 Issue No.5

CURRICULUM VITAE: INITIATIVES

Appendix C – Travel Log

Dalia Mesias provided Brother Willy's Official Travel Log. He attended global events related to his Presidency, his international leadership roles, and the Notre Dame Alumni Reunions His duties took him to six continents: Africa, Asia, Australia, Europe, North and South America.

Europe: Brother Willy in Rome with his friend Bro. Joao do Prado.

Africa: In Nairobi, Kenya

1	BRO. WILLY'S OFFICIAL TRAVELS	
2	COUNTRY	YEAR
3	AMSTERDAM	2000
4	BRAZIL	2013
5	CANADA	2007
6	CANADA	2019
7	DUBAI	2013
8	GERMANY	1999
9	GERMANY	2008
10	HONGKONG	2000
11	HONGKONG	2006
12	ITALY	2000
13	ITALY	2015
14	ITALY/ROME	2015
15	KENYA	2014
16	KOREA	2006
17	KOREA	2014
18	KOREA	2015
19	KOREA	2015
20	KOREA	2016
21	LISBON, PORTUGAL	2013
22	MACAU	2013
23	MALAYSIA	2005
24	MALAYSIA	2014
25	MALAYSIA	2014
26	MALAYSIA	2015
27	MALAYSIA	2015
28	MALAYSIA	2015
29	MALAYSIA	2016
30	MALAYSIA	2018
31	MEXICO	2006
32	MEXICO	2010
33	PERU	2019
34	ROME, ITALY	2013
35	SINGAPORE	2005
36	SINGAPORE	2010
37	SINGAPORE	2014
38	SINGAPORE	2015
39	SINGAPORE	2018
40	SPAIN	2008
41	SRI LANKA	2015
42	SRI LANKA	2015
43	SRI LANKA	2015
44	SYDNEY/BRISBANE, AUSTRALIA	2016
45	THAILAND	2009
46	THAILAND	2012
47	Thailand	2014
48	UAE/DUBAI	2015
49	UK	2017
50	USA	1999
51	USA	2001
52	USA	2003
53	USA	2005
54	USA	2006
55	USA	2007
56	USA	2008
57	USA	2010
58	USA	2012
59	USA	2017
60	USA	2019
61	VIETNAM	2019

Travel Log continued

Willy Lubrico
March 18, 2016

MARIST INTERNATIONAL COMMISSION MEETING- SIDNEY, AUSTRALIA

He stopped in Dubai to visit
Notre Dame Alumni and their family.

Willy Lubrico added 2 new photos from November 21, 2015.
November 21, 2015

World Education Congress- Rome 2015 CEAP Board Delegates

Gladys Enanoria is with **Willy Lubrico** and **Debie Peñafiel Mendoza**.

A happy meeting with the 3 presidents of the Marist schools in the Phils. ((NDDU, NDMU, NDKC) and ma'am Debie at the Universidad de M. Champagnat in Lima, PERU (bro. Manny is not in the photo).

Appendix D - Notre Dame of Dadiangas Presidents

FIFTY THREE YEARS OF LEADERSHIP
THE DIRECTORS AND PRESIDENTS
NOTRE DAME OF DADIANGAS UNIVERSITY

God bless these men who did great works "without care who gets the credit."

[Barbara Dixon, on her installation as President, Truman University Nov. 14, 2003]

Bro. Joseph Damian Teston, FMS
1st Director, 1953-56

- He is one of the Marist "Big Four" – the first group of Brothers who came to the Philippines in 1948.
- The first Marist Director of Notre Dame of Lagao in 1952 assuming from Fr. Berthrand Demers, the last OMI Director
- July 1953: With hardly any financial resources, he was determined to serve the needs of the early settlers of Dadiangas. He opened classes and held them inside the OPLGV church, then owned by the OMI Fathers. Sixty three [63] second year and ninety [90] first year students composed the first enrollment. Thus Notre Dame of Dadiangas was born and Bro. Damian Teston is considered the school's FOUNDER.

Bro. Maurus James Doherty, FMS
2nd Director, SY 1956-57

- Served NDD as Director while at the same time the District Superior of the Marist Brothers
- Purchased the four-hectare property along the National Highway where NDDC main campus is now located.

Bro. Bernard Curtin, FMS
3rd Director, SY 1957-58

Bro. Curtin's one year term was a busy one, as the Brothers

- formed the first Marist community of Dadiangas
- prepared the opening of the High School Boys Department
- constructed the first concrete building where the Michael O' Keefe building now stands
- constructed the Marist Residence inside the campus

Bro. Michael O' Keefe, FMS
4th Director, 1958-60; 1963-66

- Opened the college Department with 3 programs and 161 students: Bachelor of Arts, Bachelor of Science in Commerce, Certificate of Secretarial Science
- Official turnover of Notre Dame of Dadiangas original campus to the Dominican Sisters
- Transferred the Boys Department to the campus along the National Highway
- Brothers moved to their new residence inside the campus

Notre Dame of Dadiangas Presidents continued

Bro. Patrick Nicholas Grogan, FMS
5th Director, 1960-63

- Beginning of formal organizational structure with the appointment of first lay elementary principal and 3 other lay administrators
- Opened the Education programs
- Built the Elementary Building with donations from his family

Bro. Henry Joseph Ruiz, FMS
6th Director, 1966-72

- Enrollment reached the 1000th mark
- Two faculty members were sent for full-time study
- Constructed the Henry Ruiz Building
- Constructed the all-steel framed Covered Court
- Constructed the OND Residence inside the Campus

Bro. Herbert Daniel Dumont, FMS
7th Director, 1972-73

- Prepared the school for the implementation of Presidential Decree No. 176, the Nationalization of schools. This decree required that all private and public schools be headed by a Filipino president
- Organized the first Board of Trustees of NDDC

Bro. Samuel Geveso, FMS
8th Head, 1st President, 1973-Dec. 1975

- First Board of Trustees became functional as separate from the Marist Council
- Published the first policy manual, written by Dean of Studies, Bro. Paul Meuten
- First written constitution and by-laws of NDDC was completed and registered with Securities and Exchange Commission
- Became the first school head to use "President" as title.

Bro. Paul Meuten, FMS
9th Head, 2nd President, 1976-79

- Established the systems according to the manuals he prepared
- Prepared the school for accreditation
- Created major Academic positions – the Academic Chairmen [Deans of Colleges today]
- Strengthened the library collection

Bro. James McKnight, FMS
10th Head, 3rd President, January-April 1976, 1979-82

- Built the St. Marcellin Champagnat Chapel
- First Formal accreditation of the three programs: Arts & Sciences, Education and Business Administration [Commerce] Level II, 3 years
- Conceptualized the ND Dadiangas High School and ND Lagao merger
- Opened the Marist Technical Training Program and Small Business Advisory Council [SBMAC]

Notre Dame of Dadiangas Presidents continued

Bro. Manuel P. Uluan, FMS
11th Head, 4th President, 1982-85

- Started the NDDC Graduate School separate from NDMU with which NDDC had previous consortium.
- Completed the merger of ND Lagao and ND Dadiangas
- Opened BS Nursing and BS Engineering
- Constructed the two-storey building for the high school in Lagao
- Level II Accreditation, 5 years, for Arts & Sciences, Education and Business Administration [Commerce]

Bro. Leonard Sonza, FMS
12th Head, 5th President, 1985-86

- Opened the Board of Trustees to lay membership
- Started the Primary Health Care Program
- Expanded the Faculty Room and Academic Chairman in the one-storey building, where the Michael O'Keefe building now stands.

Bro. Crispin P. Betita, FMS
13th Head, 6th President, 1986-1992

- Started an extensive faculty development program to meet CHED & PAASCU requirement for the faculty Master's degree
- Increased substantially the salary of Master's degree holders to encourage graduate studies
- First written mission-vision
- Level III accreditation of AB, Educ. & Business programs
- Started to build scholarship funds from donations
- Started a more visible alumni activities in Lagao and Dadiangas
- Built Bro. Reginald Theodore building for the Elementary Department
- Unit Heads empowerment with them preparing and controlling their budgets
- Established the funds for the future, the development and retirement funds

Bro. Briccio J. Baynosa, FMS
14th Head, 7th President, 1992-1995

- Built the Bro. Roger Bagares Hall
- Expanded the library at HR building
- Opened Mother and Child Center
- Started the Notre Dame of Dadiangas College - Mutual Health Benefit Program that provide tremendous help for employees hospitalization
- Started admission of Girls in the Grade School

Bro. Wilfredo E. Lubrico, FMS
15th Head, 8th President, 1996-2006

- Opened 12 degree programs in College and seven programs in the Graduate School
- Had the Accreditation of Elementary, High School and the six programs in the College
- Strengthened alumni organization in the Philippines and connected with the alumni organization in the US
- Granted Deminimis benefits
- Earned Autonomous status
- Built Bro. Leonard Sonza & Bro. Michael O'Keefe Halls
- Worked on the application for University Status
- Started admission of Girls in the High School
- Opened the Espina Campus with socialized tuition
- Restructuring the Basic Education to form the Integrated Basic Education [IBED]
- Built the administration building of the High School in Lagao.

Notre Dame of Marbel Presidents continued

THE DIRECTORS AND PRESIDENTS
NOTRE DAME OF MARBEL UNIVERSITY

OBLATE FATHERS

Fr. Francis McSorley, OMI
1946-1947

Fr. William McGrath, OMI
1947-1949

Fr. Joseph Quinn, OMI
1949-1950

Fr. Matthew Casey, OMI1950-1951 No photo available

MARIST BROTHERS

Bro. Edmund Conrad Paradis, FMS
1951-1952

Bro. Herbert Dumont, FMS
1952-57, 1958-61

Bro. Joseph Damian Teston, FMS
1957-58, 1968-70

Bro. Henry Joseph Ruiz, FMS
1961-1966

Bro. Norman Roy, FMS
1966-1968

Bro. Paul Johannes Meuten, FMS
1970-1973

Notre Dame of Marbel Presidents continued

Bro. Agustin Cabrera, FMS
1973-1976

Bro. Renato Cruz, FMS
1976-1980

Bro. Wenceslao Calimpon, FMS
1980-1985

Bro. Manuel Uluan, FMS
1985-1989

Bro. Eugene Pius, FMS
1989-1993

Dr. Leonor Pagunsan
1993-1999

Bro. Crispin Betita, FMS
1999-2006

Bro. Wilfredo E. Lubrico, FMS
2006-2021

Bro. Dominador Santiago, FMS
Feb 2021-June 2021

Bro. Paterno S. Corpus, FMS
2021-Present

Appendix E – Marikina Memorial Service

UPDATES

Br. Willy's 2-day Wake at Marist School Marikina

by Marjorie Veronica Raneses

Marist School Marikina joins the Marist Brothers in mourning the passing of Br. Wilfredo E. Lubrico, FMS who succumbed to complications of prostatic cancer at the age of 68.

A visionary leader and prophetic missionary, Br. Willy held key positions in varied Marist institutions and academic organizations. He served as president of Notre Dame of Dadiangas University and Notre Dame of Marbel University for many years, the chair of the board of trustees of Notre Dame of Kidapawan College, the president of Notre Dame Educational Association, and CEAP Board Member and PEAC Program Director for Region 12.

On January 26 – 27 Br. Willy's remains lay in repose at the Our Lady of the Magnificat Chapel. The varied Marist school communities in the Philippines together with his family members and relatives paid homage to this truly endearing and inspiring Marist brother through Masses, nightly prayers, and vigil that were live streamed via Zoom and Facebook.

During the first day, Bishop Noli Buco, JCD, DD Auxiliary Bishop of Antipolo presided over the 6 PM Mass and concelebrated it with Rev. Fr. Merwin Tahad from the Diocese of Imus and Rev. Fr. Edward Bacus from the Our Lady of the Abandoned Shrine. At 8 PM a nightly prayer was led by members of the Marist Marikina Community and the family of Br. Willy.

On the second day, the 6 PM Mass was presided over by Rev. Fr. Jeffty Mendez, CP the parish priest of St Gabriel of Our Lady of Sorrows Parish, and Rev. Fr. Vivien Nuera, CP. The 8 PM nightly prayer was led by the NDMU Community. This was immediately followed by a eulogy that saw colleagues and family members expressing their fond memories with Br. Willy and giving testimonials of his admirable character as a person and as a Marist Brother.

At 3 AM on January 28 a special send-off ceremony was conducted before Br. Willy's remains were transported to Mindanao via Philippine Airlines.

Indeed, Br. Willy will be sorely missed and will always be remembered as a true champion of the Filipino youth and the Marist education and mission.

Appendix F – Posthumous Award

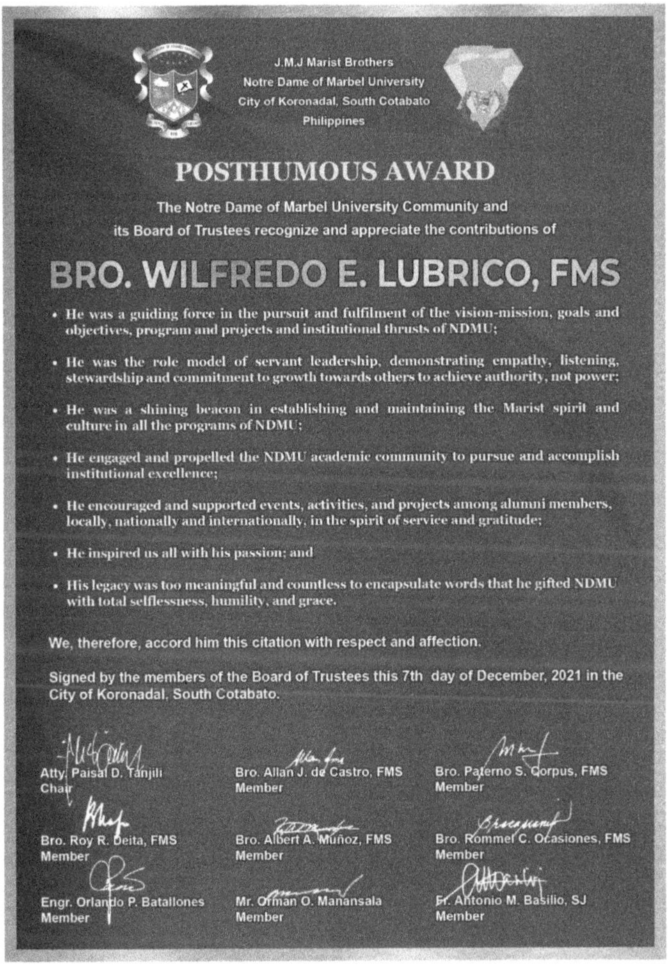

J.M.J Marist Brothers
Notre Dame of Marbel University
City of Koronadal, South Cotabato
Philippines

POSTHUMOUS AWARD

The Notre Dame of Marbel University Community and
its Board of Trustees recognize and appreciate the contributions of

BRO. WILFREDO E. LUBRICO, FMS

- He was a guiding force in the pursuit and fulfilment of the vision-mission, goals and objectives, program and projects and institutional thrusts of NDMU;
- He was the role model of servant leadership, demonstrating empathy, listening, stewardship and commitment to growth towards others to achieve authority, not power;
- He was a shining beacon in establishing and maintaining the Marist spirit and culture in all the programs of NDMU;
- He engaged and propelled the NDMU academic community to pursue and accomplish institutional excellence;
- He encouraged and supported events, activities, and projects among alumni members, locally, nationally and internationally, in the spirit of service and gratitude;
- He inspired us all with his passion; and
- His legacy was too meaningful and countless to encapsulate words that he gifted NDMU with total selflessness, humility, and grace.

We, therefore, accord him this citation with respect and affection.

Signed by the members of the Board of Trustees this 7th day of December, 2021 in the City of Koronadal, South Cotabato.

Atty. Paisal D. Tanjili Chair	Bro. Allan J. de Castro, FMS Member	Bro. Paterno S. Corpus, FMS Member
Bro. Roy R. Deita, FMS Member	Bro. Albert A. Muñoz, FMS Member	Bro. Rommel C. Ocasiones, FMS Member
Engr. Orlando P. Batallones Member	Mr. Orman O. Manansala Member	Fr. Antonio M. Basilio, SJ Member

ABOUT THE CO-AUTHOR
BRICCIO JAUD BAYNOSA

A philosophy and sociology professor in the Graduate School Department of the Holy Trinity College of General Santos City, Briccio J. Baynosa, was born on April 9, 1947, in General Santos City, Philippines. He specializes in Catechetics, English Literature, and Teaching English as a Second Language. He earned his Ph.D. in Education, Major in Educational Management at the University of Santo Tomas in Manila. He was a former member of the Congregation of the Marist Brothers of the Schools (FMS), Philippine Sector, East Asia Province. The Editor of *Fighting for Repose by Harry V. Peterson* (LifeRich Publishing 2021), he served as the President of Notre Dame of Dadiangas University 1992-1995.

FOREWORD by
DR. ROBERTO T. BORROMEO

Dr. Roberto T. Borromeo is the current President of Elizabeth Seton School in Las Pinas City, Philippines. Prior to his appointment, he served as Dean of the College of Education and Associate Professor of Educational Leadership and Management at De La Salle University (DLSU). An alumnus of Notre Dame of Dadiangas University, he finished his Master of Arts in Educational Management and Doctor of Education degrees from DLSU. As a British Council Fellow, he completed a postgraduate Diploma in Educational Planning and Management from the University of London Institute of Education and the Management Development Program (MDP) at Harvard University. Brother Willy was his student in Ph.D. classes at DLSU, and worked with Brother Willy as a resource person on Strategic Planning in Marist Institution's formation. Dr. Borromeo was a former Marist aspirant (Junior). Of his being an authority to write the Foreword, he texted, "Aside from my personal interactions with Brother Willy, of course nothing beats familiarity with the main author and her work and mastery of the genre. I am privileged to have done a bit for this tribute to Brother Willy. It has been a great learning experience for me as well".

ABOUT THE ARTIST
BUENO SILVA, Oil Painting, Cover

Bueno Silva was born in Baguio City, raised in General Santos City when his father worked for Dole Company Philippines. He attended Notre Dame of Dadiangas University. In 2005, he painted the portrait of his alma mater's founder, Brother Joseph Damian Teston, FMS who is 101 years old and lives in the Marist Hall, Bronx, New York. Bueno is a world-renowned artist best known for his commission works on Pope Paul VI, Pope John Paul II, President Ronald Reagan, President Ferdinand Marcos, King Bholkia of Brunei, Senator Dianne Feinstein, General Paulino T. Santos, John & Steve Baird of the Baird Warner Chicago, Mother Founder Maria Ignacia Del Espiritu Santo, R.V.M., and our Lady of Beaterio that was made into a National Philippine postage stamp. He resides in Chicago, Illinois, with his beloved wife Pat and their family. Bueno and Brother Willy were best of friends.

Endnotes

1 "Consecrated Persons and their Mission in Schools", Vatican Roman Curia, Congregations Documents, 2002. Retrieve from the Internet, November 2021

2 "St. Marcellin Champagnat 1789-1840", Champagnat Marist District of the Pacific Website. Retrieved from the internet February 10, 2021

3 "What is consecrated life?" Vocation Center, Catholic Archbishop of Sydney. Retrieved from the internet February 10, 2021

4 "T'nalak Weaving, Philippines", The Textile Atlas, Emily Lush, Laos Museum. Retrieved from the Internet February 27, 2021. T'nalak is a sacred cloth woven by the T'boli people in communities around Lake Sebu, Mindanao island. Traditionally made by women of royal blood, thousands of patterns that reference folklore and stories are known to the T'boli women by memory.

5 "No Greater Service (A Peace Corps Photo Memoir 1969-1974," LifeRich Publishing, 2020, Alvin J. Hower, p.316. Warp is the set of yarns or other elements stretched in place on a loom before the weft is introduced during the weaving process, regarded as the longitudinal set in a finished fabric with two or more sets of elements.

6 Capetown Diamond Museum. Lifted from the Internet, January 31, 2021.

7 "Philippine Literacy Rate 1980-2022", Macrotrends. Retrieved from Internet May 5, 2021.

8 "Homesteads on the Public Domain", ACT NO. 926, Republic of the Philippines Department of Agrarian Reform, October 7, 1903. Retrieved from the Internet, May 11, 2021

9 Elena Sagan Engane, a T'boli lady provided information about Brother Willy's uncle Melecio, the brother of his mother Maria Paz. Elena is married to Johnny Engane, a cousin of Brother Willy. Elena was my pupil in Grade 3 when I taught at the Santa Cruz Mission in June 1972.

10 "Baguio, NCR record coldest temperatures this year", Ma. Teresa Montemayor, December 5, 2021. Retrieved from the Internet, December 11, 2021.

11 The eight hectares was divided among Romeo's four living children. Only Anecito lives in the Naci farm with his family. It is sad to note, that the Sapali River have changed its course and often flooded that it now runs through six hectares of the property. The river also swept most of the arable land taking with it the rice fields and fruit trees like coconut that Tatay Pidio had planted. Anecito now raises cows, goats, and chickens to survive.

12 It is now legally called Notre Dame of Surala. The old name was derived from its location relative to the Allah River. It is located "sur" or south of Allah River. According to a reliable source, the name Surallah was inadvertently written as Surala when the school was registered at the Department of Education. It stuck and was never changed back to Surallah.

13 Interview conducted by Estrella T. Golingay. Brother Willy and Estrella were classmates from first to second year high school. They would later work together at the Notre Dame of Marbel University

14 "What is Shoktong" – Old medicinal wine made in Binondo; Philippine News. April 8, 2020. Retrieved from Internet February 17, 2021. Chinese rice "wine" or herbal liquor, believed by many Filipino women to be effective for inducing menstrual bleeding and abortions. The Spaniards called it Vino de Chino. Shoktong is a colloquial spelling in line with contemporary Filipino pronunciation.

15 Ewing is an Ilongo term for the pope's nose, the small, roundish, fatty disk at the chicken's tail where long feathers sprout. It was the favorite part of the chicken of Brother Willy's father.

16 Dinuguan is a Filipino savory stew of pork entrails using meat, vinegar, spices, and simmered in gravy of pig's blood.

17 "Was it an age of prosperity under Marcos?" Debt, Deprivation and the Spoils of Dictatorship, Philstar Global News Lab. 31 years of Amnesia. Retrieved from the Internet on July 14, 2021.

18 "New People's Army", Wikipedia. Retrieved from Internet, Oct 18, 2021

19 Eddie Garcia was a famous Filipino movie star

20 Interview of Teresa Lubrico Golveo conducted by Estrella T. Golingay

21 "St. Marcellin Champagnat". Mt. Maria College Website, Queensland, Australia. Retrieved from Internet. May 12, 2021

22 "St. Marcellin Champagnat, Founder of the Institute of the Marist Brothers, Lluis Serra Llansana, Marist of Champagnat website, Casa Generalizia Fratelli Marist. Retrieved from Internet October 26, 2021.

23 Ibid. Retrieved from Internet October 26, 2021

24 Ibid. Retrieved from the Internet October 26, 2021.

25 "Our Mentors: Oral History from our Mentors", Chris Gammon, 2011. Notre Dame of Gen. Santos City, USA website. Retrieved from May 6, 2021.

26 "Brother Bernard Curtin, FMS", Marist Archives, Deceased Brothers, Marist Brothers United States Province. Retrieved from Internet, October 28, 2021

27 Ibid. Retrieved from Internet, October 28, 2021

28 Conscientization is a social concept, grounded in Marxist critical theory, which focuses on achieving an in-depth understanding of the world, allowing for the perception and exposure of perceived social and political contradictions. Marxism is a social, political, and economic theory originated by Karl Marx, which focuses on the struggle between capitalists and the working class. Marx wrote that the power relationships between capitalists and workers were inherently exploitative and would inevitably create class conflict. Investopedia website. Retrieve May 7, 2021.

29 "Exclaustration". Wikipedia. In the canon law of the Catholic Church, exclaustration is the official authorization for a member of a religious order (in short, a religious) bound by perpetual vows to live for a limited time outside their religious institute, usually with a view to discerning whether to depart definitively. Retrieve May 7, 2021.

30 "A Tribute to Brother Willie on the Occasion of his Silver Jubilee". Brother Romulo L. Porras, FMS, Reprinted from AMIHAN, The Marist Brothers Newsletter of the Philippine Province, November-December 1997 issue under The Archivist's Corner. Brother Briccio Baynosa officially left the congregation on Dec. 10, 2015

31 Brother Renato Cruz aka Brother Rey was in the United States by February 1995. He died of leukemia on May 9, 1997, two and a half years after diagnosis of Chronic Lymphocytic Leukemia an incurable form of leukemia.

32 "Web app" or "online app" is also used in a business setting as an abbreviation for "Web application" or "online application" — meaning software that you access and use while online, via a browser, instead of software residing on your computer such as Microsoft Word.

33 ISO - The International Organization for Standardization is an international standard-setting body composed of representatives from various national standards organizations. Founded on 23 February 1947, the organization develops and publishes worldwide technical, industrial, and commercial standards. Wikipedia. Retrieved from Internet November 11, 2021.

34 "Mario Andretti Quotes", BrainyQuote Website. Retrieved from Internet, May 17, 2021

35 "Reunion...a Bridge Over Time", About Us. History of Notre Dame Schools in General Santos City". Hower, Prima. 1997. Notre Dame of Gen. Santos City, USA website. Retrieved from May 6, 2021 www.notredamegensan.org

36 “Whatsoever you do to the least of my people”, Goodsongs website, Willard Jabusch 1930-2018. Retrieved from Internet. January 21, 2021 printed with license from Oregon Catholic Publications, 2021

37 “The Blind Men and the Elephant”, Wikipedia. Retrieved from Internet. September 11, 2021.

38 Ibid.

39 “What Counts as View on YouTube, Facebook and Instagram”, Hassan Ali. Wyzowl Website. Retrieved from Internet, October 20, 2021

40 “Volunteer Service Overseas”, London, England. 1958. VSO Website. Retrieved July 17, 2021. Volunteer Service Overseas (VSO) is the world’s leading independent international development organization that works through volunteers to fight poverty in developing countries.

41 *Kamanol* is an iteration of “*manol*”. *Daw manol* is an expression that Brother Willy was very fond of saying. It is a Hiligaynon word that can be construed as lowlife, mean, rude, vulgar, etc. But in the context of what it means to Brother Willy, “bumpkin or yokel” would be the best way to translate it, which means, “an unsophisticated, naïve, or socially awkward person from the countryside.”

42 I was a beneficiary of this initiative of Brother Willy. He invited my siblings and me in 2013 to stay overnight at the Marbel Marist Convent, had supper and breakfast with the community. Initially, I declined Brother Willy’s offer. I explained that Josie Ferrariz Tizon and I were once assigned to adorn with fresh flowers the altar of our parish church and the Marist Brothers Chapel in Lagao Novitiate. We were freshman at NDL high school. Brother Bernard Curtin told us on the first day we reported at the Novitiate that we could use the faucet in the kitchen to fill our vases with water, but we were not to enter any other room. And, we were not to speak to any of the boys in the Juniorate. Brother Willy said, “That was then, this is now”. I tried to wiggle out of it and told him my siblings – Nena, Susan, Tito – and I planned to go shopping and check in at a hotel. He won’t hear of it. He drove us to the shopping mall and took us back to the convento. We shared dinner with the Marist Brothers with his Community at NDMU, enjoyed the fellowship and a basketful of fruits from the Marist farm.

43 To “ukay” literally means to “dig” from a pile. This term “Ukay-Ukay Talipapa” in the Philippines is akin to thrift shops in the United States.

44 Update: The Hower-Bates Library Network is proud to have established five Children’s Libraries; two dedicated to the Indigenous children, T’boli and Maguindanao. There is also a Reading Center for the Aetas in Olongapo displaced by the Mt. Pinatubo eruption on June 15, 1991.

As of February 2022, HBLN has shipped 75,000+ books to 52 libraries in the Philippines. It has recently partnered with Congresswoman Shirlyn Banas Nograles as part of her initiative to help supply books to Tahanan Ng Libro (House of Books) in remote barrios of South Cotabato starting at Tampakan. www.alvinandprimahower.com

CPSIA information can be obtained
at www.ICGtesting.com
Printed in the USA
LVHW112146080422
715402LV00009B/134/J

9 781489 740397